Introducing Interpreting Studi

This thoroughly revised, restructured and updated edition of Franz Pöchhacker's trusted textbook introduces students, researchers and practitioners to the fast-developing discipline of Interpreting Studies.

Written by a leading researcher in the field, *Introducing Interpreting Studies* covers interpreting in all its varied forms, from international conference to community-based settings, in both spoken and signed modalities. The book first guides the reader through the evolution of the field, reviewing influential concepts, models and methodological approaches. It then presents the main areas of research on interpreting, and identifies present and future trends in Interpreting Studies.

Introducing Interpreting Studies gives a comprehensive overview of the field and offers orientation to those undertaking research of their own. Chapter summaries, guides to the main points covered, and suggestions for further reading make this an eminently practical and user-friendly textbook. The book is complemented by The *Interpreting Studies Reader* (Routledge, 2002), a collection of seminal contributions to research in Interpreting Studies, and by the comprehensive *Routledge Encyclopedia of Interpreting Studies* (Routledge, 2015).

The updated edition features new chapters on history, discourse, and technology, and extensive new material on such topics as working memory, participation, remote interpreting and automation. With an enhanced structure and additional content, *Introducing Interpreting Studies* remains the essential textbook for all students and researchers in Interpreting Studies.

Franz Pöchhacker is Associate Professor of Interpreting Studies at the University of Vienna. He is the editor of the *Routledge Encyclopedia of Interpreting Studies* (Routledge, 2015) and co-editor of *The Interpreting Studies Reader* (Routledge, 2002) and of the international journal *Interpreting*.

"*Introducing Interpreting Studies* has been for the past 12 years the canon for interpreting studies, providing a comprehensive and insightful description of all types of interpreting. Written by a leading authority in the field, the book is well structured, well written and well referenced. This edition is an updated and improved version of an already excellent book and will undoubtedly continue to hold its place as the Interpreting textbook for many years to come."

Sandra Hale, *University of New South Wales, Australia.*

Praise for the First Edition

"This comprehensive, structured, and accessible primer will quickly become the standard textbook around which introductory courses are organized ... Its publication represents a major contribution to the field of Interpreting Studies."

International Association of Conference Interpreters (AIIC)

"This book will undoubtedly become a fixture in the recommended literature of students of interpretation around the world."

Book Review

"An ambitious, well-informed and well-researched piece of work. We can safely say that, with the new-found momentum fuelled by the publication of such a work, interpreting studies will soon establish itself firmly as a new discipline."

Perspectives: Studies in Translatology

Introducing Interpreting Studies

Second edition

Franz Pöchhacker

LONDON AND NEW YORK

This edition published 2016
by Routledge
2 Park Square, Milton Park, Abingdon, Oxon OX14 4RN

and by Routledge
711 Third Avenue, New York, NY 10017

Routledge is an imprint of the Taylor & Francis Group, an informa business

© 2016 Franz Pöchhacker

First published by Routledge 2004

British Library Cataloguing in Publication Data
A catalogue record for this book is available from the British Library

Library of Congress Cataloging in Publication Data
Pöchhacker, Franz, author.
Introducing interpreting studies / by Franz Pöchhacker. -- Second Edition.
pages cm
Includes bibliographical references and index.
1. Translating and interpreting--Research. I. Title.
P306.5.P63 2016
418'.02072--dc23
2015030312

ISBN: 978-0-415-74271-9 (hbk)
ISBN: 978-0-415-74272-6 (pbk)
ISBN: 978-1-3156-4957-3 (ebk)

Typeset in Times New Roman
by Taylor & Francis Books

Contents

Illustrations

Acknowledgements

This second edition of my introduction to interpreting studies, like the first, has come to exist only on the strength of the collective achievements of interpreting scholars past and present. By definition, I owe a great debt of gratitude to the entire community of researchers who have contributed to this field. The acknowledgements in the original edition listed over 30 colleagues who had given generously of their time and expertise to provide input and feedback on individual topics or chapters, and the value of their contributions at that time remains undiminished. For this revised and expanded edition, the number of colleagues deserving explicit acknowledgement has increased by a hundred. Indeed, it is the community of over 130 contributors to the *Routledge Encyclopedia of Interpreting Studies* (Routledge, 2015) that I have to thank for sharing their up-to-date knowledge of our field. Working with them as editor of that volume has been a great learning experience that is reflected in the presentation of selected research in this book. I am grateful to Louisa Semlyen and her team at Routledge for making this synergy possible by showing much patience with my plan for this second edition.

One special colleague and friend, who had provided encouragement and guidance throughout my work on the first edition, and whose inspiration can never be sufficiently acknowledged, is no longer there to receive the thanks she deserves. And yet, Miriam (Shlesinger) is very much present in our field, and will be for a long time to come. Her untiring efforts to give advice and support in matters of language and style have been carried on most admirably by Peter Mead, to whom I am greatly indebted for his perceptive comments and countless suggestions for improving this text. If there are still some pages where I have not managed to enhance the clarity and readability of the first edition quite as much as I had intended, the responsibility is, of course, solely my own.

Franz Pöchhacker

Publisher Acknowledgements

Grateful acknowledgement is given to copyright holders and authors for permission to use the following material:

Figures 1.1, 1.5 and 13.1, adapted from F. Pöchhacker, *Dolmetschen: Konzeptuelle Grundlagen und deskriptive Untersuchungen*, copyright © 2000, Tübingen: Stauffenburg Verlag.

Figure 1.2, adapted from G. Garzone and M. Viezzi (eds), *Interpreting in the 21st Century: Challenges and Opportunities*, copyright © 2002, Amsterdam/Philadelphia: John Benjamins.

Figure 3.1, reproduced from S. Lambert and B. Moser-Mercer (eds), *Bridging the Gap: Empirical Research in Simultaneous Interpretation*, copyright © 1994, Amsterdam/Philadelphia: John Benjamins.

Figure 4.2, adapted from J. Tseng, *Interpreting as an Emerging Profession in Taiwan – a Sociological Model*, MA thesis, 1992, Fu Jen Catholic University.

Figure 4.3, adapted from R.W. Brislin (ed.), *Translation: Applications and Research*, copyright © 1976, New York: Gardner Press.

Figure 4.4, reproduced from D. Gile, *Basic Concepts and Models for Interpreter and Translator Training*, copyright © 1995, Amsterdam/Philadelphia: John Benjamins.

Figure 4.5, reproduced from C. Dollerup and A. Loddegaard (eds), copyright © 1992, Amsterdam/Philadelphia: John Benjamins.

Figure 4.6, adapted from R. M. Ingram, "Simultaneous interpretation of sign languages: Semiotic and psycholinguistic perspectives," *Multilingua* 4 (2), copyright © 1985, Amsterdam: Mouton Publishers.

Figure 4.7, adapted from H. Kirchhoff, "Das dreigliedrige, zweisprachige Kommunikationssystem Dolmetschen," *Le Langage et l'Homme* 31, copyright © 1976, Brussels: Institut Libre Marie Haps.

Figure 4.8, adapted from C. Stenzl, *Simultaneous Interpretation: Groundwork Towards a Comprehensive Model*, MA thesis, 1983, University of London.

Figure 4.9, adapted from S. Kalina, *Strategische Prozesse beim Dolmetschen*, copyright © 1998, Tübingen: Gunter Narr.

Figure 4.10, adapted from D. Seleskovitch and M. Lederer, *Interpréter pour traduire*, copyright © 1984, Paris: Didier Érudition.

Figure 4.11, reproduced from D. Cokely, *Interpretation: A Sociolinguistic Model*, copyright © 1992 by Dennis Cokely, Burtonsville, MD: Linstok Press.

Figure 4.12, reproduced from B. Englund Dimitrova and K. Hyltenstam (eds), *Language Processing and Simultaneous Interpreting*, copyright © 2000, Amsterdam/Philadelphia: John Benjamins.

Figure 4.13, reproduced from R. Setton, *Simultaneous Interpretation: A cognitive-pragmatic analysis*, copyright © 1999, Amsterdam/Philadelphia: John Benjamins.

Every effort has been made to contact copyright-holders. Please advise the publisher of any errors or omissions, and these will be corrected in subsequent editions.

Introducing *Introducing* ...

Re-introducing ...

A dozen years after the first edition of this book, an update was clearly overdue, given the steady growth and diversification of research on interpreting. Those familiar with the 2004 version will find the book considerably changed, with many parts extensively revised and restructured, and several new chapters. And yet the basic design of the book, and certainly its aim and vision, have remained exactly the same – that is, to provide students, research-minded teachers and practitioners of interpreting as well as scholars in related fields with a broad and balanced overview of interpreting studies as an academic field of study. Therefore, the way this book is introduced here differs little from the introduction written twelve years ago. The one major difference is reference to the *Routledge Encyclopedia of Interpreting Studies* (Pöchhacker 2015), a comprehensive presentation of the state of the art that serves as an ideal complement to this textbook.

Perspective

The view of interpreting studies offered in this book is inevitably shaped by my individual perspective and some related constraints. My approach to interpreting is from the vantage point of 'Translation Studies,' the field of my **academic socialization**. On the other hand, my **professional background** and experience (as an interpreter in international conference and media settings) is rather narrow compared to the breadth of the field to be covered. Indeed, it was only in the course of my work as a researcher that I came to be involved in the field of community-based interpreting and developed an appreciation for interpreting in signed languages. Though I have done my best to expand my horizons and interact with interpreting researchers in different domains of our emerging community, it would be presumptuous to claim shared ground with all of them. What I hope we do share, though, is the aspiration toward 'unity in diversity' for our field of study.

Another constraint relating to the perspective of this book is **language**. Being limited to a small number of working languages, I have been unable to consider publications in languages like Russian, Japanese and Chinese. This has become less of a problem with the increasing use of English as a *lingua franca*, which has helped us achieve a considerable degree of 'linguistic unity in diversity' for our field. But that does not resolve the complex issue of terminological diversity and conceptual relativity, so acute in a discipline with an object as multifaceted as interpreting, which has been described from many different perspectives. Since the space available in this textbook permits only a limited degree of definitional rigor, my use of basic concepts and terms – such as 'message,' 'text,' 'language,' 'context' and 'culture,' to name but a few – is often unspecified and aims at a broad 'common denominator' so as to provide a starting point for further differentiation. With or without a definition, though, there should be no doubt in the reader's mind that conceptual choices of the kind underlying this book are invariably colored by a given analytical perspective. Hence the need to caution the would-be interpreting scholar right from the beginning against the temptation to accept 'reality' at face value, be it a definition or a concept – or a textbook for a discipline.

Much like the maker of a documentary, the writer of a textbook strives to give a meaningful account but cannot claim to know and represent what the state of affairs, or the state of the art, is 'really' like. The film-maker and the textbook author have to decide what to bring into view, what to foreground, in which light and from what angle. As much as the goal is to do justice to all the protagonists, the resulting picture is based on a great number of **choices**. Some of these may be painful (as in deciding what to leave out) and others creative (as in establishing links and relations); all of them, however, are governed by the fundamental need to impose on the subject one's own sense of **coherence** and structure.

Structure and Features

Turning to another metaphor which seems particularly appropriate here, this book is intended to be a 'map' of interpreting studies as a field of research. What is more, its individual parts and subdivisions can be viewed as mapping efforts in their own right, ultimately adding up to a multi-layered representation of the field. This section briefly describes the structure of the book, which consists of 13 chapters organized into three parts. Each chapter begins with a short lead-in and is divided into 'sections,' with numbered first-level subheadings (e.g. 3.1). Most of these sections are in turn composed of several 'subsections,' with numbered second-level subheadings (e.g. 3.1.1) following a lead-in paragraph for the section.

Part I: Foundations

Part I comprises four chapters which make up the 'synthetic' representation of the discipline. Chapter 1 reviews major **conceptual** distinctions to illustrate the breadth and complexity of the object of study and map out its theoretical terrain. The emphasis is on the construction of a coherent typological framework rather than on encyclopedic information about various forms of interpreting, as would be found in a 'handbook.' A basic level of familiarity with interpreting is thus presupposed. Where needed, such knowledge is readily available from the "Sources and Further Reading" listed at the end of the chapter.

Chapter 2 chronicles the **historical** "Evolution" of interpreting studies as a discipline. Responding to questions such as 'who?' 'when?' and 'where?,' the chapter could be said to map the sociology and geography of the field and its institutional infrastructure. Chapter 3 reviews the major **disciplinary, theoretical** and **methodological** "Approaches" to interpreting, responding mainly to the questions 'what?' and 'how?' and culminating in a map of the discipline in terms of "paradigms," or **research traditions**. Chapter 4 elaborates on the theoretical foundations by presenting "Models" of interpreting, at various levels of **modeling**.

Each of the four chapters in Part I begins with a list of the **main points** covered and concludes with a "Summary," as well as a list of "Sources and Further Reading." In addition, some "Suggestions for Further Study" are provided as a prompt for reflecting on the chapter content with regard to geographical and linguistic contexts not covered in the book.

In order to minimize redundancy and provide cross-references among major points covered in the various mapping dimensions, **text links** are used throughout the book. These forward and backward links, mostly to information in particular subsections (e.g. » 3.2.1, « 1.2.3), create interrelations within as well as between the different parts and chapters.

Part II: Topics

Building on the foundations laid in Part I by the 'synthetic' overview in terms of concepts, developments, approaches, paradigms and models, the second part of the book is devoted to a more 'analytical' presentation of the **state of the art**. In a total of eight chapters of uneven length (repackaged from the original four in the first edition), some of the prominent topics of research are introduced with reference to the relevant literature. Chapter 5, on "Language and Memory" (expanding parts of the chapter on 'Process' in the first edition), provides the foundation for Chapter 6, which focuses on "Cognitive Processes." The next two chapters deal with text and discourse, with Chapter 7 putting the emphasis on "Product and Effect" and Chapter 8 on "Discourse in Interaction." Chapter 10, on "Profession," is flanked by "History" (Chapter 9) and "Technology" (Chapter 11), both of which have been expanded from sections in the first-edition chapter on 'Practice and Profession.' Part II concludes with Chapter 12, on "Education."

All of these chapters feature landmark examples of empirical research on the topics at hand. Insofar as readability would permit, these studies are presented in the style of mini-abstracts, with special emphasis on aspects of research design such as the subjects, sample, techniques of data collection and analysis, and overall methodological strategy. Nevertheless, given the extensive nature of the territory to be covered, the review of selected research in Part II is even more reductionist than the mapping efforts in Part I, serving only as a 'roadmap,' as it were, with hardly any room for a description of the scenery. The difficult choice of what to mention, and what not, leaves these thematic reviews open to criticism from authors who may, rightly, feel that their work has been given short shrift. I hope they will understand that such lack of coverage results not from a lack of appreciation, but from the mandate to keep the book's bibliography to a manageable size. After all, the thematic presentations are essentially designed to help locate various avenues and crossroads in the overall landscape of **research topics**; getting there is only possible via engagement with the **literature**, as indicated by references in the text and also found in relevant articles in the *Routledge Encyclopedia of Interpreting Studies* that are listed, in SMALL CAPITALS, as "Further Reading" at the end of each chapter.

Part III: Directions

As a conclusion to the overview of interpreting studies provided in the two main parts of the book, Chapter 13 reviews some major trends and future perspectives of interpreting studies as a field of research. In addition to these "Directions" for the discipline, the final section of the book offers some basic orientation for those undertaking research of their own.

Sources, Authors, Subjects

Given the need to keep the **bibliography** of this book reasonably concise, the list of references reflects a priority for widely cited 'classics,' for particularly innovative and illustrative examples of recent work, and, overall, for publications which may be more readily available (and written in a language which is more easily accessible) to the readers of this book. As pointed out above, this textbook, and in particular the overview of selected topics and research, find an ideal complement in the *Routledge Encyclopedia of Interpreting Studies* (Pöchhacker 2015), whose more than 2,100 bibliography entries constitute an extraordinarily comprehensive and up-to-date list of references to the literature on interpreting. The two-part **index**, finally, permits a focus on individual members of the interpreting studies community and their work ("Author Index"), and serves as an effective tool to access key concepts and topics ("Subject Index") across the structural subdivisions of the book.

Function

The fact that this book is organized thematically, rather than by interpreting types and professional domains, reflects the underlying vision of the discipline. While recognizing that interpreting studies is characterized by an overwhelming degree of diversity and difference, this textbook reaffirms linkages, relations, and common ground in various dimensions. Though this may be of little worth to researchers and teachers who specialize in one domain or another, the added value of this **integrated approach** for the discipline as a whole would seem to justify the focus on 'unity in diversity.'

Aside from the function of this book as an introductory reference work for the interpreting studies community at large, its design and thematic scope should make obvious how it can be used as a textbook. While it can certainly stand on its own, it is most profitably used in conjunction with *The Interpreting Studies Reader* (Pöchhacker and Shlesinger 2002), all chapters of which are cited in the text, and best complemented by the *Routledge Encyclopedia of Interpreting Studies*. Ideally, teachers of introductory courses or modules on interpreting theory would consider this book essential reading for their students. If this is the case irrespective of professional domain, this second edition will continue to promote an integrated view of interpreting studies and serve its continued development as a highly differentiated – and thus all the more fascinating – field of study.

Part I
Foundations

1 Concepts

This initial chapter introduces some basic concepts and distinctions relating to interpreting as the object of interpreting studies. The set of types and terms presented here will serve as a broad foundation for what will be discussed in the course of this book.

The **main points** covered in this chapter are:

- the conceptual roots of 'interpreting'
- the definition of interpreting
- the relationship between interpreting and translation
- the social settings and interaction constellations in which interpreting takes place
- the major parameters underlying typological distinctions
- the complex interrelationships among various 'types' of interpreting
- the mapping of theoretical dimensions and domains of interpreting practice and research

1.1 Conceptual Roots

Interpreting is regarded here as **translational activity**, as a special form of 'Translation.' (The capital initial is used to indicate that the word appears in its generic, hypernymic sense.) Interpreting is an ancient human practice which clearly predates the invention of writing – and (written) translation. Many Indo-European languages have words for interpreting, and interpreters, whose etymology is largely autonomous from words for (written) translation. Expressions in Germanic, Scandinavian and Slavic languages denoting a person performing the activity of interpreting can be traced back to Akkadian, the ancient Semitic language of Assyria and Babylonia, around 1900 BCE (see Vermeer 1992: 59). The Akkadian root *targumânu/turgumânu*, via an etymological sideline from Arabic, also gave rise to the 'autonomous' English term for interpreter, **dragoman**.

The English word 'interpreter,' in contrast, is derived from Latin *interpres* (in the sense of 'expounder,' 'person explaining what is obscure'), the semantic roots of which are not clear. While some scholars take the second part of the word to be derived from *partes* or *pretium* ('price'), thus fitting the meaning of a 'middleman,' 'intermediary' or 'commercial go-between' (see Hermann 1956/2002), others have suggested a Sanskrit root. Be that as it may, the Latin term *interpres*, denoting someone 'explaining the meaning,' 'making sense of' what others have difficulty understanding, is a highly appropriate semantic foundation for 'interpreter' and 'interpreting' in our current understanding.

These etymological roots of the verb '**to interpret**' make for a semantically tense relationship with the terms 'translation' and 'translate': While one can capitalize on the polysemy of 'interpret' to argue for a meaning-based, rather than word-based, conception of Translation (» 3.2.4), it has also been common to stress the distinction between the more general hermeneutic sense and a narrowly construed translational sense of the word. This is particularly striking in the legal sphere, where lawyers view it as their prerogative to 'interpret' (the law) and expect court interpreters to 'translate' (the language) (» 10.3.2). Rather than semantic quibbling, this constitutes a fundamental challenge to our understanding of what it means to translate and/or interpret, and many parts of this book, beginning with the following section, will be devoted to attempts at finding an appropriate response.

1.2 Interpreting Defined

Within the conceptual structure of Translation, interpreting can be distinguished from other types of translational activity most succinctly by its **immediacy**: in principle, interpreting is performed 'here and now' for the benefit of people who want to engage in communication across barriers of language and culture.

1.2.1 Kade's Criteria

In contrast to common usage as reflected in most dictionaries, 'interpreting' need not necessarily be equated with 'oral translation' or, more precisely, with the 'oral rendering of spoken messages.' Doing so would exclude interpreting in signed (rather than spoken) languages (» 1.4.1) from our purview, and would make it difficult to account for the less typical manifestations of interpreting mentioned further down. Instead, by elaborating on the feature of immediacy, one can distinguish interpreting from other forms of Translation without resorting to the dichotomy of oral vs written. This is what Otto **Kade**, a self-taught interpreter and translation scholar at the University of Leipzig (» 2.3.1), did as early as the 1960s. Kade (1968) defined interpreting as a form of Translation in which

- the source-language text is presented only once and thus cannot be reviewed or replayed, and
- the target-language text is produced under time pressure, with little chance for correction and revision.

Kade chose to label the semiotic entities involved in Translation as 'texts' (» 7.1), for which one could substitute expressions like 'utterances' (in the broad sense), 'acts of discourse,' or 'messages,' subject to an appropriate definition. Whatever the terms, his definition elegantly accommodates interpreting from, into or between signed languages and also accounts for such variants of interpreting as 'sight translation' (» 1.4.2), 'live subtitling' or even the on-line (written) translation of Internet chats. This vindicates the general characterization of interpreting as an **immediate** type of translational activity, performed 'in real time' for immediate use. A definition relying on Kade's criteria, foregrounding the immediacy of the interpreter's text processing rather than real-time communicative use, could thus be formulated as follows:

> Interpreting is a form of Translation in which a **first and final rendition in another language** is produced on the basis of a **one-time presentation** of an utterance in a source language.

The criteria of ephemeral presentation and immediate production go some way toward covering our need for conceptual specification. Making our concept of interpreting hinge on the generic notion of Translation, however, leaves us exposed to the more general uncertainty of how to define that term. While the study of interpreting does not presuppose an account of Translation in all its variants and ramifications, our choice to define interpreting as a form of Translation implies that no interpreting scholar can remain aloof from the underlying conceptual issues. As George Steiner (1975: 252) put it, with reference to the German word for 'interpreter': "Strictly viewed, the most banal act of interlingual conveyance by a *Dolmetscher* involves the entire nature and theory of translation."

1.2.2 Interpreting as Translation

Given the expansive and varied theoretical territory of Translation, as covered in reference works like the *Routledge Encyclopedia of Translation Studies* (Baker and Saldanha 2009) and the *Handbook of Translation Studies* (Gambier and van Doorslaer 2014), there is a plethora of approaches on which we might draw to enrich our account of interpreting as a form of Translation. Since different scholars will define and characterize their object of study in accordance with their particular aims, experiences and interests, the basic question regarding the nature of Translation has drawn widely discrepant answers. To illustrate the spectrum of choice, let us take a look at four answers to the question 'What is Translation?' and consider their theoretical implications.

Translation is:

a   a process by which a spoken or written utterance takes place in one language which is intended or presumed to convey the same meaning as a previously existing utterance in another language (Rabin 1958)

b   the transfer of thoughts and ideas from one language (source) to another (target), whether the languages are in written or oral form ... or whether one or both languages are based on signs (Brislin 1976a)

c   a situation-related and function-oriented complex series of acts for the production of a target text, intended for addressees in another culture/language, on the basis of a given source text (Salevsky 1993)

d   any utterance which is presented or regarded as a 'translation' within a culture, on no matter what grounds (Toury 1995)

Definition (a) foregrounds the defining relationship between the source and target utterances and stipulates 'sameness of meaning' as an essential ingredient. It also introduces, albeit implicitly, human agents and attitudes in terms of 'intentions' and 'expectations.' Definition (b) describes Translation as a process of 'transfer' acting on 'ideas' in the medium of 'language.' Definition (c) introduces a number of descriptive features, such as 'situation,' 'function,' 'text' and 'culture,' and stresses the target orientation of the translational product. The target orientation is carried to the extreme in definition (d), in which the theorist relinquishes any prescriptive authority and accepts as Translation whatever is treated as such in a given community.

All four definitions accommodate interpreting, but each foregrounds different conceptual dimensions. And whatever is stipulated as an essential feature of Translation (i.e. notions like transfer, ideas, sameness, intention or culture) will carry over to our definition of interpreting and will have to be accounted for in subsequent efforts at description and explanation. We are free, of course, to formulate an altogether different definition of our own, but it would seem foolish to reinvent the wheel of Translation in order to move on with the study of interpreting. We could certainly mine the various definitions of Translation for basic conceptual ingredients, such as

- an **activity** consisting (mainly) in
- the **production** of **utterances (texts)** which are
- presumed to have a **similar meaning and/or effect**
- as **previously existing** utterances
- in **another language and culture**.

These terms can be adapted and refined in different ways. The notion of 'activity,' for instance, could be specified as a 'service,' possibly qualified as 'professional,' for the purpose of 'enabling communication' and for the benefit of 'clients' or 'users.' Similarly, we could specify 'production' (and 'communication') as taking place in a given 'situation' and 'culture,' and we could elaborate and differentiate such key concepts as 'culture,' 'language,' 'utterance' and 'meaning.' No less significant than terminological refinements, however, are the ways in which our conceptual framework reflects some key areas of theoretical controversy. These include:

- the scope of the interpreter's task ('mainly' production);
- the perspective on the translational process (target-oriented 'production' rather than source-dependent 'transfer'); and
- the normative specification of the translational product (the assumption of 'similarity' in 'meaning' or 'effect').

Whichever of these options one might wish to pursue, the definitional scaffolding set up in these terms should provide sufficient support to interpreting scholars seeking to conceptualize their object of study as a form of Translation. It should be clear, though, even – or especially – in a textbook, that any definition of one's object of study is necessarily relative to a set of underlying theoretical assumptions. In the words of Gideon Toury (1995: 23):

> Far from being a neutral procedure, establishing an object of study is necessarily a function of the *theory* in whose terms it is constituted, which is always geared to cater for certain needs. Its establishment and justification are therefore intimately connected with the *questions* one wishes to pose, the possible *methods* of dealing with the objects of study with an eye to those questions – and, indeed, the kind of *answers* which would count as admissible.

In this relativistic perspective, there can be no such thing as an objective definition fixing, once and for all, the 'true meaning' or 'essence' of what we perceive or believe something to be like. This 'non-essentialist,' postmodern approach to meaning has been reaffirmed by leading scholars as part of the "shared ground" in Translation studies (Chesterman and Arrojo 2000). Its theoretical and methodological consequences will become clear in subsequent sections of this book (» 3.3.1). In the present, foundational chapter, we now return to the concept of interpreting to review ways in which it can be further distinguished with regard to various criteria.

1.3 Settings and Constellations

If we approach the phenomenon of interpreting from a historical perspective, the most obvious criterion for categorization and labeling is the **social context of interaction**, or **setting**, in which the activity is carried out. In its distant origins, interpreting took place when (members of) different linguistic and cultural communities entered into contact for some particular purpose. Apart from such contacts *between* social entities in various **inter-social settings,** mediated communication is also conceivable *within* heterolingual societies, in which case we can speak of interpreting in **intra-social settings**.

1.3.1 Inter-social and Intra-social Settings

Some of the first mediated contacts between communities speaking different languages will have served the purpose of trading and exchanging goods, of 'doing business,' which would give us **business interpreting** as a 'primeval' type of interpreting. In one of the earliest publications discussing different types of interpreting, Henri van Hoof (1962) mentions **liaison interpreting** as a form of interpreting practiced mainly in commercial negotiations. More than thirty years later, Gentile et al. (1996) took advantage of the generic meaning of 'liaison,' denoting the idea of 'connecting' and 'linking up,' and extended the term 'liaison interpreting' to a variety of interpreting settings across the inter- vs intra-social dimensions.

Where the representatives of different linguistic and cultural communities came together with the aim of establishing and cultivating political relations, they will have relied on mediators practicing what is usually called **diplomatic interpreting**. When relations turned sour, or maybe before they were even pursued, armed conflict would have necessitated mediated communication in a military setting. Such **military interpreting**, as in talks with allies, truce negotiations or the interrogation of prisoners, thus bears a historical relationship to the diplomatic kind.

As societies became increasingly comprehensive and complex, we can conceive of multi-ethnic socio-political entities (such as the empires of Roman times or Spain's Golden Age) in which communication between individuals or groups belonging to different language communities necessitated the services of interpreters. Following the establishment of institutions for the enforcement of laws and the administration of justice, particularly in newly conquered or colonized territories, interpreters were enlisted to ensure that even those not speaking the language of the authorities could be held to account. Hence, **court interpreting**, for which specific legal provisions were enacted in sixteenth-century Spain, is a classic example of interpreting in an *intra-social* institutional context. In many jurisdictions, what is commonly labeled 'court interpreting' includes tasks like the certified translation of documents as well as interpreting in quasi-judicial and administrative hearings. One can therefore distinguish between the broader notion of **legal interpreting**, or **judicial interpreting**, and **courtroom interpreting** in its specific, prototypical setting.

Apart from the legal sphere, interpreting to enable communication between 'heterolingual' segments of a multicultural society emerged only more recently in the context of egalitarian states committed to the 'welfare' of all their citizens and residents. Once the principle of 'equal access' came to be seen as overriding expectations of linguistic proficiency, the intra-social dimension of interpreting became increasingly significant. In the US, for instance, legislation in the

1960s designed to give deaf persons equal access to the labor market gave a strong impetus to the development of interpreting services for users of signed language (» 1.4.1, » 2.1.2). With the focus of such efforts at the 'social rehabilitation' of the deaf placed on employment training and education in general, sign language interpreting in educational settings (**educational interpreting**) went on to become one of the most significant types of intra-social interpreting.

The issue of access, first to the labor market and then to a variety of public institutions and social services, was also at the heart of new communication needs arising in the context of (im)migration. While countries like Sweden and Australia responded as early as the 1960s to the demand for interpreting services to help immigrants function in the host society, others have been slow to address such intra-social communication needs. It was only in the 1980s and 1990s, in the face of mounting communication problems in public-sector institutions (healthcare, social services), that 'interpreting in the community' acquired increasing visibility. Thus **community interpreting**, also referred to as **public service interpreting** (mainly in the UK), emerged as a wide new field of interpreting practice, with **healthcare interpreting (medical interpreting, hospital interpreting)** and **legal interpreting** (including, among others, police and asylum settings) as the most significant institutional domains.

An interpreting type whose linkage to the intra-social sphere is less obvious is **media interpreting**, or **broadcast interpreting** (often focused on **TV interpreting**), which is essentially designed to make foreign-language broadcasting content accessible to media users within the socio-cultural community. Since spoken-language media interpreting, often from English, usually involves personalities and content from the international sphere, media interpreting appears as rather a hybrid form on the inter- to intra-social continuum. On the other hand, the community dimension of the media setting is fully evident when one considers broadcast interpreting into signed languages. By the same token, court interpreting can also be located in the international sphere, as in the case of war crimes tribunals.

As indicated, the activity of interpreting has evolved throughout history in a variety of settings, from first-time encounters between different tribes to institutionalized inter-social 'dealings' as well as in intra-social ('community') relations. We can therefore posit a spectrum which extends from inter- to intra-social spheres of interaction and reflects an increasing institutionalization of contacts and communication. Some of the contexts for which there is historical evidence of the interpreting function are illustrated in Figure 1.1 along the inter- to intra-social spectrum. Selected settings are grouped under the catchwords 'expedition' (= isolated *inter-social*), 'transaction' (= institutionalized *inter-social*) and 'administration' (= institutionalized *intra-social*), with the progression from the upper left to the lower right corner of the diagram indicating, ever so roughly, developments and shifts in relative importance over time.

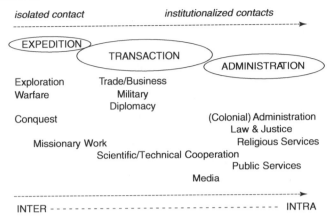

Figure 1.1 Interpreting in different spheres of social interaction

1.3.2 *Constellations of Interaction*

In addition to the categorization of interpreting types by social context and institutional setting, further significant distinctions can be derived from the situational constellation of interaction. In an early sociological analysis, R. Bruce W. Anderson (1976/2002) modeled the prototypical constellation of interpreting as 'three-party interaction' (» 4.3.1), with a (bilingual) interpreter assuming the pivotal mediating role between two (monolingual) clients. This is now commonly referred to as **dialogue interpreting**, highlighting the mode of face-to-face communicative exchange. The term is closely associated, if not synonymous, with what was previously introduced as '**liaison interpreting**' (« 1.3.1). Both of these terms foreground the bilateral nature of communication – in contrast with multilateral communication, as takes place in conferences attended by numerous individuals and representatives of different institutions, hence **conference interpreting**.

Interpreting for international conferences and organizations, in many ways the most prominent manifestation of interpreting in our time, did not emerge as a recognized specialty until the early twentieth century, when official French–English bilingualism in the League of Nations ushered in *de facto* multilingualism in international conferencing. **International conference interpreting**, which was to find its apotheosis in the policy of linguistic equality of the European Union, has spread far beyond multilateral diplomacy to virtually any field of activity involving coordination and exchange across linguistic boundaries. What is distinctive about conference interpreting is that it takes place in a particular 'ritualized' format of interaction ('conference'). It is often set in an international environment, but conference interpreting is also practiced in national contexts and institutions, such as the Belgian or Canadian parliaments.

Combining the distinction based on constellations (formats of interaction) with that of different 'spheres of social (inter)action' modeled in Figure 1.1,

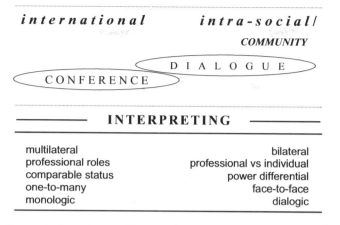

Figure 1.2 Conceptual spectrum of interpreting

we can conceive of interpreting as a conceptual spectrum extending from **international** to intra-social (**community**) interpreting. While it is tempting – and often efficient – to juxtapose conference and community interpreting, it is important to understand the difference between focusing either on the level of socio-cultural communities and their members/representatives or on the format of interaction (e.g. a multilateral conference or face-to-face dialogue). Figure 1.2 attempts to illustrate this dual spectrum.

The main idea is that the two levels allow for multiple combinations, so that dialogue interpreting in an international setting (as in a meeting of two heads of state) is equally accounted for as interpreting in a conference-like community-based setting (e.g. an assembly involving deaf participants). Even so, the descriptors at the bottom of the figure highlight characteristics that are usually or typically associated with either end of the dual spectrum – that is, international conference interpreting and dialogue interpreting in the community.

While the descriptive features are neither exhaustive nor suggestive of all-or-nothing distinctions, they point to some important differences. In particular, the nature of community interpreting is best understood by bearing in mind that one of the parties involved is an **individual** human being, speaking and acting on his or her own behalf.

The dual distinction between 'international vs community-based' and 'conference vs dialogue interpreting' is only one way of categorizing major (sub)types of interpreting. The following section will introduce additional parameters and interpreting types in order to sharpen awareness of the diversity and complexity of the phenomenon under study.

1.4 Typological Parameters

Apart from the broad classification of interpreting types by settings and constellations, there are additional and rather clear-cut criteria for a more systematic inventory of types and subtypes of interpreting, among them: language modality, working mode, directionality, technology use, and professional status.

1.4.1 Language Modality

In most of the literature on the subject, the term 'interpreting' is used generically as implying the use of spoken languages, traditionally with reference to Western European languages as used in international conferences and organizations. The more explicit term **spoken-language interpreting** gained currency only with the increasing need for a distinction vis-à-vis **sign language interpreting**, popularly known also as 'interpreting for the deaf.' Since deaf and hearing-impaired people may actually rely on a variety of linguistic codes in the visual rather than the acoustic medium, it is more accurate to speak of **signed language interpreting** (or **visual language interpreting**). This allows for the significant distinction between interpreting from or into a sign language proper (such as American Sign Language, British Sign Language, French Sign Language, etc.), that is, a signed language which serves as the native language for the **Deaf** as a group with its own cultural identity (hence the distinctive capital initial), and the use of other signed codes, often based on spoken and written languages (e.g. Signed English). Working from and into such secondary (spoken-language-based) sign systems is referred to as **transliteration**, and sign language interpreters or transliterators will be used depending on the language proficiency and preferences of the clients.

Interpreting into a signed language is sometimes referred to, loosely, as 'signing' ('voice-to-sign interpreting' or 'sign-to-sign interpreting'), as opposed to 'voicing' or 'voice-over interpreting' ('sign-to-voice interpreting'). A special modality is used in communication with deafblind persons, who monitor a signed message, including **fingerspelling**, by resting their hands on the signer's hands (**tactile interpreting**).

1.4.2 Working Mode

As in the case of language modality, the way in which interpreting was originally practiced did not require terminological qualification until the emergence of a new working mode. It was only in the 1920s, when transmission equipment was developed to enable spoken-language interpreters to work simultaneously, that it became meaningful to distinguish between **consecutive interpreting** (after the source-language utterance) and **simultaneous interpreting** (as the source-language text is being presented). It may be interesting to note that simultaneous interpreting was initially implemented as '**simultaneous consecutive**,' that is, the simultaneous transmission of two or more consecutive renditions in different output languages. Recently, another hybrid form using the same label has become feasible with the use of highly portable digital recording and playback equipment. In this modern form of simultaneous consecutive (or SimConsec), the interpreter produces a consecutive rendering by playing back and simultaneously interpreting a digital recording of the source speech (» 11.1.2).

Since consecutive interpreting does not presuppose a particular duration of the original act of discourse, it can be conceived of as a continuum which ranges from the rendition of utterances as short as one word to the handling of entire speeches, or more or less lengthy portions thereof, 'in one go' (Figure 1.3). Subject to the individual interpreter's working style – and memory skills – and a number of situational variables (such as the presentation of slides), the consecutive interpretation of longer speeches usually involves **note-taking** as developed by the pioneers of conference interpreting in the early twentieth century (» 2.1.1). Hence, consecutive interpreting with the use of systematic note-taking is sometimes referred to as **'classic' consecutive**, in contrast to **short consecutive** without notes, which usually implies a bidirectional mode in a dialogue interpreting constellation.

For sign language interpreters, whose performance in the visual channel leaves little room for activities requiring additional visual attention, note-taking is less of an option, and they work in the short consecutive or, typically, the simultaneous mode. It should be pointed out in this context, however, that the distinction between consecutive and simultaneous interpreting is not necessarily clear-cut. Since neither voice-over interpreting nor signing cause interference in the acoustic channel, sign language interpreters are free to start their output before the end of the source-language message. Indeed, even spoken-language liaison interpreters often give their (essentially consecutive) renditions as simultaneously as possible.

Whereas the absence of acoustic source–target overlap makes simultaneous interpreting (without audio transmission equipment) the working mode of choice for sign language interpreters, spoken-language interpreting in the simultaneous mode typically implies the use of electro-acoustic transmission equipment. Only where the interpreter works right next to one or no more than a couple of listeners can s/he provide a rendition by **whispered interpreting**, or '**whispering**' (also known by the French term *chuchotage*), which is in fact done not by whispering but by speaking in a low voice (*sotto voce*). This is also possible with portable transmission equipment (microphone and headset receivers) as used for guided tours. Nevertheless, simultaneous interpreting with full technical equipment (» 11.1.1) is so widely established today

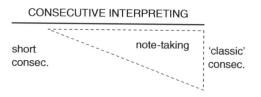

Figure 1.3 Continuum of consecutive interpreting

that the term '**simultaneous interpreting**' (frequently abbreviated to **SI**) is often used as shorthand for 'spoken-language interpreting with the use of simultaneous interpreting equipment in a sound-proof booth.'

A special type of simultaneous interpreting is the rendition of a written text 'at sight.' Commonly known as '**sight translation**,' this variant of the simultaneous mode, when practiced in real time for immediate use by an audience, would thus be labeled more correctly as '**sight interpreting**.' In sight translation, the interpreter's target-text production is simultaneous not with the delivery of the source text but with the interpreter's real-time (visual) reception of the written source text. If the interpreter is working 'at sight' without the constraints of real-time performance for a (larger) audience, sight interpreting will shade into the consecutive mode or even come to resemble 'oral translation,' with considerable opportunity for 'reviewing' and correction. A special mode of (spoken-language) simultaneous interpreting is **SI with text** in the booth. Since authoritative input still arrives through the acoustic channel, with many speakers departing from their text for asides or time-saving omissions, this variant of the simultaneous mode is not subsumed under sight interpreting but rather regarded as a complex form of SI with a more or less important sight interpreting component.

Some of these distinctions, which are represented graphically in Figure 1.4, do not hold to the same degree across language modalities. As already mentioned, signing (i.e. voice-to-sign, sign-to-sign or **text-to-sign interpreting**) is feasible in the simultaneous mode without special equipment. In contrast, sign-to-voice interpreting may be performed with or without a microphone and a booth. Simultaneous interpreting equipment is needed only where a monologic source speech in sign language needs to be interpreted into several (spoken) languages, requiring separate audio channels. In text-to-sign interpreting, the interpreter may need to alternate between reception (reading) and

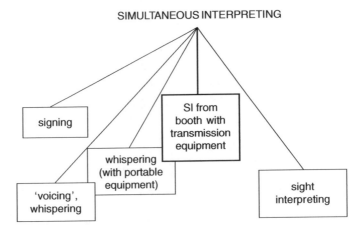

Figure 1.4 Forms of simultaneous interpreting

production (signing), thus bringing sight translation closer to the (short) consecutive mode.

1.4.3 Directionality

While the interpreting process as such always proceeds in one direction – from source to target language – the issue of direction is more complex at the level of the communicative event. In the prototype case of mediated face-to-face dialogue (« 1.3.2, » 4.3.1), the interpreter will work in both directions, that is, 'back and forth' between the two languages involved, depending on the turn-taking of the primary parties. Bidirectional interpreting is thus typically linked with the notions of 'liaison interpreting' and 'dialogue interpreting,' but it may equally occur in conference-type interaction, where interpreters may work in a 'bilingual booth,' or are said to provide 'small retour' (i.e. interpret questions and comments back into the language chiefly used on the floor).

Although it is common practice in conference interpreting, there is no special label for 'one-way' or one-directional interpreting at the level of the communicative event. Relevant distinctions are rather made with reference to the individual interpreter's combination of working languages, classified by AIIC, the International Association of Conference Interpreters (» 2.1.1), as A, B or C languages (A = native or best 'active' language; B = 'active' language spoken with near-native proficiency; C = 'passive' language allowing 'complete understanding'). The Western tradition of conference interpreting has favored simultaneous interpreting from B or C languages into an interpreter's A language. **A-to-B interpreting**, or **retour interpreting**, though widely practiced on 'local' (national) markets, has not been equally accepted for simultaneous interpreting in international organizations. In contrast, sign language interpreters, most of whom are not native signers, typically practice simultaneous interpreting as A-to-B interpreting and consider B-to-A, that is, sign-to-voice interpreting, the more challenging direction.

An issue which actually constitutes a parameter in its own right, but can be linked to the present directional context, is the directness with which the source-to-target transfer at a particular communicative event is effected. Where the language combination of the interpreters available does not allow for 'direct interpreting,' recourse is made to **relay interpreting**, that is, indirect interpreting via a third language, which links up the performance of two (or more) interpreters, with one interpreter's output serving as the source for another. Relay interpreting in the simultaneous mode was standard practice in what used to be the Eastern bloc countries, where Russian served as the *pivot* language in the multilingual Soviet Empire. The Russian relay system and its reliance on A-to-B interpreting as the standard directional mode were shunned by proponents of the Western tradition. For some UN and EU working languages, however, the combination of A-to-B and relay interpreting has played an important role, often with English serving as the *pivot* language, and has become prominent also in the enlarged European Union.

1.4.4 Use of Technology

The use of technical equipment was discussed earlier in connection with simultaneous interpreting (« 1.4.2), where it essentially functions to avoid the mixing of source- and target-language messages in the acoustic channel. Obviously though, electronic transmission systems for sounds and images also serve more generally to overcome spatial distances and 'connect' speakers (including interpreters) and listeners who are not 'within earshot' or, in the case of signing, within the range of view. Apart from their common use *in situ* (e.g. in conference halls), electroacoustic and audiovisual transmission systems are therefore employed in particular to reach far beyond a given location. In what is broadly referred to as **remote interpreting** (» 11.2), the interpreter is not in the same room as the speaker or listener. This could mean that the interpreter is in a booth or separate place on the premises, with hardwired connections. Typically, though, greater distances are involved, and bridged with different types of telecommunications equipment.

The oldest form of remote interpreting, proposed as early as the 1950s, is **telephone interpreting (over-the-phone interpreting)**, which became more widely used only in the 1980s and 1990s, particularly in intra-social settings (healthcare, police, etc.). Telephone interpreting is usually performed with standard telecommunications equipment in the bilateral consecutive mode. The emergence of video(tele)phony was of particular significance for the deaf and hard-of-hearing, who now have access in many countries to videoconference-based services known as **video relay service** (VRS). VRS allows deaf users of sign language to communicate over the phone, the call being mediated by a 'video interpreter.'

Beyond telephone calls, remote interpreting using videoconference technology can serve international and multilateral conferences as well as community-based institutional encounters. Pioneered in international conference settings several decades ago with satellite links, remote interpreting has recently expanded particularly in community-based domains, such as healthcare and legal settings. This includes encounters involving deaf persons, for which 'video remote interpreting' (VRI) is sometimes used as a distinct label.

Terminology in this area has evolved along with technology. One important distinction is made between remote interpreting proper, where the interpreter is not in the same location as the participants in the interaction, and **video-conference interpreting**, where the interpreter is on site together with one of the parties connected via 'video link.'

No less future-oriented than technology-driven forms of remote interpreting (which, despite complaints about the 'dehumanization' of interpreting, continue to rely on especially skilled human beings) are attempts at developing **automatic interpreting** systems on the basis of machine translation software and technologies for speech recognition and synthesis. While such **machine** interpreting (» 11.3.2) is unlikely to deliver 'fully automatic high-quality interpreting' in the near future, advances in mobile and cloud computing have led to impressive progress in the development of 'speech-to-speech translation' for certain applications and domains.

1.4.5 Professional Status

Whereas the parameters and interpreting types introduced so far relate to the way in which interpreting is performed, yet another crucial distinction relates to the level of skill and expertise with which the human agent performs the task. Most of the literature on interpreting presupposes a certain – and, more often than not, rather high – professional status of the activity and its practitioners. In other words, the unmarked form of 'interpreting' often implies **professional interpreting**, and 'interpreters' are regarded as 'professionals' with special skills – also in the usage of this book. Historically, it is of course difficult to clearly separate professional interpreting from **non-professional interpreting** or **natural interpreting**, that is, interpreting done by bilinguals without special training for the task.

The issue of "natural translation" has been championed since the 1970s by Canadian translatologist Brian Harris, who postulated that "translating is coextensive with bilingualism," that is, that all bilinguals have at least some translational ability (Harris and Sherwood 1978: 155). Similarly, Toury (1995) put forward the somewhat less radical notion of a "native translator," stressing the role of bilingualism as a basis for learning how to interpret (and translate). Both proposals point to the merit of studying the process by which a bilingual without special training acquires and applies interpreting skills, and both Harris and Toury agree that there exist socio-cultural translational norms which shape interpreting practices and determine the skill levels required for the activity to be recognized as such.

"The translating done in everyday circumstances by people who have had no special training for it" (Harris and Sherwood 1978: 155) has presumably been common practice throughout history. Today, too, communication with speakers of other languages often remains heavily dependent on the efforts of natural interpreters, the most significant example in community settings being bilingual children, of immigrants or deaf parents, interpreting for their family. On the whole, it was only when task demands exceeded what 'ordinary' bilinguals were expected to manage that the job of interpreter was given to people who had special knowledge (of the culture involved or of the subject matter) and skills (in memorizing and note-taking or simultaneous interpreting) as well as other qualifications, such as moral integrity and reliability (» 10.2.1). Even so, the criteria for deciding what or who is professional or not in interpreting are not always hard and fast, and the issue of the professional status of (various types of) interpreting and interpreters needs to be considered within the socio-cultural and institutional context in which the practice has evolved (» 2.1).

1.5 Domains and Dimensions

The typological distinctions introduced in the course of this chapter indicate the multi-faceted nature of interpreting as an object of study. This concluding section will present an overall view of this diversity and complexity by aligning a number of conceptual dimensions and parameters which relate to major domains of interpreting practice. The resulting 'map' of the territory of interpreting studies should provide some useful orientation for our subsequent *tour d'horizon* of the field.

The best-known and most influential attempt at charting the territory of the discipline concerned with the study of translational activity is the survey of translation studies by James S. Holmes (1972/2000), usually represented graphically as the 'map' of Translation studies (see Toury 1995: 10, Munday 2001: 10). Holmes was not primarily concerned with interpreting, which he posited far down in his branch structure as oral (vs written) human (vs machine) Translation in the "medium-restricted" theoretical domain. To put interpreting more visibly on the map, Heidemarie Salevsky (1993) proposed an analogous branch structure for the discipline of interpreting studies, with theoretical subdomains based on a list of situational variables (see Salevsky 1993: 154): varieties of interpreting (consecutive vs simultaneous); the medium (human, machine, computer-aided interpreting); language combinations; culture combinations; area/institution (interpreting in court, in the media, etc.); text relations (text type, degree of specialization, etc.); and partner relations (source-text producer vs target-text addressee).

In a synthesis of these mapping efforts and the discussion in sections 1.3 and 1.4 above, we can adopt the following set of eight dimensions to map out the theoretical territory of interpreting studies: (1) **medium**; (2) **setting**; (3) **mode**; (4) **languages (cultures)**; (5) **discourse**; (6) **participants**; (7) **interpreter**; and (8) **problem**. These conceptual dimensions are used in Figure 1.5 to illustrate the broad spectrum of phenomena to be covered by theoretical and empirical research on interpreting.

While Figure 1.5 is primarily designed to exemplify the varied nature of interpreting in the horizontal dimensions, the vertical arrangement of the dimensions is such as to suggest major subdomains of interpreting practice and research. Thus, on the left-hand side of the diagram, the features listed for the various dimensions add up to the domain of international conference interpreting, whereas a vertical cross-section on the right-hand side suggests some of the main features of community-based interpreting. Given the many facets of the diverse phenomena to be covered, the diagram cannot amount to a combinatorial map of features. On the whole, however, the interplay of the first seven dimensions serves to highlight some of the key factors in the various prototypical domains. As indicated by the use of dotted lines, the problem-oriented dimension shown at the bottom of Figure 1.5 represents not a continuum of descriptive features but a set of examples of major research concerns to date, as explored more fully in Part II of this book.

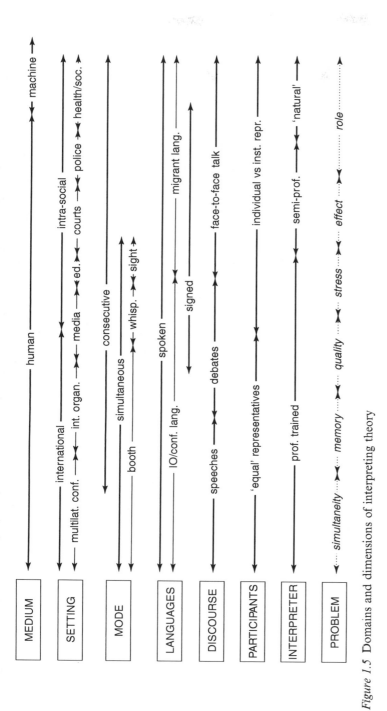

Figure 1.5 Domains and dimensions of interpreting theory

Summary

This chapter has laid the conceptual foundations for our survey of interpreting studies by defining the object of study and reviewing its typological ramifications. Acknowledging a basic dependence on theoretical approaches to the generic concept of Translation, interpreting was characterized as an *immediate* form of translational activity, performed for the benefit of people who want to engage in communication across barriers of language and culture. Defined as a form of Translation in which a first and final rendition in another language is produced on the basis of a one-time presentation of a source-language utterance, the concept of interpreting was differentiated according to *social* contexts and institutional *settings* (inter-social vs intra-social settings) as well as situational *constellations* and formats *of interaction* (multilateral conference vs face-to-face dialogue). In addition to the continuum between the prototypical domains of *international conference interpreting* and *community-based dialogue interpreting*, including *court* or *legal interpreting* and *healthcare interpreting*, a more detailed typology of interpreting practices was drawn up by applying the parameters of language modality (*signed-* vs *spoken-language interpreting*), working mode (*consecutive* vs *simultaneous interpreting*), directionality (*bilateral, B/C-to-A, A-to-B* and *relay interpreting*), use of technology (*remote interpreting, machine interpreting*), and *professional status* (*'natural' vs professional interpreting*). Finally, a conceptual orientation to the complex interplay of domains and dimensions was offered in the form of a 'map' of the theoretical territory of research on interpreting.

Sources and Further Reading

On the terms 'interpreter' and 'interpreting' in English and other languages, see Mead (1999) and Pöchhacker (2010a) as well as INTERPRETING in Pöchhacker (2015). There are few publications specifically devoted to a comprehensive conceptual analysis of interpreting. The pioneering "taxonomic survey" of interpreting put forward by Harris in the mid-1990s has remained unpublished. For typological discussions with reference to community interpreting, see e.g. Gentile et al. (1996) and Roberts (1997). For reference, see the articles under the headings of MODES and SETTINGS in Pöchhacker (2015). Most books recommended for a deeper understanding of various domains of professional practice focus only on a particular type of interpreting. These include: for conference interpreting, Herbert (1952), Seleskovitch (1978a), Jones (1998); for court interpreting, González et al. (2012), Laster and Taylor (1994); for community interpreting, Hale (2007); and for signed language interpreting, Frishberg (1990), Stewart et al. (1998). Chapter-length accounts of

"Conference Interpreting," "Court Interpreting," "Healthcare Interpreting," "Signed Language Interpreting," etc. can be found in *The Routledge Handbook of Interpreting* (Mikkelson and Jourdenais 2015).

Suggestions for Further Study

- What are the etymology and current meaning of words for 'interpreter' and 'interpreting' in other languages?
- How is the distinction between 'translation' and 'interpreting' made in other languages, in dictionaries, in academic writings and in the profession(s)?
- Do other languages offer a lexical distinction between 'interpreting,' or 'interpretation,' in the translational sense and in the sense of exegesis or explanation?
- What forms and types of interpreting are conceptually salient in other languages and national contexts, and how are they differentiated and interrelated?

2   Evolution

This chapter describes the development of research on interpreting and the emergence of interpreting studies as a discipline, with special emphasis on the sociology of the field and its academic infrastructure. Thus the 'making' and the 'make-up' of interpreting studies will be profiled in response to questions like 'who?' 'when?' and 'where?' Given the crucial role of professionalization in this development, I will first review the professional underpinnings of the discipline and then trace its evolution from profession-based writings to theory-based research.

> The **main points** covered in this chapter are:
>
> - the evolution of professional standards for interpreting as a specialized occupation
> - the beginnings of research on interpreting
> - the academic institutionalization of the discipline
> - the leading representatives and centers of interpreting research
> - the diversification and integration of interpreting studies since the 1990s
> - the state of the discipline in the twenty-first century

2.1 Socio-professional Underpinnings

Interpreting is an ancient human practice. Some fascinating evidence of the role and status of interpreters in bygone civilizations has been preserved: one early example from Ancient Egypt is a relief of a mediating figure in the Memphite tomb of General Haremhab (or Horemheb), dating from c. 1340 BCE (see Thieme et al. 1956: [7]). Through the ages and up to the twentieth century, however, interpreting was generally considered too 'commonplace' and unspectacular an activity to deserve special mention or attention, and documentary evidence of interpreting and interpreters is relatively sparse. Examples include references to interpreting officials in China's imperial records, lists of salaried interpreters in the service of the Roman Empire, sixteenth-century laws enacted by the Spanish Crown to regulate interpreting practices in its colonies, and accounts of dragomans serving diplomatic exchanges with the Ottoman Empire. These different sources indicate that interpreting has long been practiced in various regions and periods in history with at least some degree of remuneration, legal standards or special know-how, if not training. Even so, it was not until the twentieth century that interpreting gained wider recognition as a profession.

2.1.1 *International Conference Interpreting*

The Paris Peace Conference after World War I marks a fundamental turning point in the history of interpreting – and of diplomacy. Following the decision to use English as well as French as official languages (thus breaking with the tradition of using French as the diplomatic lingua franca), interpreters were recruited for the negotiations. One of these was Paul Mantoux, whom his colleague Jean Herbert (1952) respectfully called 'the first conference interpreter.' The peace agreements envisaged the creation of an international organization, the **League of Nations**, also with English and French as official languages. When this body, and its affiliate, the International Labour Organization (**ILO**), started operating in Geneva in 1920, a corps of especially skilled language professionals emerged. Faced with the need to render entire speeches, interpreters developed their own **note-taking** technique for consecutive interpreting. At the ILO, where Edward Filene's idea for a system of **simultaneous interpreting** was implemented in the late 1920s, interpreters were involved in the successful testing of this new technique.

These new skill requirements, and expanding communication needs in international politics and trade, led to the establishment of institutions providing systematic **training**, distinct from those preparing linguists for diplomatic service. The very first such school in twentieth-century Europe was a college for business translators/interpreters founded in **Mannheim**, Germany, in 1930 and subsequently transferred to the University of Heidelberg. In the early 1940s, **schools** for the training of (translators and) interpreters (T/I schools, 'interpreter schools') were also established at the universities of Geneva and Vienna. The successful use of simultaneous interpreting at the **Nuremburg Trial** (1945–6), and its subsequent adoption by the **United Nations**, gave increased momentum to the professionalization of interpreting at international conferences, and more interpreter schools were set up.

Fostered by an expanding professional market and rising numbers of graduates, national as well as international **professional organizations** of (translators and) interpreters were formed in the early 1950s. Alongside the International Federation of Translators (FIT), designed as an umbrella organization to represent T/I professionals via affiliated national associations of translators and interpreters, the International Association of Conference Interpreters

(AIIC) was created in 1953 as a professional body with worldwide individual membership. Based on a **code of ethics** and **professional standards** adopted in 1957, AIIC proved very successful in regulating interpreters' working conditions and establishing a high profile for the profession on an international scale. In the 1990s a US anti-trust action challenged fee arrangements and working conditions, and AIIC held its ground on the latter. It maintains its influence in collective bargaining with international organizations and has played a significant role in the area of training (» 2.1.3, » 12.5.2) as well as in research on vital aspects of the profession (» 10.4.2, » 10.5). The fact that the essentially self-regulating international profession has, to some extent, been brought under national jurisdiction and curtailed in its power is indicative of professional developments in other domains of interpreting. Indeed, outside the now widely recognized norms for interpreting in international organizations and conferences, the struggle for professionalization in other settings has typically been subject to national legislation and local institutional constraints.

2.1.2　Interpreting in the Community

Compared to the 'wave' of professionalization that swept conference interpreting to high international prestige after the 1950s, the professionalization of interpreting in community-based settings appears more like a pattern of ripples. Unlike the realm of international conferences and organizations, efforts to ensure professional status and recognition for interpreters in the community are by definition set in a particular national and socio-cultural context.

The type of intra-social interpreting with the strongest historical roots is interpreting in courts of law. Nevertheless, despite sixteenth-century precedents in legislation, interpreting in the courtrooms of most national jurisdictions was not linked to particular professional standards until late in the twentieth century, often with continued reliance on 'chance interpreters.' Notwithstanding early **legal provisions** for the appointment, and even testing, of 'sworn translators-interpreters' (e.g. in Denmark) as well as **associations** of court interpreters, there is little evidence of systematic training (» 2.1.3, » 12.1.2). In the US, a major impetus for the establishment of professional interpreting **standards** in (federal) courts came from the 1978 *Court Interpreters Act*, which established mechanisms for **testing and certification**, ushering in widespread progress towards professionalization at federal and state levels (» 10.2.3). Similar momentum has been generated more recently in Europe by *Directive 2010/64/EU on the Right to Interpretation and Translation in Criminal Proceedings*.

The significance of legal provisions regarding arrangements for interpreting is also evident in the professionalization of American sign language interpreters. Prompted by legislation in the 1960s which authorized the use and remuneration of interpreters for the vocational rehabilitation of deaf and hearing-impaired persons, providers of education and rehabilitation services for the **deaf** met with interpreters in 1965 and founded a national organization of interpreters, subsequently known as the Registry of Interpreters for the Deaf, or **RID** (» 9.3.2). It was this professional body that, much like AIIC, successfully established standards of professional practice and ethics for its (several thousand) members, and enforced these through its own system of evaluation and **certification**. A cornerstone for these efforts was the RID **Code of Ethics**, which became a much emulated model for subsequent attempts by spoken-language community interpreters to codify their professional standards.

Sharing the mission of facilitating 'access' to public services, but serving (im)migrants rather than deaf and hearing-impaired citizens, spoken-language community interpreting was pioneered by countries with an explicit **immigration** policy, such as Australia and Sweden, where telephone interpreting and on-site healthcare and social service interpreting were launched around 1970. While such interpreting services were also subsequently adopted in North America and Europe (e.g. in France, the Netherlands and the UK), Australia remains unique for its National Accreditation Authority for Translators and Interpreters (NAATI), which gives **accreditation** to training courses and administers tests for the recognition of different levels of vocational linguistic qualifications in nearly 100 languages.

In the UK, a professionalization initiative for **community interpreting** (in medical, social as well as legal settings) resulted in the publication of a seminal handbook (Shackman 1984) and further profession-building initiatives and publications by the country's leading professional organizations for language practitioners, the Chartered **Institute of Linguists** and the Institute of Translation and Interpreting (**ITI**). There and elsewhere, the literature on interpreting in various institutional settings received considerable input from **service providers** themselves, as reflected in a number of publications on 'working with interpreters' by medical and legal experts.

Aside from legal interpreting, which is often viewed as a separate professional domain, progress in the professionalization of community interpreting has been achieved mainly in the field of healthcare. In the US, in particular, anti-discrimination legislation has been used to promote the employment of skilled medical interpreters, thus providing a basis for the creation of **professional organizations**. On the whole, though, the great diversity of institutional settings, demographic and political circumstances, and regulatory environments in different countries has made the development of community-based interpreting as a profession highly uneven and dispersed. It was only towards the mid-1990s that community interpreting became the topic of international cooperation and exchange. Even so, much of the common ground of community interpreters worldwide has consisted in the lack, rather than the existence, of professional standards, remuneration and training, and those promoting harmonization at the national and international levels – such as Canada's 'Critical Link' (Critical Link Canada/Critical Link International), the US National Council for Interpretation in Health Care (NCIHC), the European Forum of Sign Language Interpreters (EFSLI), the European Legal

Interpreters and Translators Association (EULITA) or the European Network for Public Service Interpreting and Translation (ENPSIT) – have found it difficult to achieve substantial progress. With public-sector institutions often unable, or unwilling, to pay for professional interpreting services, there are few incentives for engaging or investing in higher-level **training**. Indeed, little training for interpreters working in community settings is offered at an academic level (» 12.1.2). This lag in the academization of the profession is one of the crucial differences between international conference interpreting and community interpreting, and has profound implications for the development of research, as discussed below.

2.1.3 Academization

Aside from the role of AIIC as a worldwide body enforcing standards of professional performance and remuneration, the high status enjoyed by conference interpreters since the 1950s is largely due to a strong market (with financially potent institutional clients) and **university-level training**. The latter has been strongly shaped by the profession, in particular by the 'school policy' of AIIC adopted in 1959. T/I schools undertaking to observe its criteria (e.g. that interpreting courses be designed and taught by practicing conference interpreters) came together in the early 1960s to form **CIUTI**, the Conference of University-level Translator and Interpreter Schools, as a select group of recognized institutions. Though foregrounding their university affiliation, CIUTI schools (including Geneva, Heidelberg, Paris, Trieste and Vienna) had a distinctly **vocational profile**, and for a long time many of them retained a separate organizational status, as reflected in designations like *École (Supérieure), Institut Supérieur, Hoger Instituut, Scuola Superiore* or *Escuela Universitaria*.

In this institutional context, pioneering professionals produced the first textbooks of interpreting (Herbert 1952; Rozan 1956; van Hoof 1962; Seleskovitch 1968), and (conference) interpreter training programs throughout the 1970s and 1980s foregrounded the professional rather than the academic dimension of higher education. Ever since the 1980s, though, there has been a trend in many institutions toward what Mackintosh (1999: 73) called "a more theory-friendly curriculum": CIUTI has come to stress the dual identity of interpreter (and translator) education as being both oriented towards professional practice and guided by **academic research**; more and more interpreter trainers have been taking an interest in research (to enhance their teaching or their academic career opportunities, or both); interpreting students have become increasingly exposed to theoretical analysis and reflection; many T/I schools have been more closely integrated with research-oriented departmental structures; and many students have completed **graduation theses** devoted to interpreting research. Most importantly, interpreting has increasingly become accepted as a subject worthy of doctoral research, and there has been a steady output of **PhD theses**, whose role in fueling the development of interpreting studies as an academic discipline can hardly be overestimated.

Whatever social and professional developments may shape the future of interpreting, it should be understood that interpreting studies as an academic discipline, and the concerns of scholars and researchers to date, have been closely connected with the field's socio-professional underpinnings since the early twentieth century. The academization of interpreter training has thus provided the crucial link between professionalization and the emergence of autonomous research. Against this background, we can now go on to review the 'making' and 'make-up' of the discipline with regard to its authors, centers, milestone events and publications.

2.2 Breaking Ground

The recognition of interpreting as a profession implies that there is a body of specialized knowledge and skills which is shared by its practitioners. This professional expertise is initially developed through experience and reflection, and subsequently tested and developed through systematic research. It needs to be made explicit, both for purposes of (re)presenting the profession to others in society and in support of the training of future practitioners. Hence the important role of publications which describe and develop the state of the art, and disseminate the specialized knowledge of the profession.

2.2.1 Pioneering Professionals

The earliest and probably best-known profession-building monograph on (conference) interpreting is *The Interpreter's Handbook* (*Manuel de l'interprète*) by Jean **Herbert**, which was published in 1952 in three languages. This 100-page book by one of the pioneers of the profession and first Chief Interpreter of the United Nations has an essentially pedagogical orientation. More specifically didactic is the booklet on note-taking in consecutive interpreting by Jean-François **Rozan** (1956), who taught at the *École d'Interprètes* in **Geneva**. Even before these now classic works in the interpreting literature, essays by leading interpreter personalities, such as André **Kaminker** and Günther **Haensch**, were published in *L'interprète*, the bulletin of the Geneva school's alumni association. Indeed, *L'interprète* stands out as the field's first specialist periodical, appearing years before *Babel*, the academic journal published by FIT.

Roger Glémet, another senior interpreter and teacher at the Geneva school, began his contribution to an early volume on *Aspects of Translation* by suggesting that "no one twenty years ago would have imagined that Conference Interpreting could become a subject for a serious paper" (1958: 105). While this remark accurately reflected the overall lack of systematic research on interpreting during the previous decades, there had been at least one exception: Jesús **Sanz**, a Spanish educator on a scholarship in Geneva, conducted a study on the work and abilities of conference interpreters there in the late 1920s, and presented his research at a Congress of Applied Psychology in Barcelona (Sanz 1930).

Conference interpreting had also been the subject of a pioneering master's thesis, completed by Eva **Paneth** at the University of **London** in 1957. Paneth, who had trained informally as a conference interpreter at A.T. Pilley's Linguists' Club in London, had collected observational data both on interpreting in practice and, in particular, on training methods at several interpreter schools in Europe (see Paneth 1957/2002). Yet her pioneering thesis, some passages of which were subsequently retracted in response to criticism from AIIC, remained an isolated example, and it was only a dozen years later that the first academic theses on interpreting were completed at the University of Heidelberg.

Further profession-building publications appeared in the course of the 1960s, mainly in Europe, but also in **Japan** (e.g. Fukuii and Asano 1961). In the same year as **van Hoof**'s (1962) comprehensive monograph on interpreting, a seminal article on conference interpreting, by Danica **Seleskovitch** (1962), was published in *Babel*. Seleskovitch, an early member of AIIC and its Executive Secretary at the time, went on to describe the theory and practice of international conference interpreting in a book which was originally published in 1968, appeared in English ten years later (Seleskovitch 1978a), and was deemed worth translating into German as late as 1988. In 1968, when *L'interprète dans les conférences internationales* first appeared, Patricia **Longley** published a similar, slim volume in London, and remained influential in the field until well into the 1980s.

Despite limited interaction between East and West during the Cold War, there were also notable early publications on interpreting in the Soviet Union, such as the books on consecutive interpreting and note-taking by Minyar-Beloruchev (1959, 1969).

2.2.2 Experimental Psychologists

During the 1960s, simultaneous interpreting attracted the attention of experimental psychologists. Pierre **Oléron**, a distinguished French professor who published extensively on deaf intelligence and education, co-authored what is credited as the first experimental study of simultaneous interpreting (Oléron and Nanpon 1965/2002). Based on observational and experimental data, the authors carried out measurements of the time delay (*décalage*) between the original and the interpreter's output (» 6.3.3) and found simultaneous interpreting to be a highly complex operation involving a number of rather elusive qualitative variables.

The first PhD thesis on simultaneous interpreting was completed in 1969 by Henri C. **Barik**, in the Department of Psychology of the University of North Carolina at Chapel Hill. Barik analyzed experimentally generated interpretation data for qualitative-linguistic features, in particular various types of 'error' (» 7.2.2), as well as quantitative-temporal characteristics, such as pausing and time lag (» 6.3.2–3). He shared these latter research interests with British psycholinguist Frieda **Goldman-Eisler** (1967, 1972/2002), who studied simultaneous interpreters' output as a form of spontaneous speech and focused on pausing as a 'window' on the process of language production. Another PhD thesis in psychology, on the feasibility of acquiring the skill of simultaneous listening and speaking through practice, was completed in 1969 at the University of Vienna by Ingrid **Pinter**, who was also an interpreter by training and later became a prolific author on interpreting under her married name **Kurz**. The issue of divided attention (» 6.3.1) was also among the topics studied by David **Gerver**, the leading representative of psychological interpreting research until his untimely death in 1981. In his 1971 PhD thesis at Oxford University, Gerver presented experiments on how simultaneous interpreting is affected by noise (» 6.4.1) and input speed (» 6.4.3), as well as on interpreters' memory performance (» 5.2.2). Based on his findings, he also formulated the first information-processing model of simultaneous interpreting (» 4.4.3). In 1977 Gerver co-organized an interdisciplinary symposium on interpreting research in **Venice** which brought together experts from a variety of scientific disciplines (including linguistics, cognitive psychology, sociology and artificial intelligence) as well as interpreter personalities such as Herbert and Seleskovitch. The proceedings volume of that milestone event (Gerver and Sinaiko 1978), though long out of print, remains one of the most comprehensive collections of papers on interpreting to date.

2.3 Laying Foundations

While scientists like Barik, Gerver and Goldman-Eisler were discovering (simultaneous) interpreting as an *object* of research in the late 1960s, a few personalities with a professional background in interpreting were also working towards establishing the study of interpreting (and translation) as a *subject* in academia.

2.3.1 Kade and the 'Leipzig School'

The most influential pioneer in the German-speaking area was Otto **Kade**, a teacher of Czech and Russian and self-taught conference interpreter, who spearheaded interpreter (and translator) training at the University of **Leipzig** from the late 1950s. In his doctoral dissertation, defended in 1964, Kade (1968) engaged in conceptual and theoretical groundwork for the systematic study of Translation (translation and interpreting); as an educator, he conducted a special training course for conference interpreters and introduced graduates into professional practice. Kade was appointed professor in 1969 and went on to complete a post-doctoral thesis in the 1970s. Though interpreting was not the primary concern for Kade and his colleagues of the so-called 'Leipzig School' of linguistically oriented translation studies, their few articles on the subject (e.g. Kade 1967; Kade and Cartellieri 1971) proved seminal to subsequent work such as that done in Germany by Hella **Kirchhoff** (» 4.3.2, » 4.4.2) in Heidelberg and Heidemarie **Salevsky** in (East) Berlin.

2.3.2   Chernov and the 'Soviet School'

In training as well as research activities, the 'Leipzig School' maintained close ties with the 'Soviet School' of interpreting research, as represented chiefly by Ghelly V. **Chernov** at the Maurice Thorez Institute of Foreign Languages in **Moscow**. In the late 1960s, between two six-year stints as an interpreter at the United Nations in New York, Chernov engaged in a research effort in cooperation with psychologist Irina **Zimnyaya** and conducted an experiment on the role of predictive understanding in simultaneous interpreting (» 6.1.2). While Chernov, who became a Professor in 1986, was not the only Russian author to publish a monograph on interpreting (see also Shiryayev 1979), his work (e.g. Chernov 1978, 1979/2002, 2004) clearly stands out as the most influential in the Russian literature on interpreting (» 4.4.3).

2.3.3   Seleskovitch and the 'Paris School'

Kade and Chernov, the two 'Eastern' practitioners whose research interests had launched them to professorial positions, had a highly prominent Western counterpart in Danica **Seleskovitch**. Having grown up with three languages (French, German, Serbo-Croat) and acquired English at school, she began her professional career in 1950 after completing a course in conference interpreting at the HEC business school in Paris. Seleskovitch started teaching in the late 1950s, published a seminal book in 1968, and completed a doctoral thesis on note-taking in consecutive interpreting in 1973 (see Seleskovitch 1975/2002). At her academic home base, the *École Supérieure d'Interprètes et de Traducteurs* (**ESIT**) of the University of **Paris** III/Sorbonne Nouvelle, she managed to establish a doctoral program in "*traductologie*" as early as 1974, thus "conquering the bastion of the Sorbonne," as she reportedly put it in her 1990 retirement speech.

The theoretical core of the research model at ESIT was the **Interpretive Theory of Translation** (IT), developed by Seleskovitch and her disciples on the basis of professional experience. This holistic theory, also known as the "*théorie du sens*" (García-Landa 1981), highlights the conceptual ('deverbalized') result of the interpreter's comprehension process, or **sense**, as the crucial stage in the translational process. Formulated as a triangular model (» 4.4.1), the IT conceptualizes interpreting as a knowledge-based process of 'making sense' rather than an operation on and between languages ('transcoding'). The IT approach was first applied by Seleskovitch to the study of note-taking in consecutive interpreting and then to simultaneous interpreting by her disciple, colleague and successor Marianne **Lederer** (» 4.4.2). Though their studies involved experimentally generated data, they were primarily informed by knowledge about successful professional practice, gained through observation and reflection with the aid of recordings and transcriptions.

This 'fieldwork' approach of the '**Paris School**,' and the simple formulation of the underlying theory, proved attractive to academically minded professionals, and a number of doctoral dissertations on interpreting were completed, most notably by Karla **Déjean le Féal**, Mariano **García-Landa** and Claire **Donovan-Cagigos**. Seleskovitch and Lederer went on to publish a volume of collected papers in 1984 (reissued in a fifth edition in 2014) and *Pédagogie raisonnée de l'interprétation* – a comprehensive account of the ESIT approach to interpreter training (Seleskovitch and Lederer 1989/2002). In the course of roughly a decade, from 1974 to 1984, the Paris School thus established itself as the leading center of teaching and research in the field of (conference) interpreting, with very close ties to the profession and to major institutional employers.

Scholarly exchange and research cooperation was still rather limited, however, even within the domain of conference interpreting. It is therefore not surprising that sign language interpreting and liaison/dialogue interpreting, which also emerged as objects of research in the late 1970s, remained outside the Paris-dominated mainstream. Both the proceedings of the Venice Symposium (Gerver and Sinaiko 1978) and the collective volume edited by Richard Brislin (1976b) contained papers on these 'other' areas of interpreting alongside contributions by Seleskovitch, apparently without generating any interaction. In particular, the appeal by Robert Ingram (1978) for sociological and social psychological studies of interpreters and their roles seems to have made as little impact as his admonition that "no description (practical or theoretical) of interpretation which fails to take account of sign language interpretation can be regarded as complete" (1978: 109).

2.4 Renewal and Internationalization

During the heyday of the Paris School, other types of interpreting, though gaining increasing recognition as fields of professional practice and/or objects of research, largely remained in the shadow of conference interpreting. It was not until the early 1990s that the (conference) interpreting research community showed clear signs of opening up to other domains (» 2.5.2). By that time, the community itself had undergone a process of transformation and renewal, with a new generation of researchers building on – and going beyond – existing foundations.

2.4.1 Regeneration

In the early 1980s, research-minded conference interpreters such as Daniel **Gile**, Jennifer **Mackintosh**, Barbara **Moser-Mercer** and Catherine **Stenzl** felt the need to move beyond the certainties and 'truths' established by the Paris School and to take a more descriptive, empirical approach to research on interpreting. Gile in particular had begun to undermine the Paris School's prescriptive idealization of the interpreting process with papers on such supposedly easily 'translatable' items as proper names and technical terms (Gile 1984) and sought to explain processing failures in terms of interpreters' management of their mental 'energy,' or processing capacity, using his **Effort Models** as an explanatory framework (» 4.4.2).

The master's theses completed by Mackintosh and Stenzl in London in 1983 similarly reflected this new outlook and proved more influential than their unpublished status would suggest. Mackintosh (1983) addressed the issue of message loss in direct as well as relay interpreting in a well-focused experimental study for which she devised a technique for scoring information content. Though Mackintosh made do with only seven items in her bibliography, two of her entries related to the theory of discourse processing as advanced by psychologist Walter Kintsch and text linguist Teun van Dijk (1978). This aptly illustrates the willingness of the 'new breed' of interpreting researchers to draw on insights gained in other fields and embrace **interdisciplinarity** as a key component of scientific work.

The MA thesis by Stenzl (1983) similarly drew on advances in text theory, with reference to the literature in German. Apart from her adaptation of a translation-theoretical model to interpreting (» 4.3.3), Stenzl undertook a lucid analysis of the state of the art, summarized as follows:

> The literature on simultaneous interpretation offers a limited range of experimental data and theoretical approaches, but practically no systematic observations and descriptions of interpretation in practice. ... It is fascinating to speculate about the mental processes involved in interpretation, but speculation can do no more than raise questions. If we want answers to those questions they will have to be based on facts rather than mere assumptions.
>
> (Stenzl 1983: 47)

Stenzl reiterated her appeal for systematic descriptive studies at the international symposium on conference interpreter training organized in late 1986 by the T/I school (SSLMIT) of the University of Trieste. It was at that meeting that many science-minded interpreter educators openly called into question some of the hallowed positions championed by the Paris School, and resolved to study them within a more rigorous framework of empirical research. Expressing the buoyant mood felt at the **Trieste Symposium**, Jennifer Mackintosh spoke of the beginning of "'The Trieste Era' in interpretation studies" (Gran and Dodds 1989: 268).

The Trieste School indeed became pivotal on several grounds. One was the interdisciplinary research conducted at the University of Trieste on the neurophysiological and neuropsychological foundations of bilingualism and simultaneous interpreting (» 5.1.2). No less important was the launching, in 1988, of a medium for continued networking and exchange after the Symposium. *The Interpreters' Newsletter* quickly outgrew the function suggested by its name and turned into a (roughly annual) specialized journal of interpreting research. With the publication of the proceedings of the Trieste Symposium (Gran and Dodds 1989) and other events and publications (e.g. Gran and Taylor 1990), Trieste became a hub for empirical research on interpreting, particularly with a (neuro) psychological as well as a text-linguistic orientation.

In 1990, the year in which Seleskovitch retired from university, Gile published an article on "speculative theorizing vs empirical research" in one of the volumes edited at Trieste (Gile 1990a). In this disputation, Gile gave credit to Seleskovitch for her eminently practical and didactically useful "ideas (or 'theories')" but drew attention to the lack of a scientific basis for numerous statements in the published text of her doctoral dissertation.

Gile's vision of progress for the field of conference interpreting research rested on a 'division of labor' between practicing interpreters engaging in research, or "practisearchers" (Gile 1994a), and specialists in the **cognitive sciences**. While identifying with the former, Gile acknowledged the superior research skills of scientists in established disciplines such as cognitive psychology, psycho-linguistics and applied linguistics. This interdisciplinary orientation was shared in particular by Barbara Moser-Mercer, who was among the first to draw on insights from cognitive psychology for a better understanding of the simultaneous interpreting process (e.g. Moser 1978) and has continued to champion the cause of interdisciplinary collaboration ever since. It was on her initiative, in collaboration with cognitive psychologist Dominic Massaro, that the first international peer-reviewed journal devoted solely to interpreting was founded in 1996. *Interpreting: International Journal of Research and Practice in Interpreting*, published by John Benjamins, reflected a distinctly inter-disciplinary orientation, but endeavored to cover interpreting in all its modes, modalities and settings.

2.4.2 Spreading Out

The new generation and research orientation that had emerged by the late 1980s had its roots firmly in the profession, but was at the same time inspired by the groundbreaking work of scientists such as Gerver. Active commitment to empirical study of this kind, which was also promoted in the framework of the AIIC Research Committee, happened to be shared by a number of individual interpreting scholars, also – and not least – in Eastern Europe. Experimental PhD theses were completed, including those by Heidemarie **Salevsky** (1987) and Ivana **Čeňková** (1988), reviving and following up on the pioneering work of authors like Barik, Chernov and Kade.

The expansion of the interpreting research community in the late 1980s and early 1990s was aided by several factors. One was the existence of *The Inter-preters' Newsletter*, which served as a platform for exchanging new ideas and research findings. The fact that it was published in **English**, the field's new lingua franca, made it widely accessible, despite its initially limited circula-tion. Another asset to international information exchange was a networking initiative launched in 1990 by Daniel Gile. His Interpretation Research and Theory Information Network (IRTIN), set up with 'nodes' in eight countries, aimed to collect bibliographic references, including unpublished MA and PhD theses, and disseminate this and other relevant information in the biannual '*IRTIN Bulletin*.' The Network grew rapidly, as did the information content of the *Bulletin* (now published electronically as the *CIRIN Bulletin*). Thanks mainly to Gile's untiring efforts, including international contacts and collaboration, the growing interpreting research community became increasingly aware of new developments, such as the founding of an Interpreting Research Association in **Japan** at the initiative of Masaomi **Kondo** in late 1990. That Association went on to publish its own semi-annual journal, *Tsûyaku-rironkenkyû*, and was later officially registered as the Japan Association for Interpretation Studies (JAIS), with its journal renamed *Tsûyaku Kenkyû /Interpretation Studies*. The special issue of *The Interpreters' Newsletter* on Japanese interpreting research, published in 1992, can serve as a perfect illustration of the field's first major wave of internationalization in the early 1990s.

As a fitting conclusion to a decade of renewal and international community-building, Daniel Gile and colleagues at the universities of Trieste and Turku co-organized an "International Conference on Interpreting" in 1994. The **Turku Conference** was designed to take stock of what interpreting research had achieved, and foregrounded various interdisciplinary orientations. Significantly, the program also included interpreting in non-conference settings (e.g. court, media), and a keynote paper by communication scholar Per Linell (1997) calling for a "dialogical approach to interpreting." While this broader scope is not reflected in the title of the Turku Conference proceedings (Gambier et al. 1997), the explicit concern with dialogue interpreting clearly foreshadows the kind of diversification that was about to emerge.

2.5 Integration and Diversification

At the Trieste Symposium, a number of participants stated that interpreting as an academic subject, however interdisciplinary in its theoretical and methodological approach, should be regarded as a discipline in its own right. It was not obvious, though, where in academia interpreting scholars might stake out their claim to a more or less autonomous field of study. The answer found in the early 1990s was based on the common conceptual and institutional ground shared by interpreting and translation, and interpreting studies came to be integrated into the wider field of Translation studies. At the same time, the scope of interpreting studies expanded to include interpreting in domains and settings beyond international conferences and organizations.

2.5.1 Linking Up

An ideal opportunity for the interpreting research community to promote its dual aspiration to interdisciplinarity and an academic home base of its own arose at the international "Translation Studies Congress," held at the University of **Vienna** in September 1992 (Snell-Hornby et al. 1994). The theme of that event, "Translation Studies – an Interdiscipline?," attracted leading scholars of translation and interpreting alike. Keynote speakers for translation included José Lambert and Hans Vermeer; the plenary address on interpreting was given by Daniel Gile, who appealed for a process of "opening up" toward other disciplines in what he referred to as "interpretation studies" (Gile 1994a). Gile's prominent use of a distinct disciplinary label was paralleled by Salevsky's in a programmatic paper, delivered several weeks later at an international conference in Prague, whose title featured the name of the discipline as "Interpreting Studies" (see Salevsky 1993). Designating the field in analogy with the term coined by Holmes (1972/2000) in his seminal paper on "The Name and Nature of Translation Studies" reinforced the identity of interpreting studies as a (sub)discipline within the broader field of **Translation studies** (» 3.1.1).

Benefiting from the emerging socio-academic infrastructure of Translation studies, interpreting scholars such as Gile gave visibility to their specialty within the European Society for Translation Studies (**EST**), which had been founded at the close of the Vienna Congress. Gile, who served the Society for many years, held office as a member of its Executive Board and Newsletter Editor and then, for two terms, as its President (2004–10). He also became a key associate of the CE(T)RA summer school in translation studies at the University of Leuven. A number of young scholars who participated in that program, particularly during Gile's turn as CERA Professor in 1993, went on to complete doctoral theses on interpreting. In particular, a group of Danish interpreters teaching at the **Aarhus** School of Business, including Helle **Dam**, Friedel **Dubslaff** and Anne **Schjoldager**, took up the torch: they edited a thematic issue on interpreting research for their school's journal, *Hermes: Journal of Linguistics* (no. 14, 1995), and, in early 1997, made Aarhus the venue for an international CE(T)RA-inspired **research training** seminar for PhD students of interpreting. The Aarhus Seminar ultimately led to the publication of a collective volume on *Getting Started in Interpreting Research* (Gile et al. 2001), and many of the participants became active members of the interpreting research community.

The institutional linking up of interpreting with translation studies during the early 1990s is also reflected in two publications from that period: the collective volume on *Empirical Research in Simultaneous Interpretation* edited by Lambert and Moser-Mercer (1994) as one of the first volumes in the **Benjamins Translation Library** (BTL) book series; and the special issue of *Target: International Journal of Translation Studies* devoted to *Interpreting Research*. Guest-edited by Daniel Gile, *Target* 7:1 (1995) provides a panorama of the field in the mid-1990s, including a profile of leading researchers and their affiliations; papers on methodological issues and on the implications of research on sign language interpreting; and essays on the evolution and state of interpreting research at the University of Trieste, in Eastern Europe and in Japan.

In terms of research content, the intertwining of interpreting and translation research proved more challenging. Vermeer's *skopos* **theory**, which gives priority to the function specified for the target text and draws on theories of action, culture and interaction (see Vermeer 1989/2000), had already been taken up by Stenzl (1983), who was in turn inspired by Kirchhoff, a colleague of Vermeer's at the University of Heidelberg. Kirchhoff had embraced the application of the functionalist approach to interpreting, and explicitly acknowledged the need to adapt the source text to "the communicative needs of receivers with a different sociocultural background" (1976/2002: 113). This was echoed by Stenzl in her appeal for a 'broader view' at the Trieste Symposium:

> we need a reorientation or perhaps more accurately a widening of our research framework so that rather than the predominantly psychological perspective we adopt a more functional approach that considers interpretation in the context of the entire communication process from speaker through the interpreter to the receiver. We have been paying too little attention to those who have been proposing such an approach for years, Kirchhoff, for example.
>
> (Stenzl 1989: 24)

Along these lines, Pöchhacker (1994a, 1994b, 1995a) used the functionalist 'theory of translatorial action' as a foundation for conceptual models and empirical analyses of interactional, situational and textual features of simultaneous conference interpreting (» 4.3.1). On the whole, though, the influence of the German functionalist school of thought remained limited to German-speaking scholars of interpreting.

The idea of target orientation, expressed by Seleskovitch as early as the 1960s (see 1978a: 9), was actually convergent with another significant current in Translation theory that came to inform research on interpreting in the 1990s. As the target-oriented paradigm of Descriptive Translation Studies, highlighting the notion of **translational norms** (Toury 1995), had become extended beyond its initial concern with literary translation, **Shlesinger** (1989a) discussed the application of norms to empirical research on interpreting.

One major implication of the target-oriented approach was an analytical interest in the textual product: the interpreter's output was no longer viewed mainly as a 'window' on cognitive processes, but as a product and instrument in the 'macro process' of mediated communicative interaction. The resulting concern with **text and discourse** drew interpreting scholars closer to various methodologies in such areas as text linguistics and discourse studies (« 3.1.3). Shlesinger herself did groundbreaking work in the mid-1990s on intonation and cohesion in simultaneous interpreting (Shlesinger 1994, 1995a), and she was the first to propose "corpus-based interpreting studies as an offshoot of corpus-based translation studies" (Shlesinger 1998). The latter has meanwhile become an important area of interpreting studies, whereas other discourse-based approaches to the study of interpreting were adopted, with little, if any, reference to translation theory, from sociolinguistics and sociology (» 8.2).

2.5.2 *Reaching Out*

From the perspective of interpreting studies in the 1990s, with its emerging identity as a sub-discipline within Translation studies, most research on professional domains other than conference interpreting remained out of sight. This included the impressive body of early work on signed language interpreting in the US, starting from the 1970s (see Roy and Napier 2015: Ch. 2 and 3), as well as studies on court interpreting in the 1980s. Scholars of interpreting in the spoken and the signed modality had come into contact at the Venice Symposium, but there was little sustained interaction. It was only more than a decade later that a convergence between the conference interpreting community and the domain of **signed language interpreting** made itself felt: French Sign Language interpreting became the topic of a doctoral thesis (by Philippe Séro-Guillaume) as well as a course language at ESIT; Seleskovitch published a keynote statement in the 1992 edition of the RID *Journal of Interpretation*, on whose Board of Editors she served in the 1990s; an English version of *Pédagogie raisonnée* (Seleskovitch and Lederer 1989) was published in 1995 by the RID; and Seleskovitch guest-edited a special issue of the Canadian T/I journal *Meta* (42:3, 1997) on signed language interpreting.

By the same token, some work on **court interpreting** had been done in the 1980s but remained rather marginal. Examples include the special issue of *Parallèles* (no. 11, 1989), the T/I journal published by the Geneva school, which also featured a six-page bibliography compiled by Daniel Gile. Much of this scholarly attention focused on famous international trials, however, and did not yet engage with the distinct realities of legal interpreting in intrasocial institutional settings. Groundbreaking work in this respect was done in **Canada**, where a two-day event on court interpreting was organized at the University of Ottawa as early as 1980 (Roberts 1981). A decade later, scholars there, most notably Brian **Harris** and Roda **Roberts**, became the driving forces behind the initiative that ultimately put community interpreting on the map.

In 1995, the "First International Conference on Interpreting in Legal, Health, and Social Service Settings" was held at **Geneva Park** near **Toronto**, Canada with the theme "**The Critical Link**." Though still grappling with basic professional issues, **community interpreting** presented itself there as a buoyant field, as reflected in the impressively varied volume of proceedings (Carr et al. 1997). Like the participants at the 1986 Trieste Symposium, the practitioners and scholars attending the landmark conference at Geneva Park were united in the belief that the field needed channels for international exchange and cooperation. Indeed, Critical Link was institutionalized as a triennial conference series, the second and third editions of which were held in Vancouver (1998) and Montreal (2001) before the Conference moved beyond Canada to such venues as Stockholm (2004) and Sydney (2007). Each conference resulted in the publication of a volume of selected papers in the Benjamins Translation Library series (e.g. Roberts et al. 2000; Wadensjö et al. 2007; Hale et al. 2009), regularly adding to an ever-increasing body of scholarly work on interpreting in the community.

Despite the heterogeneity of community-based settings, the Critical Link community has displayed a keen awareness of the common ground shared between community-based spoken-language and signed-language interpreters as well as between those working in legal, healthcare and other settings in a great variety of circumstances throughout the world. Apart from the Critical Link community's core group in Canada, educators and researchers like Holly **Mikkelson** and Cecilia **Wadensjö** emerged as leading authorities on the strength of their professional experience and academic achievements.

Wadensjö, in particular, provided vital theoretical and methodological inspiration to those wishing to study interpreting in **face-to-face** interaction. She drew on Bakhtinian dialogism and Erving Goffman's (e.g. 1981) sociological approach to the analysis of role performance in communicative interaction to establish a conceptual framework for the analysis of triadic interpreter-mediated encounters (» 8.1.1). Her discourse-analytical investigations of immigration-related, medical and media interviews yielded novel insights into the complex interplay of translating and 'coordinating' (discourse management) in **dialogue interpreting** (» 8.2.1).

Wadensjö's (1998) 'interactionist' approach became widely adopted in research on interpreting in a variety of community-based settings. It proved highly germane to the work of Cynthia Roy (2000a), who focused on **turn-taking** processes in sign language interpreter-mediated conversation within the framework of sociolinguistic **discourse studies**. Drawing on a range of discourse analytical approaches, including conversation analysis and the ethnography of communication, Roy (2000a: 66) provided evidence that "an interpreter's role is more than to 'just translate' or 'just interpret'," and highlighted the interpreter's contribution to the dynamics of the interaction.

Major contributions to this line of discourse analytical research on interpreting were also made by Ian **Mason**, who edited a special issue of *The Translator* (5:2, 1999) and a collective volume on *Dialogue Interpreting* (Mason 2001). The studies brought together in these volumes cover a broad range of modalities and settings, from courtroom interaction, police and asylum interviews to thera-peutic encounters to interaction in talk shows and over the phone. Alongside the various Critical Link volumes, they provide an impressive illustration of the diversification of interpreting studies in the course of the 1990s.

By the time the third landmark conference on interpreting to take place in Italy (after Venice 1977 and Trieste 1986) was held at the T/I school of the University of Bologna at **Forlì** in late 2000, the developments outlined above were clearly making themselves felt. Though only a 'local' initiative, com-pared to the multi-center cooperation underlying the 1994 Turku Conference, the Forlì Conference exceeded the latter in scope and diversity. Participants experienced a comprehensive overview of the field, with the concerns of sign language interpreters and mediators in courtroom and healthcare settings being voiced alongside those of interpreters working in EU institutions and the UN as well as in the media. The Forlì Conference thus provided a first snapshot of the breadth and diversity of *Interpreting in the 21st Century* (Garzone and Viezzi 2002), and of the research community that had established a disciplinary framework for studying it.

2.6 Consolidation

After a decade of groundbreaking scientific efforts from the mid-1960s, followed by a decade which laid the foundations of an academic field of study in its own right, and a decade of renewal and expansion from the mid-1980s, interpreting studies was developing into an increasingly wide-ranging discipline from the mid-1990s into the early twenty-first century. By 2004 it was coming into its own with growing assurance, asserting its place in the international scientific community. What followed can be characterized as a process of consolidation, visible in its position in Translation studies, its academic infrastructure, and its progress in terms of size, scope and sophistication. Thus 'consolidation' is understood here as a process of coming together and forming a unified whole – a process of gathering strength, and of developing a clear profile and position from which to move further ahead.

2.6.1 Interpreting in Translation Studies

By the early 2000s, after a decade of integration and linking up, there was no doubt that the study of interpreting constituted an integral part of Translation studies. A number of institutional indicators can serve as evidence of this close and uncontested (sub)disciplinary relationship. At the level of the scholarly community, it seems remarkable that Daniel **Gile**, the driving force behind the renewal and internationalization of the budding discipline of interpreting studies, served two terms, from 2004 to 2010, as President of the European Society for Translation Studies (EST). While interpreting studies had been part of the Society's remit from the outset, **EST** Congress programs and proceedings volumes in the new millennium testify to its sustained presence and status in this international community. Likewise, the closely related community-building initiative of the **CETRA** Research Summer School in Translation Studies based at the University of Leuven featured interpreting scholars among its staff, and two CETRA Chair professors with a background in interpreting (Miriam Shlesinger and Franz Pöchhacker, in 2007 and 2012 respectively).

With regard to scholarly output as reflected in the field's most important book series (i.e. Benjamins Translation Library), the number of **BTL** volumes devoted solely to interpreting has tended to increase, and totals roughly a dozen titles per decade. Books focusing on conference interpreting, court interpreting, signed language interpreting and community interpreting reflect the diversity of interpreting studies, and the breadth it adds to Translation studies as a whole. Interpreting is also covered extensively in John Benjamins's online *Translation Studies Bibliography* as well as in many entries of that publisher's four-volume *Handbook of Translation Studies* (Gambier and van Doorslaer 2014). The same applies to reference volumes by other publishers, such as the *Oxford Handbook of Translation Studies* (Malmkjær and Windle 2011) and the *Routledge Handbook of Translation Studies* (Millán and Bartrina 2013). Routledge in particular, however, has adopted Venuti's view that interpreting studies is a subarea of Translation studies "whose volume and degree of specialization demand separate coverage" (Venuti 2000: 2). Hence the publication of separate anthologies, introductory textbooks and, more recently, reference volumes such as *The Routledge Handbook of Interpreting* (Mikkelson and Jourdenais 2015) and the *Routledge Encyclopedia of Interpreting Studies* (Pöchhacker 2015). This parallel development of translation and interpreting studies keeps fueling the debate over the interrelation of translation research and interpreting research (e.g. Schäffner 2004), or what Shlesinger (2004) promoted under the heading of "inter-subdisciplinarity," aspects of which will be discussed in Chapter 3. At any rate, the dual status of interpreting studies – as a subdiscipline within the broader field as well as a separate specialized field of study on a par with that of written translation – provides fertile ground for multiple forms of interaction.

2.6.2 Going On, and Further

For interpreting studies as a discipline in its own right, the stability implied by the notion of 'consolidation' relates to the field's academic and institutional infrastructure as well as to a steady output of research. The latter presupposes the former, and there is evidence of growth and development in both dimensions. The number of institutions engaged in interpreter education and interpreting research throughout the world has continued to rise, not least as a result of the enormous expansion of this field in **China**. The number of Chinese universities offering master's degree programs in translation and interpreting (MTI) shows a tenfold increase, from 15 in 2007, when they were first authorized, to some 160 by the end of 2011. At least 100 of these offer interpreting courses, and half a dozen universities offer PhD programs in interpreting studies. Some of the most active centers include Beijing University of Foreign Studies, Shanghai International Studies University, Guangdong University of Foreign Studies and Xiamen University. These institutions have also been key players in the **National Conference on Interpreting**, a biennial conference series launched at Xiamen University in 1996 and linked up with the international interpreting research community by the addition of an 'International Forum' from its fifth edition, held in **Shanghai** in 2004.

Similar developments, albeit on a smaller scale, can be noted in other Asian countries, in particular the Republic of **Korea**, where such institutions as Hankuk University of Foreign Studies and Ewha Womans University, both in Seoul, have held international conferences, formed scholarly societies and published journals (including *Forum* and *Journal of Translation Studies*) featuring interpreting alongside translation. Beyond Asia, interpreting studies has acquired a solid profile at several universities in **Australia**, and its enormous potential is evident in **South Africa**, with its uniquely complex situation of multilingualism and coexisting cultural communities. Aspects of this complexity and potential with regard to the practice and study of interpreting are obviously present also in other countries and regions of the world; the First

Brazilian Symposium on Interpreting Studies, held at the University of São Paulo in 2013, is a case in point.

Aside from its geographical spread, making interpreting studies 'bigger' and 'broader,' its consolidated development in the early twenty-first century also reflects increasing levels of **specialization**. While the successive Critical Link conferences and proceedings volumes, together with a similar conference series on community interpreting launched at the University of **Alcalá** in 2002, and another one in **Berlin** in 2013, reflect steady progress, interpreting scholars have increasingly been drawn to international events devoted to specific topics. Examples include the two international conferences on **quality** in interpreting held at **Almuñécar**, Spain, in 2001 and 2011; the 2008 Symposium on **aptitude** for interpreting in **Antwerp**, and the two conferences held there in 2011 and 2013 in the framework of the EU-funded AVIDICUS project on **remote interpreting**; biennial conferences on **non-professional interpreting** and translation, started at the University of Bologna at **Forlì** in 2012; the first international workshop there, in 2015, on **corpus-based interpreting studies**; and the first international workshop on **multimodality** in dialogue interpreting, at the University of Surrey in 2015.

Such gatherings of specialists within interpreting studies as well as experts from related disciplines are invariably reflected in the field's published literature, in the form of proceedings volumes, peer-reviewed collections of selected papers, special issues of journals, or individual research articles. The infrastructure for reporting on research is quite readily available. The media of publication created in the 1990s, such as the BTL book series and **journals** such as *Perspectives, The Translator* and *Interpreting* (the latter having been re-launched in 2004 with a new editorial team), are now well established and have gone from strength to strength; in addition, authors of research on interpreting have access to newly founded journals, often involving interpreting scholars as members of the editorial team or advisory board. Examples include *Translation and Interpreting Studies*, the journal of the American Translation and Interpreting Studies Association (ATISA), published since 2006; *Translation & Interpreting*, an online journal launched in 2009; as well as two international journals devoted specifically to (translator and) **interpreter education** – *The Interpreter and Translator Trainer* (since 2007) and the *International Journal of Interpreter Education* (since 2009).

Needless to say, the steady increase in the quantity of publications requires major efforts at quality assurance if standards of excellence for research are to be ensured. Aside from strict **peer-reviewing** policies, the aspiration toward high scientific standards has been pursued by various **research training** initiatives. These include postgraduate conferences, where young researchers can present work in progress and receive constructive input (e.g. IPCITI, an annual collaborative effort by four universities on the British Isles), and PhD and summer schools in translation and interpreting along similar lines to CETRA (» 12.5.4).

In the light of these developments, one can safely claim that the discipline that came into its own by the early years of the twenty-first century has held

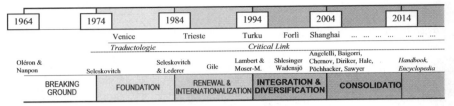

Figure 2.1 Decades of development in interpreting studies

its ground and made further progress in several respects. Not only has it become more far-reaching in terms of geographical spread and thematic scope, and strengthened its academic and institutional infrastructure, but it has also developed a sharper and more coherent profile as a dynamic and varied field of study. The *Encyclopedia of Interpreting Studies* (Pöchhacker 2015), a joint effort by more than 130 authors from some 30 different countries, aptly reflects the process of consolidation that now characterizes the discipline's development.

Figure 2.1 offers a graphic summary of the field's evolution, divided into ten-year periods from 1964 to 2014. In addition to the five roughly decade-long **phases** of development, the diagram includes **places, people** and **publications** for illustration. The place names underneath the timeline at the top refer to conferences that can be regarded as milestones in the emergence and development of the scientific community, whereas the terms '*traductologie*' and 'Critical Link' merely indicate that the early concern with the academic study of conference interpreting has been increasingly complemented by community interpreting as a more recent object of research. The space further down contains the names of authors whose publications coincide with the chronological reference points of the diagram (e.g. Oléron and Nanpon 1965, Seleskovitch 1975, Seleskovitch and Lederer 1984, Lambert and Moser-Mercer 1994, etc.); in addition, names like Gile, Shlesinger and Wadensjö are included to reflect the broader influence of these authors in the respective decade(s). On the far right, the two reference volumes mentioned above, both published in 2015, are listed as indicators of the level of consolidation achieved in interpreting studies by the mid-2010s.

Summary

Against the background of the *twentieth-century professionalization* of interpreting, with particular regard to the increasing *academization of training*, this chapter has reviewed several stages in the evolution of interpreting studies, roughly indicating *who* did *what*, and what happened *when*, and *where*. Following the groundbreaking efforts of *pioneering practitioners of conference interpreting* and *experimental psychologists* in the 1950s and 1960s, *academic foundations* for the field were laid in the 1970s, especially at ESIT in Paris under the leadership of Danica Seleskovitch. From the mid-1980s, the conference interpreting research community saw a period of *renewal* and *internationalization*, driven not least by the efforts of Daniel Gile and a new generation of like-minded researchers. Benefiting from closer links with the Translation studies community and its newly emerging socio-academic infrastructure, interpreting studies experienced *integration* as well as a *diversification* of the settings and domains in its purview in the course of the 1990s. Thanks to the Critical Link conference series in Canada and various related developments, *community interpreting,* including the concerns of previously neglected domains such as *court interpreting* and *signed language interpreting,* became prominent as an area in need of training and research. Scholars such as Cecilia Wadensjö and Cynthia Roy introduced innovative research approaches appropriate to the discourse-based analysis of interpreting in community-based domains, thus broadening the emerging discipline's theoretical and methodological scope. By the early years of the new millennium, interpreting studies had come into its own as a discipline, and since then has maintained its momentum. Fueled not least by vigorous growth in Asia, and China in particular, interpreting studies has achieved consolidation by strengthening its academic and institutional infrastructure and further extending its range of scientific interests and research output.

Sources and Further Reading

For information on the field's professional underpinnings, see the relevant chapters ("Conference Interpreting," "Community Interpreting," "Signed Language Interpreting," etc.) in *The Routledge Handbook of Interpreting* (Mikkelson and Jourdenais 2015) as well as CONFERENCE INTERPRETING, COMMUNITY INTERPRETING, LEGAL INTERPRETING, HEALTHCARE INTERPRETING and SIGNED LANGUAGE INTERPRETING in Pöchhacker (2015).

For the development and status of interpreting studies as an academic discipline, see Gambier et al. (1997), Gile (1994a, 1995a, 2000), Pöchhacker (2010b) as well as INTERPRETING STUDIES and more specific entries, such as GERVER, VENICE SYMPOSIUM, PARIS SCHOOL, SELESKOVITCH, SOVIET SCHOOL, CHERNOV, TRIESTE SYMPOSIUM, *THE INTERPRETERS' NEWSLETTER, CIRIN BULLETIN,* CRITICAL LINK and *INTERPRETING,* in Pöchhacker (2015).

Suggestions for Further Study

* What is the status of various interpreting domains in countries and regions other than those referred to in this chapter?

- What is the academic status there of interpreting and interpreter education, and how has it been changing over the years?
- How has research on interpreting evolved, in terms of publications, PhD programs, etc., in countries and languages other than those mentioned in this chapter?
- When and where does the interpreting literature in languages other than English reflect evidence of interaction between various domains of the profession, between interpreting and translation research, and between interpreters and specialists in other academic disciplines?

3   Approaches

Against the background of the evolution of interpreting studies described in Chapter 2, we now turn to the ideas and forms of inquiry which make up its substance. This chapter will first review the main disciplinary perspectives from which research on interpreting has been approached, and then discuss the major conceptual and methodological orientations of interpreting studies in terms of its memes, methods and paradigms.

> The **main points** covered in this chapter are:
>
> - the disciplinary perspectives from which inquiry into interpreting has been launched
> - the key ideas, or 'memes,' which inform past and present thinking about interpreting
> - the interplay of theory and methodology, and major methodological orientations
> - the main research traditions, or paradigms, in the study of interpreting

3.1 Disciplinary Perspectives

The field of interpreting studies has been strongly shaped by conceptual and methodological approaches from other, more established disciplines. Taking stock of its central ideas and theoretical frameworks therefore presupposes an awareness of these varied disciplinary perspectives and of the way these disciplines themselves evolved and developed over time.

3.1.1 Studying Interpreting as Translation

Having positioned interpreting studies within the wider field of Translation studies (« 1.2.2), we would naturally assume that the fundamental ideas and research approaches of translation scholars also inform inquiry into the translational activity of interpreting. And yet research on interpreting has been sourced from translation studies only to a very limited degree. Translation scholars have mostly defined their object in the narrower sense, as limited to the written medium, and have seen little need to fit their models and methods to interpreting. Indeed, the number of those who have adopted a comprehensive conception of Translation, including all and any translational activity, is very small. Scholars such as Holmes, Toury and Vermeer, who have sought, in principle, to account for interpreting in their theories, have tended to neglect it in their research practice; understandably perhaps, considering the strongly profession-based tradition and, at times, defensive attitude of the mainstream (conference) interpreting research community, and considering the elusive nature of the phenomenon, so much less convenient to study than language fixed in writing. This lack of attention from translation scholars was largely reciprocated by their interpreting counterparts, who showed little if any awareness of how they might draw on potentially relevant work dealing with written translation.

It was only in the early 1990s that influential approaches to (written) translation, including concepts like target-text function ('skopos') and translational norms, began to be explored in the field of interpreting (» 2.5.1). Toward the end of that decade efforts to reaffirm the common ground shared by the Translation studies community gathered momentum. A position paper on "Shared Ground in Translation Studies" by Chesterman and Arrojo (2000) drew numerous constructive responses, including two by leading authors in interpreting studies. This suggests that, at least at the fundamental levels of **epistemology** and **methodology**, basic insights from research on translation were being brought across into interpreting studies and helping lay down broader-based foundations for it (» 3.2.1). In more concrete terms, some methods used by translation researchers were successfully adapted to the study of interpreting. Examples include the retrospective protocols inspired by think-aloud protocols (TAPs) used in translation process research (e.g. Vik-Tuovinen 2002), and corpus-based studies of interpreting drawing on concepts, tools and insights from corpus-based translation studies, as envisaged by Shlesinger (1998). Though corpus-based interpreting studies took some time to emerge, it has since developed into a highly productive line of inquiry (e.g. Setton 2011; Straniero Sergio and Falbo 2012). On the whole, however, the evolution of research on interpreting has been shaped not so much by its sibling discipline as by research undertaken from a range of psychological, linguistic and sociological perspectives and such fields as communication studies, education and neuroscience.

3.1.2 Psychological Approaches

Among the disciplines which have some bearing on the study of interpreting, the most prominent is clearly the field of **psychology**, whose conceptual and methodological approaches have shaped the study of (simultaneous) conference interpreting. Some of the earliest studies of simultaneous interpreting (e.g. Treisman 1965) were still done in the behaviorist tradition of **experimental psychology**, measuring 'verbal behavior' in terms of 'stimulus' and 'response.' From the late 1960s, this gave way to a focus on the cognitive workings inside the 'black box.'

Under the broad heading of **cognitive psychology**, various currents can be identified: **psycholinguistics** studies how human language is acquired and used, and has tended to be most closely associated with linguistic theories (e.g. with a focus on lexical and grammar processing skills); early cognitive psychologists, including David Gerver (» 2.2.2), applied the computer metaphor to human information processing and took a special interest in storage operations and memory structures; the psychology of **memory**, and of working memory in particular (» 5.2.3), was pursued not only in a computational framework but also in the neural network (or parallel distributed processing) approach that emerged in the interdisciplinary field of **cognitive science** in the late 1980s; increasing interest was devoted to language comprehension and strategic **discourse processing** (e.g. Kintsch 1998); and the use of constructed laboratory tasks lost ground to the study of real-world fields of **expertise**, including simultaneous interpreting (Ericsson 2000).

Well into the 1990s, cognitive approaches, which typically rely on hypothetical constructs such as memory structures and strategic operations, were largely distinct from neuropsychological approaches, which center on neurophysiological activity during language processing in the brain. As **neuroscience** has advanced, however, there has been increasing convergence, leading to the emergence of cognitive neuroscience as the most sophisticated framework to date for studying language and cognition (» 5.1.3).

3.1.3 Linguistic Approaches

Complex sub- and interdisciplinary convergences and major reorientations also characterize the second broadly labeled field which is commonly viewed as a logical source for interpreting studies – **linguistics**. In the 1960s, when interest in a scientific account of translation and interpreting was emerging, linguists still seemed to be concerned mainly with the study of phonology, lexis and grammar of language as a system (or as *langue*, in Saussure's terms). This is what prompted Seleskovitch and the Paris School (« 2.3.3) to formulate an antithetical position that centered on actual language use (*parole*) in communicative contexts. Nor was there much enthusiasm among early interpreting scholars for studies in **contrastive linguistics**, most of which remained at the level of phrases and isolated sentences.

A major impetus came when the boundaries of linguistic analysis were extended beyond the sentence in the 1970s. As linguists broadened their purview to engage with text and discourse in social situations, some influential new theoretical frameworks were developed: **systemic functional linguistics** (e.g. Halliday 1985) views language as a social semiotic system and combines a text-oriented analysis (e.g. in terms of 'texture') with an account of the communicative context (using notions such as 'field' and 'tenor'); likewise, **text linguistics** (e.g. Beaugrande and Dressler 1981) studies textual features (e.g. 'cohesion') as well as parameters of text use in communicative situations. The work of Beaugrande (1980), in particular, was informed by advances in the interdiscipline of cognitive science that emerged in the 1970s. This convergence of cognitive and linguistic perspectives is aptly illustrated in collaborative work by Kintsch and van Dijk (e.g. 1978) on discourse comprehension, which had a major impact on the study of interpreting (» 6.1.2). While 'text' and 'discourse' were used in a closely related sense in the 1980s, the broader notion of **discourse studies** came to prevail over 'text linguistics.' Indeed, the notion of 'discourse' has come to be used in such a variety of fields as to defy a standard definition. By the late 1990s, discourse studies, in various ramifications, had far outgrown the realm of linguistics and was considered a multidisciplinary entity covering the study of social interaction as well as linguistic structures and processes (see van Dijk 1997a, 1997b).

The study of language use in social interaction was also pursued as early as the 1960s in the framework of interactional **sociolinguistics** as conceived by Gumperz and Hymes (1972). Viewing language as situated communication between speakers and hearers engaged in purposeful activity, these scholars laid the groundwork for the prevailing discourse-based approaches to research on interpreting (« 2.5.2). Of key concern to linguists and sociologists alike, the various approaches to **discourse analysis** that have developed from these foundations are difficult to bring under a single disciplinary label. Applied to such fields as healthcare and the law, they tend to form interdisciplinary links of their own, as in the case of **health communication** and **forensic linguistics**.

More distinctly linguistic approaches that eventually came to inform research on interpreting are **pragmatics** and **computational linguistics**, albeit again with important interdisciplinary components. A subfield of linguistics and semiotics, pragmatics is yet another early reaction to Saussurean structuralist linguistics, and focuses on the way context contributes to meaning. Key contributions include **speech act theory** and Grice's Cooperative Principle, which served as major sources of inspiration for the more recent framework of relevance theory (Sperber and Wilson 1986/1995). This in turn comes under the broader heading of **cognitive pragmatics**, which studies linguistic aspects of language use in the framework of cognitive science. The resulting interdiscipline, roughly contemporary with interpreting studies, includes the application of computer science to the study of language processing. After decades of spectacular progress in information and communication technologies, such computational applications are more accessible and powerful than ever before, and have greatly enhanced the potential of **corpus linguistics** to inform the study of interpreted text and discourse.

3.1.4 'Cultural' Approaches

Sociolinguistic approaches to the study of language use in interaction, which came to the fore in the early 1970s, were also informed by insights from **anthropology**. Thus, the **ethnography of communication** (originally labeled the 'ethnography of speaking'), developed by linguistic anthropologist Dell **Hymes**, rests on the view that the assumptions and beliefs shared by a speech community, or 'culture,' guide the way people think and (inter)act. This concept proved particularly relevant to the study of **intercultural communication**, which emerged in the 1960s in the US, spearheaded by anthropologists like Edward T. **Hall**. While of obvious relevance to the mediation of communication across cultures (see Brislin 1976a), these theoretical and methodological frameworks remained out of sight for interpreting scholars until they were brought to bear on the emerging domain of community interpreting two or three decades later (e.g. Angelelli 2000).

Beyond these roots in cultural anthropology, the more recent advent of the broadly interdisciplinary perspective of **cultural studies**, with its various historical, literary and postcolonial orientations, has had little impact on interpreting research to date. One prominent exception is the call by Michael Cronin (2002) for a "cultural turn" in interpreting studies, which also offers points of interface with more recent approaches from the field of sociology.

3.1.5 Sociological Approaches

Aside from some roots of current discourse analytical approaches, most notably the tradition of **conversation analysis** as developed by sociologist Harvey Sacks and his associates (Sacks et al. 1974), sociology as the study of human social behavior and institutions had little impact on interpreting research until the 1990s. The early contribution by Bruce Anderson (1976/ 2002), who pointed to the research potential of issues like situational constellations and role conflict as well as the power and relative status of participants, was only rediscovered two decades later. One particularly important source of influence from sociology was Erving Goffman, some of whose major works date back to the 1950s: his analysis of face-to-face interaction and participation in discourse (e.g. Goffman 1981) strongly inspired the work of Wadensjö (« 2.5.2) and became a cornerstone of the micro-sociological study of dialogue interpreting (» 8.1.1).

On the macro-sociological level, the **social theory** of Pierre Bourdieu stands out as the most influential framework. Key constructs such as habitus, field, and symbolic capital have proved attractive to scholars studying the translating profession(s) and the power and status of interpreters (and translators) in society (see Inghilleri 2005a).

All the disciplinary perspectives reviewed above have contributed to research on interpreting, either through specialists in these fields taking a direct interest in the subject or as sources of conceptual and methodological tools taken up by interpreting scholars. Clearly, then, there is an impressive variety of disciplinary vantage points which have shaped the view of interpreting as an object of study. The following section takes stock of these various conceptions in terms of the 'memes,' or recurring ideas, of interpreting studies.

3.2 Memes of Interpreting

The notion of 'memes' is used here in relation to Chesterman's (1997) account of *Memes of Translation*. The socio-biological concept of 'meme,' which was introduced in the mid-1970s, refers to ideas, practices, creations and inventions that have spread and replicated, like genes, in the cultural evolution of mankind. Chesterman applies this construct to the evolution of thinking about translation. He identifies eight stages, or memes, and associates these with metaphors illustrating particular ways of 'seeing' and **theorizing** the phenomenon.

In what follows I will similarly review the evolution of thinking about interpreting, and propose five memes or dominant ideas. Like Chesterman (1997), I will regard some of these 'ways of seeing' as so broad and pervasive as to constitute 'supermemes.' These will first be presented and briefly discussed, while also introducing the individual memes that will then be presented in greater detail (» 3.2.3–7). Two of the supermemes – **process(ing)** and **communicative activity** (» 3.2.2) – have been identified specifically for interpreting; others correspond to the five supermemes listed by Chesterman and need to be accounted for here if we conceive of interpreting as a form of **Translation**.

3.2.1 Interpreting as Translation

The five ideas which Chesterman (1997) elevates to the status of supermemes of translation are: the **source–target** metaphor, the idea of **equivalence**, the myth of **untranslatability**, the **free-vs-literal** dichotomy, and the idea that all **writing is** a kind of **translating**. The last-mentioned item reflects Chesterman's focus on (written) translation rather than Translation as a hypernym and need not concern us here, though a somewhat parallel idea will be discussed later in the sense that 'all understanding is interpreting' (» 3.2.4). The remaining four supermemes of translation are easily shown to be equally present, though not always made explicit, in theoretical approaches to interpreting. Most pervasive is perhaps the free-vs-literal dichotomy, in such terminological guises as 'meaning-based' vs 'form-based interpreting,' or 'interpreting proper' vs 'transcoding.' The issue of untranslatability would appear to be of more concrete concern to interpreters than to translators, given the real-time performance constraints which define the activity of interpreting. Nevertheless, except for some references to forms of expression which have commonly been considered unsuitable for interpreting, like poetry or wordplay, the issue of untranslatability has received little attention in interpreting studies. The idea of equivalence is not nearly as prominent in the discourse of interpreting as in translation theory, though it may be a tacit assumption underlying much work on 'accuracy' and 'errors' in conference interpreting research. The source–target metaphor, finally, is practically a *sine qua non* for interpreting, given the situational immediacy linking the two acts of discourse.

3.2.2 Process(ing) vs Communicative Activity

Viewing interpreting first and foremost as a **process** is probably the most influential supermeme in interpreting studies. While the notion of 'process' can also be construed much more broadly (see Linell 1997: 50), its use in the discourse on interpreting has largely been confined to the more specific sense of **processing** operations transforming an input into an output. Gile (1994b: 40) represents this conception as "a process P acting on an input I and producing an output O" (Figure 3.1).

The generic process structure can be instantiated for various types of input and output. Most typically, the interpreting process has been conceptualized as a process acting on 'verbal material,' as a transfer of words and structures from a source language to a target language. The notion of **verbal transfer** is thus a widespread meme of interpreting (» 3.2.3) within the broader conceptual sphere of the process(ing) supermeme. It continues to shape lay perceptions of interpreting (and translation), just as it informed early research on interpreting in experimental psychology.

As psychologists turned from observing verbal behavior to speculating about the mental operations taking place in the 'black box,' researchers' attention shifted from the verbal input–output relationship to the mental process as such. Drawing on advances in information theory and cognitive psychology, interpreting was conceptualized as a set of information processing operations rather like those in a digital data processing device (i.e. a computer). The human processor was assumed to perform a number of cognitive skills, such as speech recognition, memory storage and verbal output generation, the combination of which would account for the complex task of interpreting. This concern with **cognitive information processing skills** arguably remains the most widespread meme in interpreting studies to date (» 3.2.5).

A supermeme of interpreting which is largely complementary to the idea of process(ing) is the notion of interpreting as a **communicative activity** performed by a human being in a particular situation of interaction. In this more 'naturalistic' perspective, interpreting is seen as a combined listening and speaking activity to enable communication.

Strongly shaped by the views of practitioners in the formative decades of the conference interpreting profession, the overall idea of the interpreter's

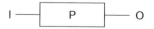

Figure 3.1 The process(ing) supermeme (from Gile 1994b: 40)

communicative activity found its most emblematic expression in the meme of **making sense**, which conceptualizes the interpreter's task as grasping the intended meaning ('sense') of an original speaker and expressing it for listeners in another language (» 3.2.4). In subsequent theorizing, the idea of interpreters actually performing a communication service appears to have been taken for granted. The communicative-activity supermeme was thus, to all intents and purposes, largely overlooked: it received explicit theoretical attention only when scholars of Translation began to enlarge their sphere of interest in the 1980s and, more importantly perhaps, when previously neglected types of interpreting first emerged as challenging objects of study. This gave rise to two more memes within the broader conceptual sphere of the communicative-activity supermeme: **text/discourse production** (» 3.2.6) and **mediation** (» 3.2.7). The former is largely shaped by theories of text, discourse and translation, while the latter is closely linked to the sociology of interaction; and both share a concern with the cross-cultural dimension of mediated communication.

The five memes of interpreting which have been introduced in this section under the umbrella of the process(ing) and communicative-activity supermemes will be discussed in greater detail in the following subsections, with regard to their prevalence in particular periods and disciplinary contexts.

3.2.3 Verbal Transfer

The most "primitive" conception of interpreting – and of Translation in general (see Chesterman 1997: 20f) – is that of a process in which words in one language are converted into words in another language. The underlying assumption of what St Jerome captured in the phrase "*verbum exprimere e verbo*" is that words contain meanings and serve as the elementary building blocks of a language. Thus a speech made up of words in one language would be reassembled by the interpreter, using target-language words with corresponding meanings, and the ease or difficulty of the task would essentially depend on the nature of the verbal material.

The view of interpreting (and translation) as an operation on and between languages makes bilingual competence seem a necessary, and sufficient, condition for performing the translational task. Conversely, it suggests that bilingualism implies the facility of switching from a word in one language to its 'other-language equivalent.' This assumption informed experimental research on the verbal behavior of bilinguals in the 1950s. Shaped by contemporary psychological approaches, bilingualism researchers measured the degree of automaticity of **word-translation** tasks by examining their bilingual subjects' response times to verbal stimuli (see Lambert 1978). Four decades later, the experimental designs of some cognitive-psychological and neurolinguistic studies on bilingual processing (e.g. de Groot 1997), though linked to a more profound understanding of the interpreting process, were nevertheless reminiscent of the traditional word-based transfer view.

The verbal-transfer meme also thrived in association with the information-theoretical mathematical model of communication, advanced in the late 1940s by Shannon and Weaver (1949). Based on the analogy of electrical signal transmission, Translation was viewed as a combined decoding and encoding operation involving the switching of linguistic code signals. The translator/interpreter, as a special type of 'transmitter' between a 'source' and a 'receiver,' was thus seen as 'switching signals' of one information-bearing 'code' to those of another. This conception of linguistic **transcoding** became firmly rooted as one of the most powerful metaphors of Translation among psychologists and linguists alike. In early psycholinguistic experiments, for instance, the focus was on the extra time required by the 'code-switching operation' in simultaneous interpreting in comparison to the monolingual repetition of verbal input known as 'shadowing' (» 6.3.3).

With regard to the 'recoding' of grammatical structures, German, with its distinct structural features among contemporary European conference languages, appeared to pose a particular challenge, and became a target for syntax-oriented studies of simultaneous interpreting. In the late 1960s, scholars at the University of Leipzig, who saw linguistics as the most promising scientific framework for the study of translational phenomena (« 2.3.1), sought to identify not only **lexical equivalence** relations but also **syntactic regularities** and correspondence rules determining the "optimum moment" for starting production in simultaneous interpreting (see Kade and Cartellieri 1971). Nevertheless, Kade and his associates also realized that the interpreter's processing of the "chain of linguistic signs" could be overridden by knowledge-based anticipation (» 6.5.2), as studied in the 1974 MA thesis by Nanza Mattern and reported by Wolfram Wilss (1978). It had thus emerged by the early 1970s that the (simultaneous) interpreting process could not be explained as a direct linguistic transfer of lexical units and syntactic structures, but was evidently mediated by some form of cognitive representation in memory.

3.2.4 Making Sense

The distinction between 'transcoding' and interpreting is central to the account of the interpreting process developed by Seleskovitch (« 2.3.3). On the strength of her professional experience in consecutive interpreting, Seleskovitch, like Herbert (1952), saw the interpreter primarily as a listener and speaker. Consequently, she regarded **understanding** ('making sense of') what had been expressed in a source language, and **re-expressing** the speaker's intended meaning, or *vouloir dire*, in a way that would 'make sense' to the target-language audience as the main components of the interpreter's work.

In what Seleskovitch termed the Interpretive Theory of Translation (*'théorie du sens'*), the interpreter, rather than rendering words ('transcoding'), combines perceptual input with prior **knowledge** (of the situational context and the subject matter as well as of languages) to derive 'deverbalized' **sense**. While

Seleskovitch (1978a: 11) would stress that "[t]o interpret one must first understand," her theory at the same time suggests that all understanding is interpreting, in the hermeneutic sense of 'interpretation.' In a broader translation-theoretical context, the sense-making vs transcoding distinction, for which Seleskovitch (1978a: 19) also offered the simile of representing an object by a painting (= an interpretation) vs a photograph (= a translation), echoes the supermeme of literal vs free translation. Indeed, the meme of making sense does not capture an aspect unique to interpreting; rather, its innovative force lies, or lay, in the prominent role attributed to context and prior knowledge at a time when pioneers in the emerging interdiscipline of cognitive science were only beginning to realize that understanding involved the activation of knowledge structures in a combination of 'bottom-up' and 'top-down' operations.

On the production side, the linkage between knowledge and making sense was given less prominent attention. It is clearly implied, however, when Seleskovitch demands that the interpreter's target-language utterance "must be geared to the recipient" (1978a: 9). If the interpreter's mission is to enable understanding, s/he must adapt the message to the audience's prior knowledge or, as Seleskovitch (1978a: 100) puts it, "cultural frames of reference," so as to ensure that it will make sense and that the target text will fulfil its **function** in the target culture. One can therefore speak of a target-oriented version of the sense-making meme, which found its most comprehensive expression in Hans Vermeer's *skopos* theory of translational action (see Vermeer 1989/2000). This 'functionalist' approach was expressly applied also to simultaneous interpreting (e.g. Kirchhoff 1976/2002) and proved influential especially among German-speaking authors. Its broader significance becomes apparent in interpreting settings beyond international conferences and organizations. In community-based domains, the primary parties are typically of unequal social status and highly discrepant educational backgrounds. In such situations, the demand to use "the verbal form best suited to understanding by the audience" (Seleskovitch 1976: 109) becomes a critical challenge. If what the interpreter says must make sense against the listener's horizon of socio-cultural knowledge, and if the interpreter is the only person capable of assessing that knowledge, s/he may well have to paraphrase, explain or simplify in order to achieve the **communicative effect** desired by the speaker (» 7.3).

3.2.5 Cognitive Information Processing Skills

Whereas behaviorist psychologists had scorned any theorizing about internal processes in favor of observing behavioral responses, cognitive psychologists hypothesized various **mental structures and procedures** responsible for the processing of verbal data, mostly by drawing on analogies with digital data processing. With the **computer** as a metaphor of the human information processing system, Gerver (1971: viii) defined the interpreting task as "a fairly complex form of human information processing involving the reception, storage, transformation, and transmission of verbal information." In this conceptual framework, some of the dominant research issues have included the **processing capacity** of the human information processing system, the possibility of dividing attention over various tasks (**multi-tasking**), and the structure and function of its **memory** component(s). To make the complex task amenable to experimental study, language processing as such is further decomposed in the information processing approach into such subtasks or **component skills** as phoneme and word recognition, lexical disambiguation, syntactic processing ('parsing') and knowledge-based inferencing. Many insights into these issues in 'natural language processing,' which constitutes a major field of interdisciplinary research in cognitive science, have been brought to bear on the study of simultaneous interpreting and its component processes (see Moser-Mercer et al. 1997).

With the emergence of the 'connectionist' or parallel distributed processing approach in cognitive science, individual language processing tasks have increasingly been implemented in **neural network** models. As an alternative to computer-like **symbol processing**, the 'subsymbolic' approach has also been applied to cognitive skills in simultaneous interpreting (e.g. MacWhinney 1997; Paradis 2000). Irrespective of the cognitive architecture posited to explain the language processing skills involved in interpreting, the meme of cognitive information processing has proved highly influential, not only for the construction of models of the interpreting process (» 4.4.3) but also for various pedagogical applications.

3.2.6 Text/Discourse Production

Whether it is viewed as a process or a communicative activity, there can be little doubt that interpreting is a production-oriented activity. The question, then, is how the output produced by the interpreter can best be characterized in analytical terms. Herbert (1952: 23) likened the interpreter to "a good public speaker," which would suggest **rhetoric** as a framework of analysis; psycholinguists would study the interpreter's output as **speech**, with particular attention to temporal features such as pauses; and cognitive psychologists have focused on aspects like information or **propositional content**. As long as linguists remained preoccupied with lexical meaning and syntactic structure, they had little to say about the interpreter's output beyond these restricted categories. It was only with the reorientation of linguistics in the 1970s towards language use in communication that more holistic conceptualizations of language production came to the fore (» 3.1.3). The notion of **text** as a complex web of relations guided by a communicative intention, as developed in particular in the text-linguistic approach of Beaugrande and Dressler (1981), was readily adopted by scholars of Translation. Interpretations, too, have been described as texts in terms of standards of **textuality**, such as cohesion, coherence, and intertextuality (» 7.1.2). Those wishing to foreground the **orality** of the interpreter's output (» 7.1.3) have tended to draw on related theoretical frameworks with a stronger focus on oral language, such as

Halliday's (1985) systemic functional linguistics and a range of other approaches centered on the notion of **discourse**. The conceptual distinction between 'text' and 'discourse' is anything but clear, and is sometimes a matter of geolinguistic tradition and intellectual preference. Whatever the designation and analytical framework, though, the dual text/discourse meme of interpreting has proved a highly significant guiding idea which also underlies **corpus-linguistic methods**.

An important point about the idea of text processing is that, while it remains a focal point of cognitively oriented approaches to discourse, it tends to reflect a **monologic** bias; that is, a view of discourse in which a text is produced by an active speaker and received by an audience. This view has proved useful as a reflection of the typical constellation at international conferences, but it is less suitable for the analysis of communicative settings where the adoption of speaker and listener roles is much more dynamic, and the immediate co-presence of the interlocutors in face-to-face communication favors an inherently interactive flow of discourse. It is this **dialogic** view of discourse as a joint activity which informs the work of Wadensjö (1998) on dialogue interpreting (» 8.2). And yet, Wadensjö's distinction between "talk as activity" and "talk as text," which highlights the dual nature of the text/ discourse production meme, suggests not a contradictory but a complementary way of conceptualizing the interpreter's activity, since the two approaches correspond to different levels of analysis (1998: 21). Indeed, her description of what else happens, other than text production, at the level of interpreting as an "(inter)activity" points to yet another way of seeing interpreting: what Wadensjö analyzes as **discourse management** in triadic interaction will be discussed here under the heading of 'mediation.'

3.2.7 Mediation

Like the meme of making sense, the mediation meme is, in many ways, a 'basic' idea associated with interpreting, and can indeed be traced to its deepest etymological roots (« 1.1). Prototypically, the interpreter, whether professional or not, is "the man (or woman) in the middle" (Knapp-Potthoff and Knapp 1987) – an **intermediary**, not so much between the languages involved as between the communicating individuals and the institutional and socio-cultural positions they represent. The interpreter's two clients, as incumbents of particular roles, have their own intentions and expectations in the communicative interaction. More often than not, these will come into conflict and will force the interpreter to take action as a 'mediator' – not as a broker or conciliator in a negotiation, but as an agent regulating the evolution of understanding. An apparently simple example of speaker conflict is simultaneous or overlapping talk. This requires the interpreter to impose priorities on the primary parties' **turn-taking** behavior and to structure the flow of discourse in a **gatekeeping** capacity, 'coordinating participation' in the interaction (» 8.2.1). In the more critical case of one party signaling a lack of understanding, the interpreter's mission of communication is at stake and may require some form of

intervention. Indeed, Knapp-Potthoff and Knapp (1986) found that a lay interpreter performing "linguistic mediation" would often shape the mediated interaction as an active **third party** rather than remain **neutral** and 'invisible.' Such findings have shone the spotlight on the complex issue of the interpreter's **role** – that is, the question of what (else), other than relaying messages, the interpreter is expected and permitted to do in order to facilitate understanding in a communicative event (» 10.3.2).

The discussion of role issues has been associated in particular with dialogue interpreting in community-based settings, where the constellation of interaction is typically characterized by unequal power relations and widely discrepant socio-cultural backgrounds between which the interpreter is charged to mediate. And yet mediation as part of the interpreter's role and task is no less relevant, in principle, to international conference interpreting (see Kirchhoff 1976/2002: 113; Seleskovitch 1978a: 100). Jones, writing from many years of professional experience, argues that conference interpreters may need to intervene actively, for example "by providing the requisite explanations or even changing the original speaker's references" (Jones 1998: 4), in order to overcome "cultural difficulties." Thus, on the assumption that the interpreter's output must be adapted to the communicative needs of the target-cultural audience, the interpreter is, by definition and necessity, a **cultural mediator** (see Kondo and Tebble 1997; Pöchhacker 2008).

3.2.8 A Map of Memes

As with any discourse on ideas, the level of abstraction at which the memes of interpreting are regarded as separate, or subsumed under a single label, is open to question. Nevertheless, the five memes seem distinctive enough to reflect both the evolution of thinking on interpreting over time and the relative dominance of key conceptual dimensions. This is illustrated in a map of memes (Figure 3.2), which shows how the key ideas informing scholarly and everyday discourse about interpreting are related within a matrix of four basic conceptual dimensions.

All memes relate, more or less closely, to the concepts of **language, cognition, interaction** and **culture**. These are shown in Figure 3.2 as separate poles, but also combine in various ways to form dimensions (e.g. language–culture, language–cognition, cognition–culture) within which the memes take their positions. Within this matrix, the five memes have been plotted in such a way as to suggest their conceptual proximity to the four poles. Though certainly no more than an intuitive visualization, this map of memes should help to give a better picture of the conceptual signposts that have guided the process of theoretical inquiry into interpreting.

The various 'ways of seeing' reviewed here in terms of pervasive and influential ideas about interpreting constitute a basic form of **theory**, as defined by Chesterman (1997: 1f) with reference to the Greek etymology of the word: *theoria*, meaning both 'a looking at,' 'a viewing' and 'contemplation,' 'speculation.' More elaborate forms of such theorizing are expressed in models,

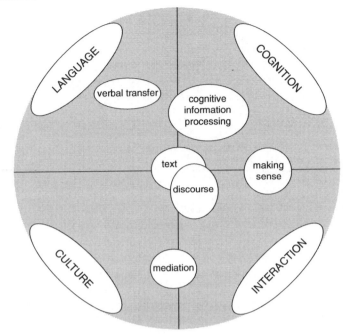

Figure 3.2 Map of memes in interpreting studies

which will be treated separately in Chapter 4. Models as well as ideas about interpreting should be tested, so as to turn speculation into knowledge. The next part of this chapter will review how this can be done, by using various ways of 'doing science' and embracing various 'ways of knowing.'

3.3 Methodology

While forming ideas about an object of study is essential to the process of inquiry, gaining more detailed knowledge requires some form of engagement with its empirical manifestations. The various options for doing **empirical research** are the subject-matter of methodology, a key domain in the philosophy of science. Methodology as the study of method is part of epistemology (i.e. the theory of knowledge), which underlies all methodological considerations (» 3.3.1). In a more specific sense, methodology also refers to the body of methods and procedures employed in a particular branch of study (» 3.3.2). Both the former (philosophical) and the latter (practical) aspects of methodology will be briefly discussed below in relation to interpreting studies.

3.3.1 'Ways of Knowing'

Science, understood as an **agreement** on what is known or accepted to be true, has long rested on the belief in ascertainable **facts** about an objective **reality**.

This epistemological stance, known as **positivism**, constitutes the bedrock of the natural sciences and has gained widespread acceptance in many other disciplines. An early opposing position was Dilthey's notion of 'human sciences,' suggesting that in the arts and humanities, as they are nowadays called, understanding through human sensory experience is an interpretive (hermeneutic) process shaped by the understanding individual embedded in a particular socio-cultural and historical context (see Pöchhacker 2011a). Nevertheless, the 'empiricist' position remained largely unshaken despite the acknowledgement that supposedly objective aspects of reality are subject to perceptual distortions and different individual interpretations. The positivist approach to science was ultimately called into question by 'postmodern' (postpositivist) – and, in particular, by **constructivist** – epistemologies, according to which there is no objective reality, and all experience is subjectively constructed. Adopting this kind of epistemological position in research on interpreting means that there is no such thing as 'natural data.' As Chesterman and Arrojo (2000: 152) point out, **data** are not 'there' as a given, but are ultimately 'taken' by the analyst, with a particular idea and purpose in mind.

In the case of interpreting studies (and Translation studies in general), most of the data are of a **qualitative** (non-numerical) rather than **quantitative** nature. Qualitative data (such as texts, images, interview transcripts or introspective protocols) will often be turned into numbers (quantified) in some way, but even then, and whenever measurements are taken in numerical form (e.g. in rating tasks), the numerical data are ultimately derived through acts of judgment and subjective interpretation. It therefore seems appropriate to consider interpreting studies a human science, with special affinity to the social sciences, which relies on multiple interpretive processes and is well-served by a social-constructivist epistemology.

Adopting a relativistic view of reality and knowledge, researchers strive for insights which hold up to **intersubjective** examination while continuously reflecting on the inescapable human limitations of scientific inquiry. This makes objectivity a **social** endeavor, informed by our individual subjectivity (see Babbie 1999: 36); hence the need for researchers to make explicit their theoretical perspective and conceptual as well as methodological choices. The latter include the choice between a **deductive** vs **inductive** approach, and the overall methodological strategy and method(s) of inquiry.

3.3.2 Strategies and Methods in Interpreting Studies

Ever since the period of renewal began in the mid-1980s, interpreting researchers have aspired to high(er) scientific standards in designing and carrying out empirical research. Nevertheless, only a relatively small share of the total research output has conformed to the canonical scientific method of **hypothesis testing**, in which existing theory is used, in a process of deduction, to formulate a new claim that can be tested against empirical data. Such testing requires **operationalization** of the claim, or hypothesis, by defining all relevant variables and specifying measurable indicators, and this may be one reason why this type of **explanatory** research is not abundant in interpreting studies. In order to identify causal links between variables, a study must have a highly structured design, informed by a thorough understanding of all relevant factors. For many topics in interpreting there is not enough well-established theory to allow this kind of analytical approach. The **purpose** of inquiry in many studies is therefore **descriptive**, or even **exploratory**. Thus, much research on interpreting is designed to answer questions such as 'What is this like?' or 'What is involved?' in order to explore a new phenomenon, and questions like 'How?,' 'How often?,' 'How many?' or 'Under what circumstances?' in order to describe (better) what is, in principle, a known part of the object of study.

Exploratory studies, in particular, suggest moving from data to theory through a process of induction, and gaining theoretical insights by identifying relationships and patterns in the data. This way of generating theory grounded in the data ('**grounded theory**') is closely associated with the **qualitative research** approaches (e.g. Denzin and Lincoln 2000), which have become established as an alternative to the quantification-oriented **hypothetico-deductive model**, and have also gained ground in interpreting studies.

Notwithstanding the need to be aware of these fundamental distinctions in the overall research process, most interpreting scholars would typically face methodological choices of a more concrete nature. These will be introduced here under the headings of 'strategy,' on the one hand, and 'method' of data collection, on the other.

Choices in **research design** can be categorized in various ways. One broad distinction which has been used frequently in interpreting studies, particularly by Gile (e.g. 1998), is between **observational** and **experimental** approaches, that is, between studying a phenomenon as it occurs, 'naturally,' as it were, 'in the field,' and making a phenomenon occur precisely for the purpose of studying it. Another, threefold categorization posits three different overall research **strategies** – fieldwork, survey research and experiments (see Robson 1993). '**Fieldwork**,' in a very broad sense, means collecting data on people or occurrences in their real-life context, often by studying a particular 'case' (**case study**); **survey research** consists of collecting data in more or less standardized form from a larger group of 'sources'; and **experimental research** involves measuring the effect of **manipulating** a particular 'independent' (explanatory) variable on a 'dependent' (outcome) variable. All three of these basic research strategies have been adopted in research on interpreting, as can be illustrated even with reference to the very first studies on the subject. The pioneering thesis by Paneth (1957/2002) on conference interpreter training, which was based on visits to several training institutions and involved the observation of teaching practices as well as interviews, is a good example of fieldwork; the early study by Sanz (1930) also involved observation in the field, but was mainly designed as a survey among twenty professional interpreters with the help of a questionnaire; and the groundbreaking study of simultaneous interpreting by Oléron and Nanpon (1965/2002) was largely based on data from an experiment, after the authors had found their fieldwork data all too 'messy' for their analytical purpose.

Survey research has been a popular strategy particularly for profession-related issues such as user expectations (» 10.4.2), role perceptions (» 10.3.2), working conditions and stress (» 10.5.2) and job satisfaction and professional status (» 10.1.2). Fieldwork, in contrast, played a surprisingly minor role until scholarly attention shifted to interpreting in community-based settings. Whereas very little large-scale fieldwork has been done on conference inter-preting (e.g. Pöchhacker 1994a; Diriker 2004), the real-life complexities of dialogue interpreting in institutional contexts have made fieldwork a strategy of choice (e.g. Wadensjö 1998). By the same token, experimental research has been the preferred research strategy for more controlled and less contextualized translational tasks. But experimenting with interpreting has been controversial from the outset and is fraught with many issues of **validity**. David Gerver himself, who could be said to have imprinted conference interpreting research with his early experiments, was keenly aware of the methodological problems that have plagued many experimental studies on interpreting to this day, and pointed to the critical challenges of

> defining and isolating both the independent and dependent variables, as well as being able to find experimental designs capable of handling the multiplicity of factors involved and the relatively small numbers of suffi-ciently skilled interpreters available at any one time in any one place with a particular combination of languages.
>
> (Gerver 1976: 167)

For these and other reasons, many experiments have been carried out with students of interpreting, raising further issues of validity. Indeed, Daniel Gile had cautioned early on against the methodological pitfalls of experimental studies and recommended "giving priority to observational research" (1990a: 37), not least to prepare the ground for experimental hypothesis testing. More recently, Liu (2011) points out that many studies adopting an 'experimental' approach (in the broader sense of generating data for the purpose of analysis) do not involve the manipulation of an independent variable, or the random assignment of participants to treatment and control groups, and should therefore be labeled, strictly speaking, as '**pre-experiments**' and '**quasi-experiments**', respectively.

In addition to the broad distinction between different overall strategies, choices in research design relate to the particular **method(s)** or techniques used for data collection and analysis. For research on interpreting, three basic options can be summarized as **watch, ask** and **record**. In standard social-science terms, this corresponds to **observational methods**, which range from informal participant observation to highly structured coding grids; **interviews and questionnaires**, which can be more or less structured and variously adminis-tered; and the collection of **documentary material** (from historical records to transcriptions of authentic discourse) for analysis.

These various methods will be amply illustrated in the review of research on selected topics offered in Part II of this book. The same applies to the different strategic orientations, including examples of research designs that defy clear-cut categorization, such as **simulations** and **action research**. Moreover, interpreting scholars are increasingly drawing on multiple sources of data and combining different methods, which is referred to as **triangulation**. Increasingly, this involves mixing qualitative and quantitative designs, and such **mixed methods research** seems highly appropriate for a discipline like interpreting studies that is both distinctly empirical and inherently interpretive in its methodological approach.

3.4 Paradigms

Building on the overview of the field's evolution (Chapter 2) and of its theoretical and methodological approaches, this final section of Chapter 3 summarizes the main research traditions in interpreting studies with reference to the notion of 'paradigm' as introduced by Thomas Kuhn.

3.4.1 *The Notion of 'Paradigm'*

According to Thomas Kuhn's (1962/1996) analysis of scientific disciplines and change processes, scientific thought and research are shaped by 'paradigms,' which are made up of the **basic assumptions, models, values and standard methods** shared by all members of a given scientific community. Working within the prevailing paradigm, researchers will design further studies and refine theories so as to account for as many aspects of the phenomenon as possible in a cumulative process. Eventually, though, a paradigm may prove incapable of dealing with 'anomalies' in the data, and new conceptual and methodological approaches come to the fore, pushing the old paradigm into crisis and taking its place. Thus Kuhn saw **paradigm shifts** as an overthrow of the old by a new paradigm, a process of revolutionary rather than evolutionary change.

Kuhn's 'radical' account of scientific progress was developed with reference to the natural sciences, but has spread far beyond this original context. Kuhn had assumed that the humanities and social sciences were more amenable to different paradigms, or 'ways of seeing,' coexisting within a single scientific community. This tenet will be examined in relation to interpreting studies below.

3.4.2 *Forging a Paradigm*

As long as research on interpreting was carried out from the perspective (and by members) of other disciplines (« 2.2.2), it was in a 'pre-paradigmatic' stage, lacking a broader consensus on basic assumptions, models and methods, or even a claim to a shared object of study. This claim was put forward by

Seleskovitch and the **Paris School** (« 2.3.3), together with distinct preferences regarding basic theoretical assumptions, values and methods. In many respects, the Paris School's position was antithetical, defined by what it was *not*: interpreting was *not* translating words ('transcoding'); interpreting research was *not* concerned with language as a system (*langue*) or language-pair-specific differences, and *not* founded on linguistics, *nor* did it use the methods of experimental psychology or psycholinguistics. More affirmatively, the Paris School shared the view, and values, of (conference) interpreting as a **profession** and sought to explain how professional interpreters succeeded in accomplishing their task. At the center of its explanatory account was the idea of **making sense**, formulated as the **Interpretive Theory** of Translation (IT). The paradigm established by the Paris School in the 1970s can thus be referred to as the **IT paradigm** and characterized as a 'bootstrap paradigm' – a first effort to lift the study of interpreting (and translation) to scientific status in academia on the strength of its own (limited) resources.

While both Seleskovitch (1975) and Lederer (1981) used experimentally generated data, the IT paradigm did *not* envisage scientific experimentation as a necessary or even valid approach to inquiry into interpreting. Aside from introspection, preference was given to the observation and largely qualitative analysis of successful professional practice on the basis of recordings and transcriptions. The IT paradigm can therefore be credited with promoting **fieldwork** on conference interpreting, even though systematic description was neglected in preference for the (largely speculative) explanation of mental processes. Experimentation remained a major bone of contention, and controversy over standards of empirical research fueled the challenge that was raised against the IT paradigm on mainly methodological grounds.

3.4.3 Turning to (Cognitive) Science

The charge leveled against the Paris School paradigm by Daniel Gile (e.g. 1990a) and other research-minded professionals was supported in particular by Barbara Moser-Mercer, who described the conference interpreting research community as divided into two largely incompatible camps:

> The first group prefers explorations which require precision of logical processes, and where members are interested in the natural sciences and quantification; the second group prefers explorations which involve the intellect in a less logically rigorous manner, where members are interested more in a liberal arts approach and general theorizing.
>
> (1994a: 17)

Moser-Mercer's (1994a) account is explicitly based on the Kuhnian notion of paradigm and cites Seleskovitch and Lederer as best representing the (less logically rigorous) "liberal arts community," whereas Gerver, Moser, Lambert,

Gile and Fabbro are all assigned to "the same natural science paradigm" (Moser-Mercer 1994a: 20). Though Moser-Mercer's broad-brush account blurs some relevant distinctions, it presents those challenging the IT paradigm as united in an aspiration to more stringent **standards of scientific research** and an openness toward other theoretical and methodological approaches, and indeed other disciplines.

In its theoretical approach, the science-minded community was guided by the meme of **cognitive information processing skills**, as elaborated by Gerver (1971, 1976) and Moser (1978) in their cognitive process models (» 4.4.3) and by Gile in his **Effort Models** (» 4.4.2). Given its central concern with cognitive processing (CP), the **CP paradigm** was mindful of the pioneering work done by Gerver (« 2.2.2, » 6.4.1, » 6.4.3) and his disciple, Sylvie Lambert (1989), and generally shared the broad agenda of **cognitive science** to explain the interplay of **language and cognition**. In fact, though, Gerver's influential definition of (simultaneous) interpreting as human information processing (« 3.2.5) had also included a crucial admonition to take account of factors beyond the cognitive mechanics as such: "Furthermore, linguistic, motivational, situational, and a host of other factors cannot be ignored" (Gerver 1976: 167). This broadens the agenda of the CP paradigm even further and highlights the need for interdisciplinary collaboration.

While research in the CP paradigm has generally been receptive towards methods and findings from other disciplines, interpreting scholars have embraced the principle of **interdisciplinarity** to a variable extent. Among the most decidedly interdisciplinary of them is Moser-Mercer, whose early interest in cognitive science was as influential as her recent work on the neural substrates of language control in collaboration with neuroscientists (e.g. Hervais-Adelman et al. 2011). Such work on the **neurophysiological foundations** of processing two or more languages in the brain goes back to the period of renewal in the mid-1980s and was first showcased at the Trieste Symposium (« 2.4.1). Spearheaded by neurophysiologist Franco Fabbro in cooperation with Laura Gran of the T/I school at the University of Trieste, neuropsychological evidence was collected to study the organization of **language(s) in the brain** in bilinguals in general, and interpreters in particular (Fabbro and Gran 1994). In a similar vein, Ingrid Kurz (1994, 1996) worked with neurophysiologist Hellmuth Petsche at the University of Vienna, using EEG mapping to visualize differential patterns of cerebral activation, and Jorma Tommola teamed up with neuroscientists at the University of Turku, using positron emission tomography (PET) to study "the translating brain" (Rinne et al. 2000). Tommola (1999) presented this 'neuro' approach as a research model *sui generis*, in contrast to the 'cognitive-behavioral approach' which is here labeled as the CP paradigm. One could therefore speak of a neurophysiological/neurolinguistic or **NL paradigm** in interpreting studies.

The NL paradigm, which had lost some of its original momentum by the turn of the century, is closely linked to – and dependent on – advanced neuroscientific **brain imaging** techniques (see Tommola 1999), among which functional magnetic resonance imaging (fMRI) has emerged as particularly promising (e.g. Hervais-Adelman et al. 2014). Given the complex technologies involved and its specialized theoretical assumptions and models, the NL paradigm is arguably the most sophisticated research paradigm for the study of interpreting to date. At the same time, there has been increasing inter-disciplinary convergence between cognitive and neurophysiological approaches. The neuro approach therefore need not be viewed as strictly separate from the much broader CP paradigm; rather, the two research orientations share an essentially cognitive interest in language processing, as pursued in the highly interdisciplinary field of **cognitive neuroscience**: cognitive psychologists define and study issues in the interplay between language and memory, increasingly with the help of imaging techniques, and neuroscientists can supply evidence relating to cognitive processes, such as executive control.

3.4.4 Focusing on Interaction

The three paradigms identified so far could all be said to center on the study of consecutive and simultaneous conference interpreting with a more or less cognitive orientation. The radically new 'way of seeing' that emerged in the early 1990s was different with regard to both the primary object of study and the theoretical and methodological frameworks (« 2.5.2). Rather than monologic conference speeches, the focus of interest shifted to interpreting in dialogic situations, for which the view of interpreting as target-text production, or cognitive information processing, seemed to be of little explanatory value. The groundbreaking studies by Cynthia Roy and Cecilia Wadensjö on **dialogue interpreting** thus mark a new conceptual and methodological departure. In her 1989 PhD thesis, Roy (2000a) performed a **qualitative analysis** of a videotaped 15-minute student–teacher meeting mediated by a sign language interpreter. With a focus on the dynamics of **interactive discourse**, and special regard for **turn-taking** processes, Roy draws on the methods of **conversation analysis** (ethnomethodology) and **discourse analysis** (interactional socio-linguistics, ethnography of communication). Along similar lines, but with an even more distinctly sociological approach, Wadensjö (1998) carried out discourse-based **fieldwork** on Russian–Swedish immigration and medical interviews mediated by state-certified Swedish dialogue interpreters. Drawing on Goffma-nian models to analyze role constellations and behavior in interpreter-mediated encounters (» 8.1.1), Wadensjö highlights how and why interpreters do more than 'just translating' and are actively engaged in 'coordinating' the primary parties' utterances.

The highly compatible work of Roy and Wadensjö supplied both a coherent conceptual approach to (dialogue) interpreting and a broad base of discourse-analytical methodology, thus launching a new paradigm for the study of interpreting as **dialogic discourse**-based **interaction**. The **DI** (dialogic interac-tionist, or discourse-in-interaction) **paradigm** gathered considerable momentum in the course of the 1990s, at a time when **community interpreting** was becoming increasingly recognized as a significant field of professional practice and a fruitful area of research. Given its essentially descriptive rather than prescriptive orientation, the DI paradigm has also proved amenable to the study of **non-professional interpreting**, which has emerged as a topic of interdisciplinary interest.

3.4.5 *Unity in Diversity*

The present review of interpreting studies in terms of 'paradigms' has identified several conceptually and methodologically distinct research traditions. As surmised by Kuhn (1962/1996) for the humanities and social sciences, the various paradigms coexist and are even partly interrelated, largely complementing rather than competing with one another. The only exception may be the fraught relationship between the IT paradigm and the CP and NL paradigms, which marked the renewal phase of interpreting studies (« 2.4.1): this can be seen as a paradigm shift, which was mainly brought about on methodological grounds.

In an intuitive visualization, one might depict the various paradigms as a cluster situated between the spheres of professional practice and training on the one hand, and the cognitive, linguistic, and social sciences on the other (Figure 3.3). The dominant CP paradigm may be considered as a science-oriented extension of the profession-based original IT paradigm. The CP paradigm reaches well into the domain of the cognitive sciences, where the NL paradigm stands out as the most specialized interdisciplinary research model for interpreting. The DI paradigm, in contrast, links aspects of profession and training with significant areas of the linguistic and social sciences. At the base of the cluster is yet another paradigm, labeled the 'TT paradigm,' which stands for target-text-oriented translation-theoretical approaches (see Pöchhacker 2004: 77). Since these reflect the view of interpreting as Translation and seek to study the phenomenon within a broader translation-theoretical framework (« 2.5.1), the TT paradigm is depicted here as part of the wider disciplinary

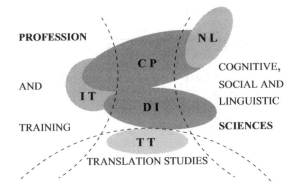

Figure 3.3 Cluster of paradigms in interpreting studies

Table 3.1 Summary table of paradigms in interpreting studies

	IT	TT	CP	NL	DI
SUPERMEME	communicative activity + process(ing)	Translation	process(ing)	process(ing)	communicative activity
MEME	making sense	making sense + text production + mediation	cognitive information processing	cognitive information processing	discourse production + mediation
INFLUENTIAL MODEL/THEORY (THEORIST)	Interpretive Theory (Seleskovitch)	translational norms (Toury), *skopos* theory (Vermeer)	Effort Models (Gile), working memory (Baddeley, Cowan)	lateralization (Fabbro), neural activation (Paradis)	participation framework (Goffman)
LEADING MEMBERS	Seleskovitch, Lederer	Shlesinger, Pöchhacker	Moser-Mercer, Gile, Setton	Fabbro, Tommola	Wadensjö, Roy
PARADIGM CASES	Seleskovitch 1975, Lederer 1981	Shlesinger 1989b, Pöchhacker 1994a	Moser 1978, Gile 1999a, Liu et al. 2004	Fabbro and Gran 1994, Hervais-Adelman et al. 2014	Wadensjö 1998, Roy 2000a
INTERDISCIPLINARY ORIENTATION	(psychology)	Translation and discourse studies	cognitive psychology	neurophysiology, neuroscience	sociology, sociolinguistics
METHODOLOGICAL STRATEGY	fieldwork	fieldwork, survey	experiment, fieldwork	experiment	fieldwork
INTERPRETING TYPE (MODE)	conference (consec. + SI)	conference (SI + consec)	conference (SI + consec.)	SI	dialogue

space of Translation studies, which is viewed as providing a broad foundation for the more specialized approaches in the (sub)disciplinary space of interpreting studies.

The account of paradigms presented here is intended as a compromise between viewing interpreting studies as a field of scattered, isolated efforts lacking theoretical and methodological consensus, and idealizing it as a discipline united by a single, generally shared paradigm. This vision of unity in diversity for interpreting studies can be illustrated with reference to interpreting scholars who have done substantial work in more than one paradigm: Kurz, for instance, a pioneer of psychological experimenting with interpreters (» 6.3.1), also engaged in collaborative research in the NL paradigm (» 5.1.2) and discussed empirical findings in a translation-theoretical framework; Pöchhacker did fieldwork on conference interpreting in a general translation-theoretical framework, as well as case studies within the DI paradigm; and Shlesinger not only made pioneering contributions to the TT paradigm (1989a, 1989b), but also carried out sophisticated experimental research in the CP paradigm (» 5.2.3).

If any major shift is to be identified in the evolution of interpreting research approaches to date, it is the extension of scholarly interest to include interpreting activities in intra-social settings, which has been associated with the adoption of sociolinguistic and sociological concepts, methods and models. On the whole, though, interpreting scholars need all these various approaches to their multi-faceted object of study – as highlighted by the variety of models of interpreting reviewed in the following chapter.

Summary

Approaches to research on interpreting have been reviewed in this chapter with regard to the disciplinary frameworks, guiding ideas, and methodological orientations that have shaped this field of study. Whereas the sibling discipline of translation studies has had little impact beyond basic *theoretical foundations*, the study of interpreting has been sourced by a variety of (inter) disciplinary frameworks under such broad headings as *psychology, linguistics, sociology*, and *cultural anthropology*. These disciplinary vantage points have shaped the way researchers have conceptualized the phenomenon of interpreting. Beyond such pervasive ideas about interpreting as *processing* and *communicative activity*, five *memes* have been found to characterize the evolution of thinking about interpreting in various periods and disciplinary contexts: *verbal transfer, making sense, cognitive information processing skills, text/discourse production* and *mediation*.

Complementing the theoretical cornerstones of inquiry, a review of fundamental issues in *methodology* has identified interpreting studies as a *human science* that relies on interpretive techniques and is well served by a constructivist epistemology. Embracing empiricist *hypothesis testing* as well as *qualitative research* approaches, interpreting researchers have employed a range of overall *strategies (fieldwork, survey research* and *experiments)* and *methods* for data collection and analysis. By its various methodological orientations and distinct 'ways of seeing,' interpreting studies can be seen as a set of related *paradigms*, including the CP (cognitive processing), NL (neuroscientific/neurolinguistic), DI (dialogic interactionist) as well as TT (translation-theoretical) paradigms. While these form distinct research traditions, they are united by a multifaceted but shared object of study.

Sources and Further Reading

On disciplinary perspectives, see COGNITIVE APPROACHES, PSYCHOLINGUISTIC APPROACHES, NEUROSCIENCE APPROACHES, LINGUISTIC/PRAGMATIC APPROACHES, DISCOURSE ANALYTICAL APPROACHES, SOCIOLINGUISTIC APPROACHES and SOCIOLOGICAL APPROACHES in Pöchhacker (2015).

For memes in Translation studies, see Chesterman (1997); for the meme of making sense, see INTERPRETIVE THEORY in Pöchhacker (2015); for the text/discourse meme of interpreting, see Hatim and Mason (1997/2002) and Roy (2000a); for the mediation meme, see Pöchhacker (2008) and MEDIATION in Pöchhacker (2015).

For epistemological foundations in Translation studies, see Chesterman and Arrojo (2000) and the subsequent discussion documented in *Target* (especially 13:1, 2001); for epistemology and methodology in interpreting studies, see Pöchhacker (2011a) as well as EPISTEMOLOGY, METHODOLOGY and INTERDISCIPLINARITY in Pöchhacker (2015); for research methods, see INTERVIEWS, SURVEY RESEARCH, EXPERIMENTAL RESEARCH, MIXED METHODS RESEARCH and ACTION RESEARCH in Pöchhacker (2015); for further guidance on methods in interpreting research, see Hale and Napier (2013).

On paradigms in interpreting studies, see Moser-Mercer (1994a), Shlesinger (1995b) and Setton (1999, Chapter 2) as well as PARADIGMS in Pöchhacker (2015).

Suggestions for Further Study

- What contributions to the literature on interpreting in languages other than English have been made by Translation scholars as well as specialists in cognitive/linguistic and socio/cultural disciplines?
- What other ideas and assumptions about interpreting could be considered for meme status in interpreting studies, and how have they manifested themselves in the literature?

- How do textbooks on methodology in other languages and fields categorize various research strategies and methodological approaches?
- How have geopolitical, linguistic and institutional factors influenced the development of different paradigms in interpreting studies?
- Viewing the various paradigms as points of reference in a much wider and diverse disciplinary landscape, what other influential approaches can be identified, and how do they relate to the research traditions accorded paradigm status in this chapter?

4 Models

Various conceptions of interpreting with different focal points on the map of memes (« 3.2.8) have been elaborated in the form of models. Proceeding from the broader levels of social context to the intricacies of cognitive processes, this chapter reviews a number of modeling approaches and discusses a range of selected examples.

The **main points** covered in this chapter are:

- the nature and purpose of modeling in the process of inquiry
- the conceptual dimensions in which the phenomenon of interpreting can be modeled
- interaction-oriented models of interpreting
- process-oriented models of interpreting
- tests and applications of models

4.1 On Modeling

4.1.1 Nature, Form and Purpose

A model can be described as some form of representation of an object or phenomenon. Models usually indicate the type and number of components which are assumed to form part of the object or phenomenon under study, and reflect the way in which the components fit together and relate to one another. In essence, then, a model is an assumption about what something is like and how it functions, so that modeling can be regarded as a particular form of theoretical endeavor. Such theoretical models can take various forms of representation, from verbal description to imagery and mathematical formulas. More often than not, the desire to 'reflect' and 'represent' a phenomenon suggests recourse to graphic forms of expression, and indeed most of the models presented in this chapter are visualized as diagrams.

Models can be used for various purposes of inquiry. As a basic form of **theorizing** they can express intuitive assumptions and ideas (memes) about a phenomenon. Models constructed on the basis of more immediate observations and empirical data are used for the purpose of **describing** some aspect of 'reality,' bearing in mind that a model, by definition, is an incomplete representation, one which singles out features and relationships that are of particular concern to the analyst. Where models seek to capture a dynamic relationship, such as a sequence over time or a relation of cause and effect, they can be used for **explaining** how or why a phenomenon occurs. On the assumption that a model includes, at a sufficient level of detail, all factors and relationships which may have an impact on the phenomenon under study, it can be used for **predicting** the occurrence of future phenomena, as in a controlled experimental setting. The latter is one way of **testing** the model and its underlying assumptions, others being continued observation and computer simulation, always with a view to further theoretical elaboration and refinement.

In principle, models of interpreting can be envisaged for any of these purposes. As evident from the evolution of ideas about interpreting, however, the phenomenon is of such complexity as to elude attempts at constructing a comprehensive predictive model. Most models of interpreting are therefore of the descriptive kind and are pegged to a particular level of analysis.

4.1.2 Levels of Modeling

With the conceptual space for theorizing about interpreting extending from the more micro-process-oriented cognitive sphere all the way to the socio-cultural dimension of the macro-process of communication, modeling implies a choice of one or more conceptual levels to be foregrounded in the representation. Which, then, are the levels of analysis that one can distinguish as potential conceptual reference points for models of interpreting?

With a view to the role of interpreters in the history of intercultural relations, one could conceive of a broadly **anthropological** model of interpreting and its role in the history of human civilization. With less abstraction and historical depth, and a more specific focus on societal structures, one would arrive at a **socio-professional** conception of interpreting; that is, a model of interpreting as a profession in society. Narrowing the focus to particular social institutions, such as international organizations, parliaments or courts, would highlight the **institutional** function of interpreting, while setting one's sights on a particular type of communicative event, like a conference or interview, would foreground the **interactional** aspects of interpreting as an activity taking place in and, at the same time, shaping a particular situation. Concentrating on the text as the material instrument in the communicative process, the analyst would view interpreting primarily as a **textual** or **discursive** process, whereas an interest in the mental processes underlying language use would give rise to **cognitive** models of interpreting. Finally, the material substrate of mental processes can be targeted with models of cerebral organization and brain activity at the most fundamental, **neural** level of inquiry.

Bearing in mind that these seven levels of analysis are meant as variable focal points rather than rigidly separable categories, they can be visualized as a set of concentric circles, extending from the 'outer' spheres of social context to a neuro-cognitive core, or, more pointedly, from **socio-cultures** to **synapses** (Figure 4.1).

Not all the dimensions suggested in the multi-level model have attracted a similar degree of analytical interest in interpreting studies. Indeed, as indicated in the diagram by variably shaded rings, modeling efforts to date have focused mainly on the level of cognitive processes, with some consideration also given to the level of interaction. These preferential focal points, which once again reflect the two supermemes of interpreting, process(ing) and communicative activity, also shape the presentation of selected models that follows.

4.2 Socio-professional and Institutional Models

While a model of interpreting in the **anthropological** dimension, with reference to intersocietal relations and cultural identities in the course of history, has not been put forward as such, the model of interpreting in various societal contexts

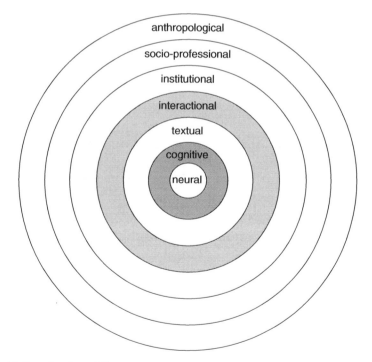

Figure 4.1 Levels of modeling

depicted in Figure 1.1 (« 1.3.1) could be cited as an illustration of the kind of issues which models at this level might address. Another example can be found in Cronin's (2002) account of "heteronomous" and "autonomous" systems of interpreting in the context of colonial empires and travel (see 2002: 393f).

A **socio-professional** model which focuses on interpreting as a recognized occupation in society was developed by Joseph Tseng (1992) with reference to conference interpreting in the social context of Taiwan. The model describes four phases in the process of **professionalization**, from "market disorder" to "professional autonomy" (Figure 4.2).

Tseng's model has been applied to other professional domains and countries (e.g. Mikkelson 1999). In more general terms, Uldis Ozolins (2000) has modeled different stages of interpreting service provision with reference to key determinants of professionalization.

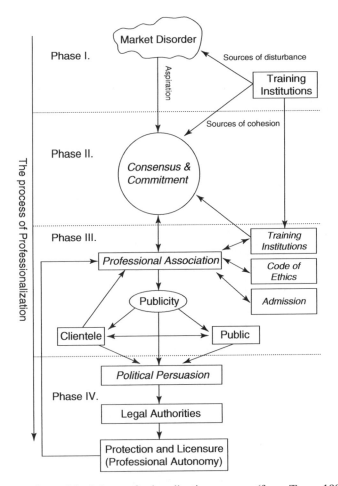

Figure 4.2 Tseng's model of the professionalization process (from Tseng 1992: 43)

More specifically still than at the level of a given society or socio-culture, the development, function and economics of interpreting can also be modeled at the **institutional** level. An example is the study by Michal Schuster (2013), who applies a five-stage sociological model for the development of language access to public institutions to the creation of Israel's first medical interpreting service.

While these examples highlight the importance and potential of modeling the phenomenon of interpreting in a broader socio-institutional dimension, interpreting scholars to date have expended relatively little effort on models of interpreting in history, society or in specific institutions. Rather, interpreting models tend to relate to the domain of **interaction** (» 4.3) or, much more so, focus on the complexities of cognitive **processing** (» 4.4).

4.3 Interaction Models

Interaction models represent the social, situational and communicative relations obtaining between the various parties involved in the process of interaction. They can be broadly subdivided into those which model the **constellation** of interacting parties as such (» 4.3.1) and those which focus on the process of **communication** (» 4.3.2) or, more specifically, the role of **text** or **discourse** in communicative interaction (» 4.3.3).

4.3.1 Constellation

The basic constellation, or **type case**, of interpreter-mediated interaction was modeled by **Anderson** (1976/2002) as a monolingual speaker of language A communicating with a monolingual speaker of language B via an interpreter commanding both languages (Figure 4.3).

Anderson's linear constellation model is one way of highlighting the pivotal position of the bilingual interpreter in the mediated exchange. Other authors have sought to express this by using a triangular representation in which the interpreter is depicted at the apex. Such models have become the default representation in the domain of community interpreting (e.g. Gentile et al. 1996; Erasmus 1999), which has been referred to by some authors as 'three-cornered interpreting.' They take account of the communicative interaction between the primary parties and foreground the **role of the interpreter** as a

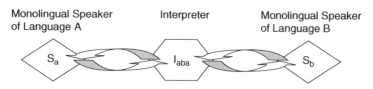

Figure 4.3 Anderson's 'type-case' model of three-party interaction (from Anderson 1976: 211)

more or less active participant in the interaction rather than a mere 'switching station' (» 10.3.2).

The basic three-party interaction model can be and has been extended in various ways to account for more complex constellations. Anderson (1976: 211) himself modeled variant forms including a negotiation with two interpreters, one for each side, and an interpreted lecture, with a larger number of speakers of language B adopting a listener role in an essentially one-directional process of communication. Similarly, Wong Fook Khoon (1990: 112) depicts several complex constellations of interpreting in Malaysian **courtrooms**, with one or two bilingual interpreters or a trilingual interpreter mediating between a judge, a defendant and a witness speaking different languages or dialects.

A simple model of the interactional constellation in **conference settings**, where a monolingual speaker addresses a more or less numerous audience, part of which cannot comprehend the language of the original speech, was suggested by Gile (1995b: 24) and is shown in Figure 4.4.

Though not necessarily involved directly in the interaction process, the "client" in Gile's model plays a significant role at the conference level. This dimension could be specified further by accounting for a range of human agents who may have an impact on the interpreter's working conditions, such as conference organizing staff, document services, and technicians. Similar considerations apply to colleagues in the interpreting team, especially in the case of relay interpreting.

An illustrative case of institution-specific complexity is the set of models discussed by Delia Chiaro (2002) for various constellations in **TV interpreting**, where mediated face-to-face communication combines with 'one-to-many' communication as typical of the mass media. Such models of the interaction constellation in an interpreted communication event also go some way toward addressing the institutional level of modeling which has hitherto received little attention.

Models of interpreted interaction, whether reflecting a 'one-to-one' or a 'one-to-many' constellation, can thus be extended and specified by adding further participant positions. At the same time, they can also be refined to reflect relevant features of the interacting parties. This is the aim of Pöchhacker's (1992) model of the interpreting situation, which hinges on the "perspective" of the individual **interactant** on the communicative event (Figure 4.5).

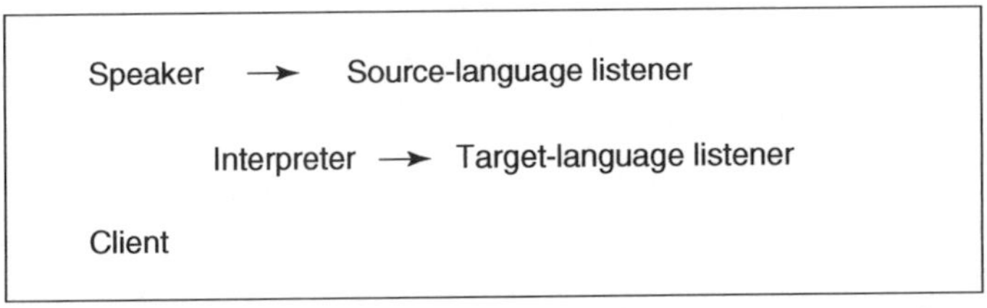

Speaker ⟶ Source-language listener

Interpreter ⟶ Target-language listener

Client

Figure 4.4 Gile's interaction model of conference interpreting (from Gile 1995b: 24)

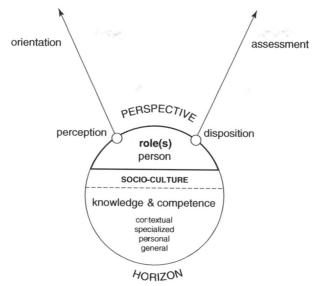

Figure 4.5 Pöchhacker's interactant model of the interpreting situation (adapted from Pöchhacker 1992: 216)

The interactant model of the situation foregrounds the "role(s)" taken on by the communicating "person" in the interaction. It suggests that the interactant's "perspective" on the situation, constituted by a continuous "assessment" of and intentional "orientation" toward the other interactants and their behavior, is essentially shaped by the individual's socio-cultural 'background,' or "horizon," made up of various types of cognitive competence and experience. In other words, the situation, in the more cognitive sense, exists only 'in the eyes of' (i.e. as seen from the perspective of) the interactant. Modulated by psycho-physical factors relating to "perception" and "disposition," the individual's orientation and assessment (including factors like motivation, emotional attitude, expectations and, not least, intentions) thus determine 'what the situation is like' and how it should be acted upon.

While the individualized interaction model applies both to the 'one-to-many' constellations typical of conference settings (see Pöchhacker 1994a: 144) and to triadic interaction in mediated face-to-face communication, it addresses positions and roles at the level of the speech event as such rather than the utterance-level dynamics of the communicative exchange (see Pöchhacker 2012: 51). In the terminology of Goffman as applied to interpreting by Wadensjö (1998), the interactant model highlights "activity roles" within a "situated activity system" in which individuals interact to perform a single joint activity (see Wadensjö 1998: 84).

Further analytical distinctions for the macro-level of mediated encounters have been proposed by Bistra Alexieva (1997/2002). In her multi-parameter model of interpreting constellations, she outlines a proto-**typology of** interpreter-mediated **events** on the basis of seven scales, most of which relate to the socio-situational constellation of the interacting parties. The parameters which bear directly on the constellation of interactants are:

- "distance" vs. "proximity" (between speaker, addressee and interpreter);
- "equality/solidarity" vs. "non-equality/power" (related to status, role and gender of speaker and addressee, as well as the interpreter in some cases);
- "formal setting" vs. "informal setting" (related to number of participants, degree of privacy, and distance from home country);
- "cooperativeness/directness" vs. "non-cooperativeness/indirectness" (relevant to negotiation strategies); and
- "shared goals" vs. "conflicting goals"(Alexieva 1997/2002: 230).

Alexieva applies her multi-parameter model to an assessment of interpreter-mediated events in terms of their degree of "culture-specificity," thus reaffirming the role of "culture" in the conception of interpreting as interaction.

4.3.2 Communication

Rather than conceptualizing interaction between human beings, early communication models of interpreting were largely shaped by the mathematical theory of communication as 'signal processing' (Shannon and Weaver 1949). The classic information-theoretical model of communication, in which a 'message' originating from a 'source' is 'encoded' and 'transmitted' through a 'channel' for 'decoding' by a 'receiver,' has been variously applied also to interpreting.

An early model of interpreting based on the standard communication model was developed in the 1970s by Ingram (see 1985). Originally conceived for sign language interpreting, Ingram's model goes beyond a verbal-linguistic conception of 'message transfer' and represents "messages in a multiplicity of interwoven codes" (Ingram 1978: 111). The idea of **multiple codes** is the distinctive feature of Ingram's semiotic model of interpreting as depicted in Figure 4.6.

Ingram's model is clearly reminiscent of the classic linear model of sender–receiver communication and, despite explicit reference to "context," essentially depicts the interpreter as a 'code-switching' station in the 'channel.' A more elaborate representation, though still founded on the assumption of language as a code and hence language processing as 'encoding' and 'decoding,' was drawn up by Kirchhoff (1976), as represented in an English adaptation in Figure 4.7.

Kirchhoff posits a **dual system of communication** in which a message (M1), composed of both "verbal" and "nonverbal" signals, is encoded by a primary sender (S1) in a given situation and socio-cultural background for reception by a primary receiver (R1) in a target-language context. The two parts of the communication system are linked together by the interpreter, who is depicted

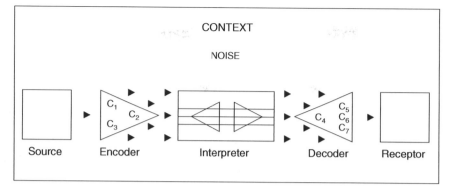

Figure 4.6 Ingram's semiotic communication model of interpreting (from Ingram
1985: 98)

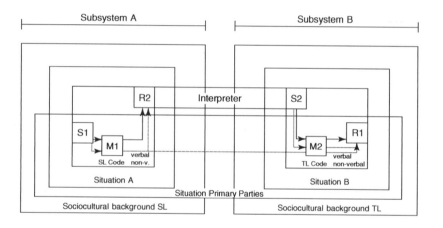

Figure 4.7 Kirchhoff's three-party bilingual communication system model (from
Kirchhoff 1976: 21)

as a 'side participant' outside the situation of the primary parties and serves
as both a secondary receiver (R2) of M1 and a secondary sender (S2) of M2
in the target-language code.

An elaboration of Kirchhoff's model which adds feedback mechanisms
between the three interactants and foregrounds the ideational or concept level
of communication has been described by Kondo (1990: 61, 2003: 81). Comparable, albeit less detailed, models were developed independently by other
authors. With special reference to communication studies, Erich Feldweg
drew up several variants of a basic communication model to account for
increasingly complex constellations of communicating parties and information flows in consecutive and simultaneous conference interpreting (e.g.
Feldweg 1996: 223).

While both Kirchhoff and Feldweg conceive of interpreted communication as a 'multi-channel phenomenon,' their account of the sign systems involved in the interpreting process is sparse compared to the ambitious semiotic model developed by Fernando Poyatos (1987/2002). Poyatos represents the verbal and nonverbal systems involved in (spoken-language) simultaneous and consecutive interpreting in the form of a matrix cross-tabulating acoustic and visual sign-conveying systems with various constellations of auditory and/or visual co-presence (see Poyatos 1987/2002: 237). The matrix model by Poyatos does not cover whispered interpreting or simultaneous sign language interpreting, but nevertheless remains the most sophisticated such analysis to date.

4.3.3 *Text/Discourse*

Ever since the 'pragmatic turn' in linguistics in the late 1970s, a number of authors have focused on the notions of text and discourse in their efforts to model mediated interaction. One of the earliest attempts in interpreting studies to use insights from text theory and translation theory for a model of interpreting as an interaction process was made by Stenzl (1983). Elaborating on a **text-theoretical model** of the translation process, Stenzl gives an account of the **communicative information flow** in (simultaneous) interpreting which centers on text processing by the speaker, interpreter and target text receiver. The key features of her model, as shown in Figure 4.8, are communicative "intention" (and, on the receiver side, "function"), "situation," "socio-cultural context," "knowledge" and "text."

According to Stenzl's (1983: 46f) description of the fifteen stages, or "steps," in the flow of communication, a speaker from socio-cultural context A defines the communicative intention I_1, assesses the receiver's situational and textual knowledge (step 1), and constructs and utters (steps 2 and 3) the source message. The latter consists of linguistic as well as para- and extra-linguistic elements (e.g. intonation, gestures, visual means, etc.) and is linked to the receiver's presupposed knowledge. The acoustic and visual signals of the source message are perceived by the interpreter (step 4) and processed together with situational and textual information (step 6) to yield I_2 (step 7), the interpreter's communicative intention as a reflection of I_1. Assessing the receiver's situational and textual knowledge (step 8), the interpreter constructs and emits the target message (steps 9 and 11), which consists of linguistic and paralinguistic elements and may also include elements transferred from the source text with minimal processing (step 10). The receiver processes the target text – as well as some information perceived directly from the speaker (step 15) – by drawing on situational and textual knowledge (step 13) and performs the communicative function F (step 14).

Although designed for simultaneous interpreting, Stenzl's model covers considerable ground as a general account of the communicative flow in interpreting. The model depicts processing stages as a number of discrete "steps," but Stenzl (1983: 47) points out that these are characterized by

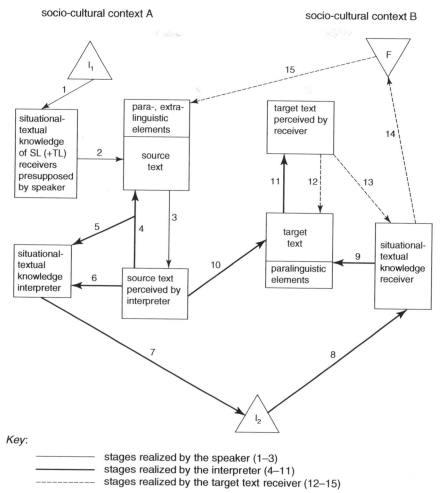

socio-cultural context A

socio-cultural context B

Key:

———————— stages realized by the speaker (1–3)

———————— stages realized by the interpreter (4–11)

– – – – – – – stages realized by the target text receiver (12–15)

Figure 4.8 Stenzl's communicative information flow model (from Stenzl 1983: 45)

"considerable interaction and simultaneity." Indeed, her dynamic flow model is as much an interaction model as it is a processing model, representing not only the 'interactants' and what is going on *between* them, but also (some of) the processes going on *within* the interpreter.

A related conception of knowledge-based text production and comprehension in interpreting was proposed by Sylvia Kalina (1998). Inspired by discourse models of monolingual communication, Kalina's model focuses not so much on the dynamic but on the **cognitive** dimension of **text processing**. It represents "communicative mediation" as a text/discourse-based process which begins with a speaker's mental discourse model and leads to a mental discourse model constructed by a target-language addressee on the basis of linguistic knowledge and world/situation knowledge (Figure 4.9).

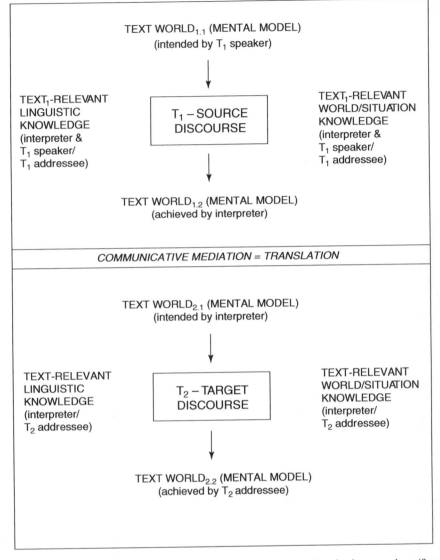

Figure 4.9 Kalina's model of comprehension and production in interpreting (from Kalina 1998: 109)

Concepts of text and discourse processing have been applied to interpreting also by Basil Hatim and Ian Mason (1997). As part of their general discourse framework for the analysis of Translation, Hatim and Mason use three key concepts of discourse theory for a tripartite model to distinguish different types of interpreting: the dimensions of "texture," "structure" and "context" are seen, respectively, as most significant to input processing in simultaneous, consecutive, and liaison interpreting (1997/2002: 256f).

4.4 Processing Models

While many models at the interactional and textual levels are not necessarily geared to a particular type of interpreting, processing models have mostly been designed for the simultaneous mode. Whether addressing the issue of **multiple task** performance in general (» 4.4.2) or the specific **processing stages** and **mental structures** involved (» 4.4.3), reference is made mainly to the process of simultaneous interpreting. An exception can be found in early models of the interpreting process whose focus is on the nature of the **translational process** (» 4.4.1).

4.4.1 Translational Process

The earliest and most general description of the processes assumed to take place in interpreting goes back to Herbert (1952: 9), who asserted that "interpretation really consists of three distinct parts: (*a*) understanding; (*b*) conversion; (*c*) delivery." However, Herbert's discussion of the central translational component was limited to language-related issues and questions of interpreting technique, with little reference to the underlying mental processes.

The interpreter who most famously ventured into a more cognitive analysis of the task was **Seleskovitch**. In an essay published ten years after Herbert's *Handbook*, Seleskovitch (1962: 16) posited that the 'mechanism' of (consecutive as well as simultaneous) interpreting was "a triangular process," at the pinnacle of which was the construct of **sense** (Figure 4.10).

According to this model, the essential process at work in Translation is not linguistic "transcoding" (which is limited to items with fixed correspondences like proper names, numbers and specialized terms) but the interpreter's understanding and expression of "sense" (« 3.2.4). "Sense," according to Seleskovitch (1978b: 336), is (1) "conscious," (2) "made up of the linguistic meaning aroused by speech sounds and of a cognitive addition to it" and (3) "nonverbal," that is, dissociated from any linguistic form in cognitive memory. The idea that translational processes are essentially based on language-free ("deverbalized") utterance meaning rather than linguistic

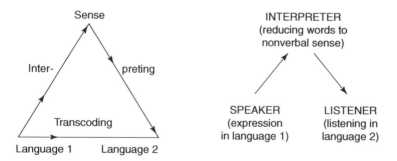

Figure 4.10 Seleskovitch's triangular model (two versions) (from Seleskovitch and Lederer 1984: 185, 168)

conversion procedures ("transcoding") is the cornerstone of the Interpretive Theory of Translation championed by the Paris School (« 2.3.3).

Given its high level of abstraction as a general model of Translation, the triangular process model by Seleskovitch left ample room for further elaboration (see e.g. Laplace 1994: 230). With reference to psycholinguistic research, García-Landa (1981) fleshed out the triangular model as two **acts of discourse** linked together by the principle of "equivalence of sense," that is, the speaker's intention for the original act of discourse equals the interpreter's perception of the intended sense, which in turn becomes the interpreter's intention for the target discourse, which equals the client's perception of the intended sense. (For a more elaborate pseudo-mathematical formulation of this equation, see García-Landa 1998.) García-Landa (1981) offers an enriched conceptualization which involves attention thresholds, memory structures (working memory, long-term memory activation), discourse components and situational variables to reflect the processes of discourse comprehension and production. In a similar vein, Betty **Colonomos** (see Ingram 1985: 99) drew up a model centered on the **formless** conceptual **message** and featuring various (short-term and long-term) memory, monitoring and feedback operations. The model by Colonomos, which was complemented by a variant representing the process of transliteration, proved influential particularly in the American sign language interpreting community and its training initiatives (see Baker-Shenk 1990).

4.4.2 Multiple Tasks

Starting, as did García-Landa (1981), from the triangular process model of the *théorie du sens*, Lederer (1981) developed a more detailed model of simultaneous interpreting involving **eight mental operations**, with two or more running concurrently at any time. Lederer (1981: 50) distinguishes three types of operations depending on their manifestation over time:

- Continuous successive and concurrent operations

    - listening
    - language comprehension
    - conceptualization (i.e. constructing a cognitive memory by integrating linguistic input with prior knowledge)
    - expression from cognitive memory

- Continuous 'underlying' operations with intermittent manifestation

    - awareness of situation
    - self-monitoring

- Intermittent operations

    - transcoding
    - retrieval of specific lexical expressions

While Lederer also relates the main processing stages – perception of linguistic input, conceptualization, expression – to the function of working memory and long-term memory, her model of the interpreting process and its main components is rather holistic. The same can be said about the model of simultaneous interpreting proposed by Kirchhoff (1976/2002: 112). Couched in the terminology of information theory, the basic process model includes "decoding," "recoding," "production," and "monitoring." In addition, Kirchhoff posits a more complex variant involving short-term storage of input segments in memory, particularly to account for syntactic divergence between the source and target languages. In this respect, and on the whole, Kirchhoff's **multi-phase model** reflects a concern with linguistic surface structure, in stark contrast to the focus on conceptual processing in the *théorie du sens*. What is more, Kirchhoff's aim is not to model the process of 'interpreting at its best' but to account for psycholinguistic **processing difficulties**. Relating her multi-tasking model to the psychological processing constraints of the interpreter, Kirchhoff's analysis focuses on such notions as "cognitive load" and "processing capacity." On the assumption that individual task components require a certain (and variable) amount of processing capacity, Kirchhoff discusses instances in which the interpreting process yields less than perfect results, involving linguistic infelicities, distortions and loss of information: "Multiple-task performance becomes a problem if task completion requires cognitive decisions which, in sum, reach or even exceed the individual's processing capacity limit" (1976/2002: 118).

This issue is also at the heart of the **Effort Models** of interpreting formulated by Gile (1985, 1997/2002). Assuming three basic efforts, labeled "listening and analysis" (L), "production" (P), and "memory" (M), Gile (1985) originally used his effort model of simultaneous interpreting to express the basic tenet that there is only a limited amount of mental "energy" (or processing capacity) available for the interpreter's processing effort, and that the sum of the three efforts must not exceed the interpreter's processing capacity:

$$(L + P + M) < C_{apacity}$$

In subsequent refinements of the model, a "coordination effort" (C) was added, and the relationships between the model components were expressed in a set of formulas as follows (see Gile 1997/2002: 165):

1 $SI = L + P + M + C$ 'Simultaneous interpreting modeled as a process consisting of the three main efforts plus a coordination effort.'

2 $TR = LR + MR + PR + CR$ 'Total processing capacity requirements are a (not necessarily arithmetic) sum of individual processing capacity requirements.'

3 $LA \geq LR,$ 'The capacity available for each effort

4	MA ≥ MR,	must be equal to or larger than its
5	PA ≥ PR, and	requirements for the task at hand.'
6	CA ≥ CR	
7	TA ≥ TR	'Total available capacity must be at least equal to total requirements.'

Gile uses his effort model of simultaneous interpreting as well as the variants formulated for consecutive interpreting and simultaneous interpreting with text (see Gile 1997/2002: 167ff) to account for a number of processing difficulties and failures. On the assumption, also known as the "tightrope hypothesis" (Gile 1999b), that interpreters, particularly in the simultaneous mode, usually work at the limit of their processing capacity, Gile uses his model to explain the effect of "problem triggers" such as proper names, numbers and compound technical terms, which may result in "failure sequences" and require special "coping tactics" (see Gile 1995b; 1997/2002; 2009).

The models reviewed here, all of them developed by interpreters rather than cognitive scientists, are at an intermediate level of specificity, between models of the basic translational process and more detailed representations of psycholinguistic operations. They focus on the simultaneity of task components and do not make specific claims regarding the ontology and 'architecture' of their components, that is, the existence and interplay in the brain of particular mental structures and procedures. The latter are the mainstay of language processing research in the cognitive sciences, which has provided foundations for various detailed models of the complex psycholinguistic processing operations in (simultaneous) interpreting.

4.4.3 *Complex Operations*

The very first psychological processing model for simultaneous interpreting was developed by Gerver (1971). On the basis of his experimental findings regarding interpreters' time lag, memory use and output monitoring, Gerver drew up a **flow-chart model** of the **mental structures and procedures** involved in input processing and output generation. (For a graphic representation, see Gerver 1975, 1976 or Moser-Mercer 1997/2002: 151.) The model features memory structures (short-term buffer store, long-term memory system, output buffer) and procedures at the control of the interpreter, such as discarding of input, pretesting of output, output monitoring and 'back-tracking' (reprocessing) to improve previous output. Source-language input is received in buffer storage and subjected to "input routines" depending on the state of the buffer store and on the interpreter's segmentation strategy. Through a process of "active reinstatement," linguistic knowledge in the interpreter's long-term memory becomes available in a short-term "operational memory" or "working memory" which serves the processing operations involved in source-language "decoding" and target-language "encoding." Maintenance in operational memory is also a prerequisite for monitoring and self-correction procedures which Gerver views as integral parts of the process and as particularly vulnerable to temporary shortages of processing capacity.

Gerver's model, which aims at a psychological rather than a linguistic description of the interpreting process, is not very explicit about translational processes as such. Even so, Gerver clearly distinguishes linguistic surface elements (sounds, words, sentences) from the "deep" level of meaning as understood by the interpreter, and suggests that grasping the relational meaning structure (subject, predicate, object) may be crucial to the translational task. While not incorporating it as an explicit feature in his model, Gerver also acknowledges the potential role of expectation-based processing, which is central to the model by Chernov (1978) discussed below.

Another model of **memory structures and processing operations** in simultaneous interpreting was devised by Barbara **Moser** in the mid-1970s. (For a graphic representation, see Moser-Mercer 1997, 1997/2002: 152f.) Moser's (1978) model, which is based on a psycholinguistic model of speech comprehension, devotes considerable attention to input processing stages up to the level of meaningful phrases and sentences, but also reflects the assumption of a close interaction between the input-driven sequential process and knowledge in long-term memory. Pivotal features of Moser's model are the search for the "conceptual base" and the construction of a prelinguistic meaning structure with the help of various types of knowledge (conceptual network, contextual knowledge, general knowledge). The conceptual meaning base then serves to activate target-language elements for syntactic and semantic word and phrase processing on the way to output articulation. The model posits a number of decision points at which processing is either moved on or looped back to an earlier stage. One of these decision points concerns "prediction," which allows for the elimination of all processing stages except feature detection up to the activation of target-language elements. Moser (1978) assumes a high degree of interaction between bottom-up and top-down processes (» 6.1) and also discusses trade-offs between the operations or stages competing for available processing capacity.

More than any other author, Chernov (1978, 1979/2002) viewed expectation-based processing, or prediction, as fundamental to the (simultaneous) interpreting process. Using the redundancy of natural languages as his point of departure, Chernov emphasizes the distinction between message elements that are new ("rhematic") versus those that are already known ("thematic"), and argues that the interpreter's attention is focused on components that carry new information. Such "information density peaks" are processed by marshaling available knowledge in a mechanism of **probability prediction** which operates concurrently on different levels of processing – from the syllable, word, phrase and utterance to the levels of the text and situational context. In Chernov's model, redundancy-based anticipation of sound patterns, grammatical structures, semantic structures and message sense is the essential mechanism underlying the comprehension process. On the production side, Chernov posits an analogous mechanism of **anticipatory synthesis**, which dovetails with the knowledge-based processes of comprehension. This focus on message sense construed with the help of knowledge-based expectation patterns suggests a basic compatibility of Chernov's model with both the *théorie du sens* and models such as Moser's which incorporate insights on knowledge structures from cognitive science.

The fundamental importance of knowledge-driven ('top-down') processing is also reflected in the sequential model by Cokely (1992a), which gives explicit consideration to the modality of input and output (spoken or signed) as well as to various **sociolinguistic** and **cultural** as well as **psychological factors** involved in the interpreting process. Cokely posits a total of seven major processing stages leading from message reception to production (Figure 4.11).

Aside from the main process sequence ("message reception" – "preliminary processing" – "short-term message retention" – "semantic intent realization" – "semantic equivalence determination" – "syntactic message formulation" – "message production"), Cokely devotes considerable space in his model to the many types of knowledge in long-term memory which are brought to bear on the various processing stages. Thus the stages of semantic and syntactic output generation involve such factors as "cross-linguistic awareness," "cross-cultural awareness," "linguistic markers" and "social markers," which Cokely (1992a: 125f) admits have yet to be subjected to more detailed analysis and validation.

Validation and testing (» 4.5), which constitute a fundamental challenge for theoretical models, come naturally, as it were, to models designed for a **computer-based implementation** of interpreting operations. The simultaneous interpreting system designed by Artificial Intelligence researcher Deryle Lonsdale (1997) comprises a limited-capacity working memory, comprehension and production modules for generating "semantic trees" and "parse trees" and an inter-lingual mapping system. Though focusing on low-level processing operations such as parsing and ambiguity resolution, Lonsdale also envisages a "dialogue processing system" in the form of a database of pragmatic factors (knowledge about the speaker and the situation, cooperative maxims, etc.) which provides context for the processing of individual utterances.

A full-scale implementation of dialogue interpreting was described by Hiroaki Kitano (1993), whose speech-to-speech automatic translation system DMDIALOG was designed to handle simple telephone conversations. The model assumes a high degree of interaction between a central knowledge base and the various processing stages (discourse processing – analysis – generation – voice synthesis), and foregrounds the role of hypothesis-building in speech processing. Kitano's is a hybrid system comprising both a symbolic (information-processing) component (for rule-based operations like sentence parsing) and a connectionist network for top-down processing in the form of pattern matching against previously encountered phrases and sentences stored in a database. Kitano (1993) characterizes his model as a "massively parallel" system, thus highlighting the connectionist aspect of its architecture (see also Moser-Mercer 1997; Setton 2003).

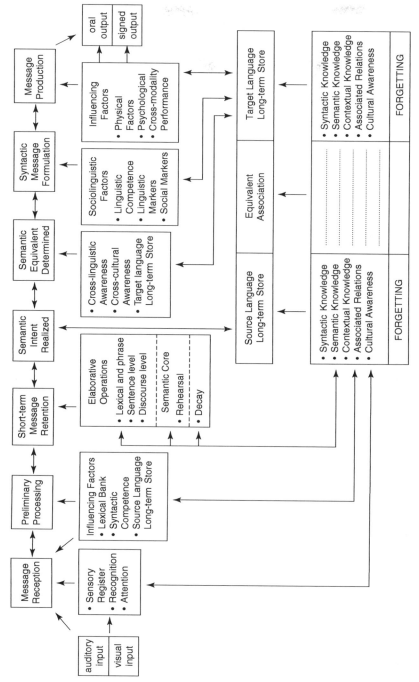

Figure 4.11 Cokely's sociolinguistically sensitive process model (Cokely 1992a: 124)

Connectionism (« 3.2.5) also underlies the theoretical model described by González et al. (2012) in their comprehensive textbook on court interpreting. Taking note of the models by Gerver, Moser and Cokely, the authors propose an updated human information-processing model which seeks to account for unconscious processing operations and multiple simultaneity. Their highly complex "non-linear" conceptualization of "simultaneous human information processing" is an attempt to reconcile connectionist neural models of cognitive functions with the specific translational norms of court interpreting.

A connectionist model backed by findings from neurolinguistic research, particularly on bilingual aphasia, was proposed by Michel Paradis (1994). His model of simultaneous interpreting (Figure 4.12) features memory buffers (circles), processing mechanisms (squares) and non-linguistic mental representations (diamonds), and highlights the **multiple simultaneity** of segment-by-segment processing operations at any given point in time.

The flow-chart representation of phrase processing in simultaneous interpreting shows each chunk (i.e. syntactic phrase and/or semantic unit) passing through eight steps: echoic memory, linguistic decoding, meaning representation, target-language encoding, target-language output, own output in echoic memory, linguistic decoding of own output, and meaning representation of own output (for comparison with the meaning constructed from source-language input). What is not evident from Paradis's parallel sequential flow-chart representation are the connectionist neurolinguistic assumptions underlying his model – the so-called "subset hypothesis" and the "activation threshold hypothesis" as well as the distinction between implicit linguistic competence and metalinguistic knowledge (» 5.1.3).

A process model which is largely compatible with both connectionist and rule-based computational approaches but essentially focuses on the level of **intermediate** cognitive **representation** of meaning was proposed by Setton (1999) in his relevance-theoretic ("cognitive-pragmatic") analysis of simultaneous interpreting. Characterized by its author as "a hybrid of best available theories" (Setton 1999: 63), Setton's processing model incorporates a range of cognitive-scientific research to address all relevant aspects of comprehension, memory and production in the interpreting process (Figure 4.13).

Though depicted as a sequential structure, from the sensorimotor level of audiovisual input processing (bottom-left) via concurrent meaning assembly and formulation controlled by a (working-memory-based) "Executive" (top center) on to output parsing and articulation (bottom-right), Setton conceptualizes all the processes as variably superimposed. Most importantly, "context" (i.e. all accessible knowledge) is assumed to play an integral part at all stages of cognitive processing, hence the pivotal role of the "task-oriented mental model" in adaptive memory. The mental model, which is sourced by both situational and world knowledge, shares with the "Assembler" a "language of representation" which encodes meaning in terms of propositions and attitudes. It is this operationalization of intermediate representations that permits Setton (1998/2002, 1999) to carry out a "blow-by-blow micro-analysis"

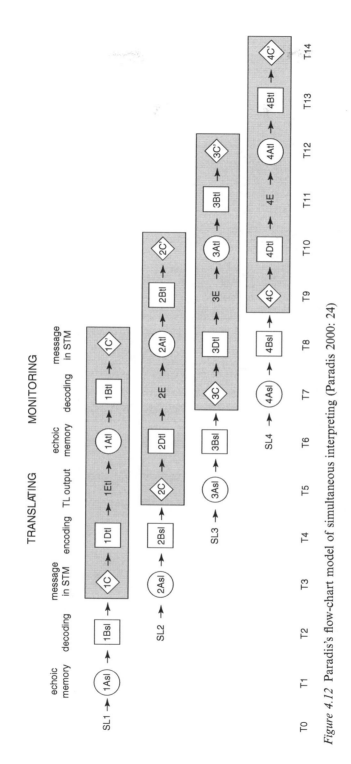

Figure 4.12 Paradis's flow-chart model of simultaneous interpreting (Paradis 2000: 24)

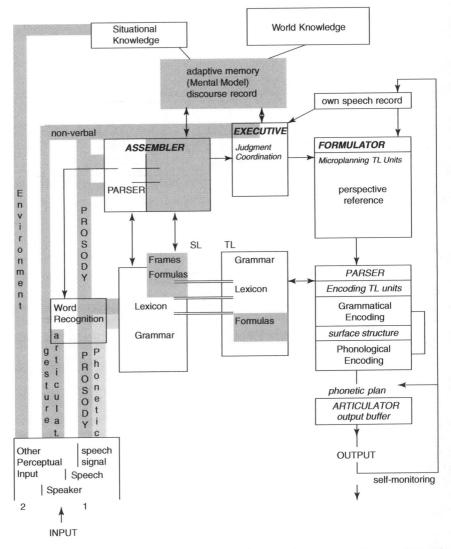

Figure 4.13 Setton's processing model for simultaneous interpreting (Setton 1999: 65)

of various discourse phenomena which had been left unaccounted for in previous cognitive (rather than cognitive-linguistic) processing models of SI.

4.5 Models, Tests and Applications

The models reviewed here, although representing only a selection of the modeling efforts in various conceptual dimensions, testify to the complex and multi-faceted nature of interpreting. Aspects of society and culture, social institutions, settings and situations, purposes of interaction, features of text and discourse, mental structures and neurophysiological processes are shown to be involved in interpreting as a communicative activity and process. Therefore, no single model, however complex and elaborate, could hope to be validated as an account for the phenomenon as a whole, that is, for 'interpreting as such.' This holds true for descriptive as well as explanatory models, and all the more so for predictive models which, as stated at the outset, need to account for all relevant variables at a sufficient level of detail.

Depending on the type of model and on the scholar's, or researcher's, epistemological position, a model can be 'tested' conceptually or in relation to specific empirical data. For predictive models, in particular, experimental testing is often viewed as the method of choice, even though it confronts the researcher with a paradoxical difficulty: given the complexity of the phenomenon, models should be as 'complete' as possible; the more complete the model, though, the more difficult its experimental validation. Cokely, for instance, whose model of seven main processing stages is complemented by a long list of highly abstract "subprocesses" (see Figure 4.11), points out that "it is not clear that the procedure used to validate the major stages in the process would be the appropriate one to use in validating sub-processes" (1992a: 125f). This problem is also acknowledged by Setton:

> It is fair to say that in the current state of knowledge, our assumptions about the workings of peripheral systems, like word recognition and articulation, are more secure than those concerning central processes, which are less accessible to experimentation.
>
> (1999: 64)

Rather than experimentation in the classic sense of hypothesis testing in a controlled laboratory environment, the methodological option for models chosen by authors such as Cokely and Setton is therefore close observation and analysis of a textual corpus generated in authentic or simulated interpreting sessions. Considering the numerous variables involved in real-life data, however, such analyses cannot strictly 'test' the model. Rather, they will serve to demonstrate the usefulness of the model in guiding the researcher's description and explanation of the empirical data.

A more stringent approach to the testing of models is to instantiate them as computer programs. The simulation by Lonsdale (1997) highlights the potential of computer modeling as well as its limitations, particularly regarding the role of knowledge-based processes and the multi-medial nature of discourse. More holistic models, such as the Seleskovitch triangle or Gile's Effort Models, have been applied successfully to experimentally generated empirical data. Clearly, though, such studies (e.g. Seleskovitch 1975; Gile 1999b) can validate only the principle underlying the model, which after all is not detailed enough to reflect real-time processing events.

Generally speaking, experimental hypothesis testing, which is the method of choice in disciplines like cognitive psychology and psycholinguistics that have provided the foundations for most processing models of interpreting, does not seem to be a viable option for testing 'full-process' models of interpreting as a whole; hence the importance of 'partial models' which single out particular aspects and components for specific analysis. Since there are likely to be as many of these submodels of interpreting as attempts to tackle particular research problems, it would be impossible to offer even a selective overview. Some of the prime examples are models of comprehension processes (» 6.1) and working memory (» 5.2.3), as covered in subsequent chapters.

Apart from their application to experimental research and corpus-based fieldwork, models have also played a prominent role in interpreter training. Indeed, several models, most notably Gile's, were originally conceived for didactic purposes and applied to research only later. Conversely, models such as Moser's were initially developed in the context of 'basic research' and subsequently came to be applied to pedagogical issues such as aptitude testing (» 12.2.2) and skill acquisition. Regardless of their nature and orientation, however, models clearly play a crucial role in the process of systematic inquiry. The present review of selected models and modeling approaches, which concludes Part I of this book, should therefore serve as an ideal point of departure for the more detailed exploration of selected topics and research in Part II.

Summary

Models, as representations of a phenomenon made up of components and relations holding between them, can be devised for interpreting in various conceptual dimensions, ranging from the broader *anthropological, socio-professional* and *institutional* levels to the *interactional* and *textual* levels and the 'internal' levels of *cognitive* and *neural* processes. Efforts to model interpreting date back to the 1970s and reflect a primary concern with aspects of communicative *interaction* and cognitive *processing*. In the former dimension, *constellation* models (e.g. by R.B.W. Anderson, Gile, Pöchhacker, Alexieva) seek to represent the interactants and the relations holding between them in the communicative event, whereas models such as those by Kirchhoff, Ingram and Poyatos focus on the nature and flow of *communication* signals, and Stenzl's and Kalina's foreground the role of knowledge and *text* in communicative interaction. Models focusing on cognitive processes, on the other hand, are aimed either at a more or less holistic representation of processing phases or *tasks* (e.g. Seleskovitch, Lederer, Kirchhoff, Gile) or at a detailed breakdown of psycholinguistic operations in terms of hypothesized *mental structures and procedures* (e.g. Gerver, Moser, Cokely, Paradis, Setton). Given the complexity of the phenomenon, models of interpreting can hardly be comprehensive and are thus difficult to 'verify' by their predictive power. Rather, most models of interpreting primarily aim to describe and explain, and are thus 'validated' by their usefulness in guiding teaching and further inquiry.

Sources and Further Reading

For a review of (processing) models in (conference) interpreting, see Part 3 of *The Interpreting Studies Reader* (Pöchhacker and Shlesinger 2002) and Setton (2003) as well as MODELS and EFFORT MODELS in Pöchhacker (2015).

Suggestions for Further Study

- To what extent can models foregrounding a given conceptual dimension (e.g. interactional, textual) be said to be compatible with conceptualizations at other levels of modeling?
- Which features of different interpreting models, in the sphere of inter-action as well as cognitive processing, can be identified as shared conceptual ground?
- How does the meaning of key concepts such as 'speaker,' 'situation,' 'role,' 'context' or 'knowledge' differ from one model to another?

Part II

Topics

5 Language and Memory

Interpreting as a form of language use to enable interlingual communication suggests language(s) as an obvious focus of interest. Given its crucial dependence on individual bilingual performance, interpreting can be studied in relation to bilingualism and the way two or more languages are organized and controlled in the brain. From a cognitive perspective, bilingual language use relies on various memory resources, the nature and function of which constitute another major area of research into the neurocognitive foundations of interpreting.

5.1 Bilingualism

The use of two (or more) languages (bilingualism, polyglossia) is a phenomenon which is open to a range of linguistic, psychological and sociological research perspectives. A distinction is usually made between the use of two or more languages in a society ('societal bilingualism') and bilinguality in the individual (e.g. Hamers and Blanc 2000). The latter, which involves such aspects as second language acquisition, bilingual processing and language switching, was explored early on with reference to translation and interpreting, and is now considered an important domain of psycholinguistics in which the perspectives of cognitive psychology and neuroscience converge on the study of complex processes of neurocognitive control.

5.1.1 Linguistic Dominance

As early as the 1950s, Canadian psychologist Wallace E. Lambert measured the reaction time of bilinguals on word-translation tasks to establish the degree of automaticity of **verbal behavior** in either language (usually French and English) and thus distinguish between **balanced** vs **dominant** bilinguals. Unlike other experimental tasks, facility of translation yielded a contradictory pattern of results, with some subjects translating faster into their acquired (non-dominant) language. Lambert et al. (1959: 81) speculated that this effect might be due to an individual's **active** vs **passive** approach to second language acquisition (as also reflected in the AIIC classification of conference interpreters' working languages), and pointed to the significance of motivational, attitudinal and cultural factors shaping a person's bilinguality. In more recent psycholinguistic experiments with word translation to address the issue of 'translation asymmetry' (e.g. de Bot 2000), reaction times were found to be consistently longer for translation from the dominant into the weaker language, and the effect of the direction of translation diminished with increasing proficiency in the acquired language.

An early acquisition-related hypothesis which has been applied to bilinguality and translation is the distinction between **compound** and **coordinate** bilinguals. This theory holds that compound bilinguals, who learned both their languages in a single context of acquisition, have two sets of linguistic signs for a single set of representational meanings, whereas coordinate bilinguals have separate sets of linguistic signs as well as somewhat different sets of representational meanings resulting from different socio-cultural contexts of acquisition. According to some psychologists, the latter configuration is typical of "true bilinguals" and a prerequisite for "true cross-cultural translation" (Ervin and Osgood 1965: 143). In one of the few empirical contributions on the subject, Christopher Thiéry, in his 1975 doctoral dissertation, surveyed four dozen fellow AIIC members with a double-A language classification and analyzed the acquisition histories and language-use patterns of thirty-four respondents. Thiéry (1978) concluded that **true bilinguals** have two 'mother tongues,' acquired before or at puberty, and need to make a conscious effort to retain their true bilingualism in adult life.

5.1.2 *Cerebral Lateralization*

Another approach to bilingualism in the individual which bears on the issue of linguistic dominance centers on the neural and **neurophysiological foundations** of linguistic functions. Departing from the fact that the left cerebral hemisphere is specialized for language (in right-handed individuals), research since the late 1970s has sought to establish whether individuals with a command of more than one language, including interpreters, exhibit a characteristic pattern of cerebral **lateralization**. Neuropsychological studies have yielded some, albeit contradictory, evidence of a more balanced neurolinguistic representation (i.e. of greater right-hemisphere involvement in bilinguals and polyglots) associated with factors like the age of acquisition (i.e. early vs late bilinguals), relative language proficiency, sex, and spoken vs signed language (e.g. Corina and Vaid 1994). For interpreters, in particular, Franco Fabbro and associates (Fabbro et al. 1990) found more bilateral cerebral involvement during verbal processing in the simultaneous mode. The overall picture, however, is clouded by statistical limitations and uncertainties regarding experimental tasks and designs. Results achieved for certain subject groups with experimental techniques such as dichotic listening or 'finger-tapping' (see Fabbro and Gran 1994) are difficult to compare with findings from electro-encephalographic analyses (e.g. Petsche et al. 1993) or brain imaging studies (e.g. Rinne et al. 2000). In one of the most methodologically rigorous studies in this paradigm, Green et al. (1994) found no evidence to support the hypothesis, fielded by Fabbro and associates, that simultaneous interpreters may develop a different, less asymmetrical pattern of cerebral lateralization. Rather, evidence of more right-hemisphere involvement has been explained by attentional strategies and recourse to nonverbal (pragmatic) knowledge, particularly when using an acquired language.

5.1.3 Neurolinguistic Mechanisms

Apart from neuropsychological experimentation, neurolinguists have used clinical data on aphasia (i.e. linguistic impairment caused by cerebral lesions) in bilingual and polyglot individuals to develop explanatory hypotheses for translational behavior (see Fabbro and Gran 1994). Paradis (2000: 20), speaking out against the "fruitless search for a differential cerebral asymmetry," has advanced the so-called **subset hypothesis**, according to which a bilingual's two languages are served by two subsystems of the larger cognitive system known as "implicit linguistic competence." Each of the two separate networks of connections can be independently activated and inhibited, and the **activation threshold** of a given trace in linguistic memory is assumed to be a function of the frequency and recency of activation (see also the "gravitational model" by Gile 1995b). Paradis cites neurolinguistic evidence to suggest that interpreting involves at least four neurofunctionally independent systems – one for each language involved and one for each direction of translation – and that the process may be either conceptually mediated or based on direct linguistic correspondence. In the neural-network account proposed by Paradis (2000), as in the similar application of the language-mode theory by Grosjean (2001), simultaneous interpreters thus have to acquire a peculiar state of inhibition/ activation for each of the linguistic component systems involved so as to permit concurrent use with a minimum of interference.

Converging evidence from the fields of psycholinguistics, neuropsychology and cognitive neuroscience suggests that the mechanisms involved in **language control** through selective activation and inhibition of a bilingual's sub-lexicons are not specific to language processing. Rather, they are assumed to be 'domain-general,' that is, to underlie the regulation of behavior of all sorts, known as cognitive or **executive control** (de Groot 2015).

5.2 Memory

Linguistic sign systems as well as all other forms of signals encountered in human interaction with the environment must have some type of mental representation. The modern conception of 'memory' for the representation of sensory input in the brain emerged in the mid-twentieth century, when psychologists developed the hypothesis of a temporary 'storage' system distinct from a more durable form of storage based on networks of neurochemical traces or activation patterns. Various models of memory allowing for 'short-term' and 'long-term' storage have since been proposed, and short-term memory resources, more generally referred to as 'working memory,' have emerged as a central concern in research on interpreters' cognitive processing. Most research in this area focuses on simultaneous interpreting (SI), even though consecutive interpreting with note-taking is similarly reliant on working memory, in addition to being the most obviously memory-dependent form of interpreting.

5.2.1 Long-Term Memory

The role of long-term memory in interpreting has attracted little specific research interest. Sanz (1930) listed 'good verbal memory' among the mental abilities his professional respondents considered essential for interpreting, and devoted a special section of his research report to the **knowledge** required: knowledge of languages, general knowledge, and knowledge of the subject matter. These knowledge resources are 'stored' in long-term memory, defined by Kintsch (1998: 217) as "everything a person knows and remembers." Aside from 'semantic memory' (concepts and world knowledge in general), this includes personal recollections of events in their particular context, referred to as 'episodic memory.' Further distinctions are made between 'explicit memory,' or 'declarative knowledge,' which is conscious, and 'implicit memory,' or 'procedural knowledge,' which is the unconscious memory of how to perform automatized tasks and skills. While all these types of knowledge in long-term memory are of obvious relevance to the receptive and productive processes in interpreting (» 6.1, » 6.2) and have invariably been considered key components of aptitude for interpreting (» 12.2), there is little evidence to date of specific long-term memory skills in interpreters.

The main exception, though little studied, is the development of efficient storage and retrieval operations in consecutive interpreting. Ever since the earliest writings on the topic (e.g. Rozan 1956), the process has been described as operating on ideas ('sense') rather than words. In the listening phase, conceptual structures are formed by semantic **chunking** of input and optionally captured on the interpreter's notepad (e.g. in the form of symbols or abbreviations). These external storage devices subsequently serve as **retrieval cues** for recall of memorized semantic structures from long-term memory. In the pioneering study of note-taking by Seleskovitch (1975, 1975/2002), a dozen professional interpreters produced a consecutive rendition of two speeches and subsequently commented on their notes. Her findings emphasize the role of notes as minimal cues, in whatever form, for retrieving a maximum of conceptual content. This account can be linked to the influential notion of **long-term working memory**, developed by Ericsson and Kintsch (1995) to explain expert comprehension. They posit so-called retrieval structures, which make available a subset of long-term memory that is linked to a cue in the short-term store. In contrast to the limited capacity of (short-term) working memory (» 5.2.3), long-term working memory is constrained only by the extent and nature of the retrieval structures, which depend on efficient chunking strategies when processing input for long-term memory storage.

Seleskovitch (1975) also highlights the need for interpreters to divide their attention between the conceptual processing of input and the taking of notes, and warns that the latter must not detract from the attention needed for comprehension processes (» 6.3.1). It is this issue of memory storage under the processing constraints of divided attention that has been investigated in a line of research using recall from long-term memory as an indicator of different cognitive processes in various types of interpreting.

5.2.2 Storage and Process

Early studies of cognitive operations in language processing by interpreters tested subjects for recall after interpreting and related tasks. Gerver (1974a), in an experiment with nine trainees and scripted texts, found that recall (as measured by content questions) was better after listening than after SI or shadowing, and identified simultaneous listening and speaking as the cause of impaired memorization. This view was corroborated in subsequent work by Isham (1994), who concluded from the differential performance of signed- and spoken-language interpreters that post-task recall was not only a function of the interpreting process itself but reflected the impact of modality-related processing interference (see also Ingram 1992: 114).

Gerver's (1974a) conclusion that better recall after interpreting than after shadowing reflected more complex, deeper processing operations in inter- preting was followed up in a 1983 PhD thesis by Sylvie Lambert (1989). In the theoretical framework of the **depth-of-processing** hypothesis, put forward as a unitary model of memory in the early 1970s, Lambert compared the recall and recognition scores of sixteen subjects (eight professionals, eight trainees) following SI, consecutive interpreting, shadowing and listening. While she found a less clear-cut pattern of results than Gerver (1974a), with recall scores yielding no significant differences between listening and the two interpreting conditions, shadowing resulted in significantly lower recall than listening and consecutive interpreting. Lambert found that a similar relationship held for recognition scores, particularly with regard to the post-task recognition of semantic (rather than lexical or syntactic) source-text information. In a comparable study with 11 professional sign language interpreters, Ingram (1992) found significantly lower semantic recognition scores for listening than for English–ASL interpreting as well as for transliterating, even though the latter had been hypothesized to be a 'shallow,' form-based processing task analogous to shadowing (see Isham 1994). Ingram (1992: 115) therefore concluded that "transliteration is not simply a programmed sensorimotor task but a task like interpretation that involves complex and deep cognitive processing."

The depth-of-processing hypothesis was also used by Maurizio Viezzi (1990) to compare information retention after two forms of interpreting in the simultaneous mode – sight translation and SI. In an experiment involving 18 professional and 24 student interpreters working from English or French into Italian, Viezzi found that recall scores were lower after sight translation than after SI only for the morphosyntactically dissimilar language pair (English–Italian). For structurally similar languages like French and Italian, recall after the simultaneous processing tasks was as good as after listening. Viezzi (1990) explained this deviation from previous findings (Gerver 1974a; Lambert 1989) as being due to the impact of morphosyntactic transformations on processing resources, but left unclear why this effect should obtain only for the simultaneous rendition of visual input.

The original depth-of-processing view of memory has largely been superseded by a multiple-systems approach. In particular, the online interaction between fresh input and knowledge stored in long-term memory is seen as crucially mediated by short-term storage and processing resources generally referred to as **working memory**. Research into working memory in interpreters initially focused on memory capacity (» 5.2.3), whereas more recent studies have put the emphasis on processing and attention management (» 5.2.4), highlighting that the concept of working memory goes far beyond the simple time-related distinction between long-term and short-term storage and relates in no small part to processing and the control of attentional resources.

5.2.3 *Working Memory*

The most influential conception of working memory, dating back to the mid-1970s, was put forward by British psychologist Alan Baddeley (e.g. 2000). His model, which underlies several studies of memory in SI, posits a limited-capacity attentional system ('Central Executive') which controls a 'slave system' for holding and dealing with speech-based information ('phonological loop') and another one for visual or spatial information ('visuo-spatial sketchpad'). Baddeley's original model was subsequently complemented by a third slave system, the so-called episodic buffer, to account for short-term storage of integrated (verbal, spatial, visual, temporal) units. An alternative account that is largely compatible with Baddeley's multi-store model, but emphasizes the linkage between short-term and long-term memory, was put forward by Nelson Cowan (1995). Like Ericsson and Kintsch (1995), Cowan conceives of working memory as an activated part of long-term memory and assumes that only a small number of items in working memory are in the **focus of attention** and hence available for processing.

As most cognitive process models of SI envisage a short-term storage function (« 4.4.3), SI skills can be assumed to be related to **working memory capacity**. In a first study using standard tasks to test the hypothesis that experience in SI is associated with enhanced working memory, Padilla et al. (1995) measured memory capacity in four groups of ten subjects (trained interpreters, beginning and advanced interpreting students, and bilingual controls) and found that the professional interpreters clearly outperformed the other groups on the digit span task (i.e. memorizing auditorily presented series of up to nine digits) and on the more complex phrase span task. A similar study by Christoffels et al. (2006) using the reading span task confirmed the superior performance of interpreters, while the experiments by Liu et al. (2004) and Köpke and Nespoulous (2006), using the listening span task, did not. Despite some methodological doubts, including the effect of the modality of test administration and different scoring techniques, there is some evidence from these and other investigations of a relationship between experience in SI and working memory capacity as measured with complex (i.e. storage and processing) tasks.

A related question explored in studies of this kind concerns the relationship between working memory capacity and performance levels in SI as measured in terms of accuracy. Using the reading or listening span task and participants at various levels of skill, including untrained bilinguals, these studies have yielded a mixed pattern of results. Liu et al. (2004) found no significant differences between student interpreters and professionals in relation to working memory capacity; others found evidence that better SI performance was linked to higher working memory spans, but only at lower levels of skill (i.e. with students and untrained bilinguals). It is not clear, therefore, whether the differences found between interpreters and control groups result from extended practice of the skill or from a priori variations in cognitive abilities.

Aside from working memory span as measured in terms of the number of units held in memory, working memory is also subject to **time limitations**. In Cowan's (1995) model, activated memory decays within 10 to 30 seconds unless it is refreshed by being moved into the focus of attention, which holds approximately four items. Baddeley (2000), on the other hand, assumes that the phonological loop can hold approximately two seconds' worth of verbal material. To prevent decay of the memory traces, they must be refreshed through a process known as subvocal rehearsal. In SI, the need for concurrent articulation makes such rehearsal impossible – an effect known as articulatory suppression – so that the time constraint on working memory can be assumed to be particularly critical. Specifically, linguistic input which demands longer storage and structural transformations must be expected to overload the capacity of the short-term store. This prediction was investigated by Shlesinger (2000a) in an experimental study with 16 professionals who were asked to interpret simultaneously, from English into Hebrew, texts containing high-load-inducing input strings (each made up of four adjectives preceding a noun, e.g. "clumsy, stylized, heavy, stilted language"). Since Hebrew is a head-initial language requiring post-modification, subjects were forced to carry out storage and restructuring operations that severely taxed their working memory capacity. Memory load was varied in terms of word length and presentation rate. The main hypothesis that slow delivery rates would result in poorer performance as a result of greater decay of unrehearsed memory traces in the short-term store was largely borne out by the experimental findings. However, Shlesinger's professional subjects generally retained only few modifiers, or none at all, in their target-language renditions, presumably as a result of performance norms licensing the omission of 'minor' linguistic items. Thus, aside from supplying highly relevant evidence of the temporal limitation of working memory capacity in SI and highlighting the methodological complexities of using strictly controlled input materials for an experimental task, Shlesinger's (2000a) study points to the importance of strategies in interpreting (» 6.5), which also include the way available cognitive resources are utilized.

5.2.4 Attention Management

In the simultaneous mode, in particular, working memory is crucial not only for its short-term storage and processing functions but also for its executive functions, allowing flexible control and allocation of **attentional resources**. One basic example of such attentional coordination is the ability to ignore distracting information, or to remain focused on a listening task despite concurrent articulation, as in the case of SI. This was investigated in the above-mentioned study on working memory capacity by Padilla et al. (1995), who tested their four groups of subjects on free recall after memorizing visually presented word lists with and without concurrent articulation of the syllable "bla." Only the trained interpreters remained unaffected by the concurrent vocalization task and achieved significantly higher recall scores than the rest of the subjects, thus demonstrating a more efficient allocation of attentional resources.

The research by Liu et al. (2004), also mentioned above, likewise focused on attention management skills in relation to levels of training and experience. With the aim of establishing to what extent expertise in SI was a function of general cognitive qualities (such as working memory capacity) rather than task-specific skills acquired through training and professional practice, Liu designed an experiment involving a total of 36 native Chinese subjects (professional interpreters, advanced and beginning students of interpreting). Apart from taking a comprehension and a listening span test, subjects were asked to simultaneously interpret three (11–17-minute) English texts, each of which contained 20 'critical sentences' followed by a continuation sentence, the first words of which were essential for a full and correct understanding. Cognitive load in the critical sentences was manipulated in terms of readability and presentation rate. Unlike Padilla et al. (1995), Liu et al. (2004) found that working memory span scores did not differentiate between the three groups of subjects. Rather, professional interpreters outperformed students only on the interpreting task as such, in which they demonstrated superior (selective) semantic processing skills in the critical sentences and more efficient **attention management** as reflected in significantly higher correctness scores for continuation sentences and markedly better quality ratings for meaningfulness, smoothness and naturalness of output.

The role of **attentional control** is also foregrounded in the study on working memory and SI by Timarová et al. (2014). In a highly sophisticated research design, a total of 28 conference interpreters with an average of twelve years of professional experience completed a set of working memory tasks focusing on cognitive control and interpreted three English texts into their A language (20 Czech, eight Dutch). The test battery included visually presented tasks measuring resistance to interference, response inhibition, updating and task-switching, as well as a test of general cognitive abilities. The main (20-minute) experimental text contained 30 sentences manipulated for syntactic and semantic complexity and the presence of numbers; the two shorter texts each contained two types of lists, either presented as such or embedded in full sentences. The authors found one working memory function – resistance to interference – to be related to interpreting experience, permitting higher accuracy in rendering lists of items, though not of numbers. Overall, the findings from this complex study suggest that some measurable aspects of SI (such as coping with lists, speed, numbers or negatives) are related to the central executive functions of working memory, though the pattern of relations is not straightforward, and different working memory functions are found to predict different subprocesses of SI.

Further Reading

Bilingualism

See BILINGUALISM and NEUROSCIENCE APPROACHES in Pöchhacker (2015).

Memory

See MEMORY and WORKING MEMORY in Pöchhacker (2015).

6   Cognitive Processes

Analyzing interpreting from a cognitive perspective suggests a simple distinction between cognitive structures and cognitive processes. As evident from the state of the art on research into working memory (« 5.2.3), however, the difference between the two is anything but clear-cut. Thus, while the focus of this chapter is on cognitive processes, it should be understood that these are closely inter-dependent with memory 'structures' and linguistic resources as described in Chapter 5. Beyond the basic distinction between receptive and productive processes (» 6.1, » 6.2), the present chapter also covers topics that have received special attention in research on interpreting, mainly with a focus on (spoken-language) simultaneous conference interpreting.

6.1 Comprehension

A key prerequisite in the interpreting process, language comprehension as a crucial topic at the interface of language and cognition is an important area of study in the cognitive sciences. A basic distinction is made in research on language understanding between 'bottom-up' (i.e. input-driven) and 'top-down' (i.e. knowledge-based) operations, both of which are required for a full account of comprehension, defined here as the act of building a mental representation of language-mediated meaning.

6.1.1 Language Understanding

Psycholinguistic research on spoken language understanding has long reflected a particular concern with the initial stages of the comprehension process. Component operations like phoneme identification, word recognition, lexical disambiguation and sentence parsing, which have been modeled in the serial information-processing as well as the connectionist paradigm of cognitive science (« 3.2.5), are naturally relevant, though hardly unique, to interpreting. Indeed, with the significant exception of speech recognition research in the context of automatic interpreting (» 11.3.1), very little interpreting-specific work has been done on the so-called **low-level processes** in language comprehension. An interesting approach was taken from the perspective of second-language acquisition research by McAllister (2000), who studied (inferior) comprehension performance in an acquired language; another is psychological research on interpreters' specialized **lexical skills** in tasks like word identification and categorization, for which Bajo et al. (2000) found a presumably training-related superiority among interpreters in contrast to bilingual controls. In general, however, interpreting scholars, particularly in the IT paradigm, have shown little interest in the lower-level stages of language understanding as studied in the psycholinguist's laboratory. Their main interest has rather been in the way interpreters comprehend utterance meaning ('sense') in situated discourse by drawing on their contextual, situational and encyclopedic knowledge.

6.1.2 Knowledge-Based Processing

It is now an established fact that comprehension is not a passive, receptive process but depends crucially on what is already known. Processing new information thus requires the active construction of some form of mental representation by integrating the input with various kinds of pre-existing knowledge – lexical, syntactic, pragmatic, encyclopedic, etc. The so-called **cloze technique**, developed in the early 1950s, is based on such a knowledge-based conception of comprehension: confronted with gaps in verbal structures, subjects will use their lexical and grammatical knowledge to fill in what is missing by a process of anticipatory reconstruction or pattern-based 'closure.' The fact that prior knowledge serves to generate **expectations** which guide the comprehension process was demonstrated early on for SI. Chernov (« 2.3.2) had 11 professional interpreters work on realistic 20-minute speeches (United Nations speeches, lectures) that had been manipulated to include meaningless (i.e. semantically anomalous) sentences and unpredictable turns of phrase (i.e. utterances which defied the phrasal expectations generated by their preceding context). Most subjects omitted or mistranslated the anomalous sentences and rendered the unpredictable utterances according to the contextually prompted expectation (see Chernov 1979/2002: 100, 2004: 189, 195). Chernov thus identified the principle of subjective redundancy and, hence, **predictability** of contextualized utterances as fundamental to the comprehension process, and made "probability prediction" the core of his processing model of SI (« 4.4.3).

Using the linguistic notions of theme and rheme to refer to 'given vs new' information, Chernov modeled the semantic level of comprehension as a process of "cumulative dynamic analysis" resulting in "sense structures." On the whole, he described the dynamic process of **understanding** as covering (1) the gradual addition of rhematic components to those already fore-grounded; (2) the bridging of sense gaps; (3) the combination of rhematic and thematic components to form more complex configurations; and (4) the molding of the resulting sense structure to fit the situational context and the hearer's knowledge (see Chernov 1979/2002: 104f). Chernov's approach is largely compatible with psychological models of discourse comprehension, such as the Construction-Integration Model developed by Walter Kintsch (1998). With reference to the influential model by van Dijk and Kintsch (1983), for instance, Chernov's account can be related to (1) building a **propositional textbase**; (2) **inferencing**; (3) building **macro-structures** (macro-processing); and (4) building a **situation model**. These notions have been applied in various studies on comprehension in interpreting.

In one of the most extensive experimental studies on the topic, Dillinger (1994) used a proposition score to compare comprehension processes in untrained bilinguals and professional interpreters. His study, which addressed a number of relevant input variables – such as text type and information density (» 6.4.4) – yielded little evidence of interpreting-specific comprehension skills, possibly for reasons of experimental design. Beyond a quantitative propositional approach, Mackintosh (1985) pointed to the relevance of macro-processing operations such as 'deletion,' 'generalization' and 'construction' in both simultaneous and consecutive interpreting, and Pöchhacker (1993) discussed interpreters' use of **knowledge structures** like 'frames,' 'scripts' and 'MOPs' in building a mental representation of message content. Isham and Lane (1994), who investigated comprehension in signed language interpreting by using a cloze task requiring inferences, found that subjects who had interpreted (rather than transliterated) the English input passages and thus processed them at a more conceptual level were better able to draw the necessary inferences.

Just what level or **conceptual depth** of comprehension is required for interpreting remains a moot point, not least because of the methodological difficulty of measuring the level of "operational comprehension" (Gile 1993: 67) during interpreting. One of the few attempts to address the contentious dichotomy between language-based 'transcoding' and 'deverbalization'-based interpreting on the basis of experimental research was made by William Isham (1994), who replicated the so-called Jarvella effect (i.e. the impact of syntactic boundaries on verbatim recall of the most recent clause) in a study involving nine English/French professional interpreters and twelve bilingual controls. Isham found that some of the interpreters displayed a similar recall pattern to listeners, whereas others showed inferior verbatim recall and appeared to be oblivious to syntactic boundaries. He concluded that both a more **form-based** approach and a **meaning-based** strategy may be viable in particular language pairs.

Mindful of these choices, an integrative account of the dynamic process of 'meaning assembly' in interpreting was developed by Setton (1998/2002, 1999) in the framework of **cognitive pragmatics** (more specifically, relevance theory). Based on the relevance-theoretic assumption that cognitively available **context** plays a key role in complementing linguistic signals, Setton analyzes (simultaneous) interpreting as an inferential process in which interpreters must derive – and give access to in their audience – meanings that are 'optimally relevant' in their cognitive environment, that is, yield maximum cognitive effects for minimum processing effort. He shows how the interpreter's **mental model** of the source speech is enriched by information that is accessible, or inferrable, in the situation of interaction and how this mental representation informs executive decisions on output production in the target language.

6.2 Production

Compared to the substantial body of language-processing research focusing on comprehension, production processes have received rather less attention, both in cognitive science in general and in the CP paradigm of interpreting studies (« 3.4.3). In the DI paradigm (« 3.4.4), in contrast, where the emphasis is on language use in interaction, researchers have shown a keen interest in 'speaking' as a situated activity. This is reflected in different lines of research relevant to interpreting as 'text/discourse production' (« 3.2.6): one which studies 'speaking' as the production of linguistic utterances as such (» 6.2.1), and another which studies utterances as tools in the interactive creation of discourse (» 6.2.3, Chapter 8).

6.2.1 From Intention to Articulation

Ever since Herbert (1952: 59) demanded that "A good interpreter must be a trained public speaker," conference interpreters, particularly when working in the consecutive mode, have foregrounded their professional skills of expression (e.g. Déjean le Féal 1990: 155). On the assumption, however, that the interpreter's speech process would be the same as that of any (native) speaker (see Seleskovitch 1978a: 97), the explanation of production processes was left to psycholinguists, who have indeed managed to elucidate the process over the course of decades of experimental research. One of the most widely accepted and influential models of production is the three-stage model of *Speaking* by Willem Levelt (1989), in which a **conceptualizer** generates 'preverbal messages,' a **formulator** encodes them as 'internal speech,' and an **articulator** produces 'overt speech.' This model has been adopted, among others, by Setton (1999) and de Bot (2000), whose account of bilingual language use and SI includes a critical discussion of production in early process models (« 4.4.3). One of these is the model by Gerver (1971), who was the first to stress that **monitoring** and correction are an integral part of the process of SI (see Gerver 1976: 202). Indeed, with the ideational component largely inaccessible to research, components of the production process such as output planning and monitoring, as manifested in self-corrections and false starts, have been of particular interest to psycholinguists and interpreting researchers alike.

6.2.2 Hesitation and Correction

Psycholinguistic research on spontaneous speech as undertaken by Goldman-Eisler since the late 1950s focused on hesitation, in particular pausing, as a 'window' on the cognitive planning activity intrinsic to speech production. Ever since Goldman-Eisler's 'pausological' approach to SI, **silent** and **filled pauses** ('ums and ahs') have been acknowledged as significant features both of the process of output generation and of the interpreter's output as a textual product (» 7.1.3). Lederer (1978/2002, 1981) and Setton (1999), for instance, discuss SI output in their corpora with reference to the interpreters' pauses as reflected in their transcriptions, and Setton (1999: 246) suggests that various types of hesitancy phenomena correspond to different levels of attention.

Applying the study of pauses and hesitations to consecutive interpreting, Peter Mead, in a PhD thesis completed in 2002, analyzed a large corpus of consecutive interpretations (English/Italian) with regard to both the quantitative incidence of **disfluencies** and his 45 subjects' retrospective explanations of their pausing behavior. On the basis of precise software-assisted measurements, Mead (2000) found an average proportion of pause time of 11 seconds for professionals working into their A language, compared to more than 20 seconds for student interpreters working into their B. In a similar vein, Tissi (2000) described student interpreters' experimental output in terms of **stalls** – that is, silent and filled pauses and lengthened syllables – and other disfluencies, such as repetitions, corrections and false starts. In a process-oriented perspective, such phenomena have been conceptualized not so much as faults and imperfections, but as typical features of orality (» 7.1.3) and **impromptu speech** (Enkvist 1982) and thus of the 'spontaneous' production required of the interpreter (see Lederer 1981: 41; Pöchhacker 1995b).

The strategic nature of **repairs** in SI was demonstrated in a corpus-based study by Petite (2005), who examined authentic interpretations by eight professional interpreters and identified different types and degrees of repair. Aside from 'mid-articulatory' (i.e. within-word) repairs, she found instances of overt **error correction** as well as repairs undertaken to achieve greater **appropriateness** (in terms of precision, disambiguation or coherence). The latter were sometimes made even when the repair did not seem to justify the additional processing cost incurred, thus placing listener orientation above the interpreter's own need to minimize cognitive effort.

6.2.3 From Utterance to Interactive Discourse

While the process leading from ideation to utterance is the focus of psycholinguistic studies of production in and by a speaking individual, research on speaking from a sociolinguistic perspective essentially investigates how two or more speakers use utterances in the process of conversational interaction. This approach to interactive discourse implies a fundamental concern with **contextual factors**, as listed early on in the mnemonic SPEAKING model (Situation – Participants – Ends – Act sequences – Key – Instrumentalities – Norms – Genres) by Hymes (« 3.1.4), which has been adopted in various domains of interpreting research. Within the 'dialogic' conception of discourse underlying the DI paradigm, production is viewed as a joint activity, or **inter-activity**, involving all participants as speakers and hearers in the interaction (» 8.1.1). Central to the discourse-analytical view of production is the notion of **turn-taking** as foregrounded in conversation analysis (» 8.2.1). The study of turn-taking behavior in particular highlights the role of **non-verbal features**, and **multimodality**, in discourse production by the interpreter and the primary participants (» 8.2.2).

6.3 Simultaneity

Ever since the introduction and spread of simultaneous conference interpreting sparked off scientific interest, the issue of simultaneity has been a key topic in processing-oriented research. While simultaneity in the form of 'overlapping talk' and the interpreter's multiple involvement in the interactivity of discourse also plays a significant role in dialogue interpreting research (» 8.2.1), the focus here is on the 'classic' view of the problem in terms of dividing attention over receptive and productive processes, and the degree of synchrony of psycholinguistic operations.

6.3.1 Divided Attention

Early cognitive psychologists in the 1950s and 1960s, such as Donald Broadbent and Alan Welford, worked on the long-standing assumption that **attention-sharing** is possible only for habitual, largely automatic tasks. In an experiment requiring subjects simultaneously to listen and respond to simple questions, Broadbent found that "the saying of even a simple series of words interferes with the understanding of a fresh message" and concluded that "we cannot attend perfectly to both the speech of others and to our own" (Broadbent 1952: 271ff). This was questioned in the 1969 PhD thesis by Ingrid Pinter (« 2.2.2), whose experiment with beginning and advanced students of interpreting as well as experienced conference interpreters clearly demonstrated the effect of practice on proficiency in the skill of simultaneous listening and speaking (see Kurz 1996). Welford's suggestion, in turn, that interpreters learned to ignore the sound of their own voices so as to avoid interference, was refuted by Gerver (1971), who pointed to self-corrections in interpreted output as evidence that simultaneous interpreters were indeed monitoring their own voices.

Gerver endorsed proposals by contemporary psychologists to replace the notion of a fixed (single) channel of limited capacity by that of a "fixed-capacity central processor," whose activity could be distributed over several tasks within the limits of the total **processing capacity** available (see Gerver 1971: 15f). This capacity-sharing approach has proved fundamental to processing models of interpreting (« 4.3) and is at the heart of recent studies on working memory in SI (« 5.2.4). While the principle of attention-sharing in the interpreting process is now beyond doubt, the details of interpreters' selective allocation, if not switching, of their attentional resources remain unclear.

6.3.2 Pauses and Synchrony

Both interpreters and psycholinguists have suggested that the simultaneous interpreter might take advantage of pauses in the source speech to avoid the simultaneity of listening and speaking. The idea that interpreters would try to crowd as much of their output as possible into the speaker's pauses (see Paneth 1957/2002: 33; Goldman-Eisler 1967: 128) was tested in the 1969 PhD thesis by Barik (« 2.2.2). Although he found support for the hypothesis in his experimental data, Barik (1973: 263) conceded that interpreters' speech activity during source-speech pauses might also be an epiphenomenon of the task as such rather than a strategy to aid performance. These doubts were confirmed by Gerver (1975, 1976) on the basis of pause-time analyses of authentic conference speeches. Employing a pause criterion of 250 milliseconds, he found that most pauses in his sample (71% of 804 pauses) lasted no more than 750 milliseconds and only 17% were longer than one second. As for the interpreter's strategic behavior, Gerver (1975: 123) concluded that "there is obviously not much he can fit into most pauses, but then neither can he avoid filling them if he is already speaking." Further evidence of the essential simultaneity of speaking and listening in SI, which had also been studied by Soviet authors (e.g. Chernov 1978; Shiryayev 1979), was supplied by Ivana Čeňková in her 1985 PhD research. Based on an oscillographic analysis of 29 minutes of fieldwork data involving Russian and Czech, Čeňková (1988) reported a ratio of concurrent activity of roughly 90% for source speeches delivered at a speed of over 200 syllables per minute.

Apart from the comparative study of pause times, which has seen a revival thanks to the availability of computer-assisted speech data analysis (e.g. Lee 1999; Yagi 1999; Tissi 2000), the synchrony of source and target speeches in SI has also been studied by comparing speech and articulation rates, the number and duration of 'speech bursts' or 'chunks' of speech between pauses, and the number of source–target 'overlap events.' The findings from such analyses are rather varied, however, given the differences in measurement techniques, pause criteria, language pairs, discourse types, and skill levels.

6.3.3 Time Lag and Segmentation

The central aspect of synchrony in SI is the 'time lag,' also known as *décalage*, between the original speech and the interpreter's output. Paneth (« 2.2.1), stressing that "the interpreter says not what he hears, but what he has heard" (1957/2002: 32), measured lag times in fieldwork data and found average values between two and four seconds. These stopwatch measurements were confirmed by Oléron and Nanpon (1965/2002), who employed special equipment to analyze time delays on parallel visual tracings. They found mean values of two to three seconds for various language combinations in a range between 0.5 and as much as 11 seconds. While time lag measurements depend on a number of methodological choices (see Timarová et al. 2011), the average of two to three seconds, or four to five words at average presentation rates (see Gerver 1969/2002), has proved quite robust for spoken as well as signed languages. Cokely (1992a) reported average onset lag times of 2.8 seconds (min. 1 second, max. 8 seconds) for English–ASL interpretation while pointing to a considerable spread of average lag times (min. 1.7 seconds, max. 4.8 seconds) among the six interpreters in his sample.

Time lag is relevant also in other forms of simultaneous processing, such as sight translation and respeaking, and even in consecutive interpreting. Andres (2002) used time-coded video-recordings to study lag times in note-taking and found that average lag times for 14 professional subjects working from French into German were between three and six seconds. The 14 student interpreters in her study, by contrast, tended to fall behind in their note-taking by more than six seconds, and to catch up by leaving gaps in their notes which showed up directly as omissions in their target-language output. Such evidence of processing overload as a result of note production competing with comprehension processes for scarce attentional resources (« 6.3.1) highlights the link between temporal variables and underlying cognitive activities, as explored also in early experiments on SI.

In an experiment involving constructed 100-word passages of English and French and an essentially word-based analytical approach, Anne Treisman (1965) measured the **ear–voice span** (EVS) of (untrained) bilingual subjects during **shadowing** (i.e. immediate verbatim repetition of the input in the same language) and simultaneous interpreting. She found the EVS to be greater for the interpreting task (four to five words versus three words in shadowing) and attributed this to "the increased decision load between input and output" (1965: 369). This differential performance on a shadowing and an interpreting task was demonstrated for professional subjects by Gerver (1969/2002) and subsequently confirmed in a more ecologically valid experiment by Linda Anderson (1994), who found an average EVS of 1.4 seconds for shadowing compared to nearly three seconds for SI.

With a focus on lag time at the beginning of new utterances, EVS has been taken to reflect segmentation of the input into 'chunks' serving as **units of translation**. From an experiment involving six professionals interpreting short (three to six minute) speeches in three language combinations, Goldman-Eisler (1972/2002) concluded that EVS units were not of a lexical but of a syntactic nature. EVS units mostly consisted of at least a complete predicative expression (noun phrase + verb phrase), with the verb phrase (predicate) playing a crucial part. Having identified propositional meaning units as the main psycholinguistic correlate of EVS, Goldman-Eisler nevertheless observed that interpreters' **chunking** behavior in output production did not follow the sequence of the input segments. Rather than "identity" between input and output chunks, Goldman-Eisler (1972/2002) found the onset of the interpreter's output to lie either before the end of the (pause-delimited) input segment ("fission") or after two or more chunks of input ("fusion"). Apart from her detailed consideration of the **language factor**, Goldman-Eisler (1972/2002: 73) briefly made reference also to factors like the "nature of the message" and the interpreter's capacity or **preference** for storing or **anticipating** input information (» 6.5.2). The fact that simultaneous interpreters might opt for various patterns of timing as a matter of personal preference, technique or strategy had been suggested early on by Paneth (1957/2002) and was found also in studies with sign language interpreters (Llewellyn-Jones 1981; Cokely 1992a). Without doubt, however, the 'nature of the message' has as strong an impact on the interpreter's processing activity as his or her preferred approach to dealing with the challenges arising from the input.

6.4 Input Variables

The complex interplay of attention, comprehension and production in the interpreting process is variously affected by a number of 'external' factors. These relate primarily to the nature of the source message which serves as the immediate 'input' to the interpreter's mental processing operations. Prior to source-text processing as such is the issue of acoustic and/or visual access and perception.

6.4.1 *Sound and Vision*

In interpreting from a spoken language, an essential condition for the viability of the process is the **acoustic quality** and perceptibility of the input. In face-to-face consecutive interpreting without technical equipment, various background noises and unsuitable positioning, for instance, can impair the interpreter's perception and thus comprehension of the original speech, but the interactive setting usually offers ways of resolving such problems. Not so in simultaneous interpreting, whether in the whispering mode, from spoken to signed languages, or in spoken-language SI with electro-acoustic transmission systems. Since simultaneous interpreters are assumed to be working at the limit of their processing capacity (see Gile 1995b, 1999b), the issue of sound quality is particularly acute. Gerver (1971, 1974b) investigated this in a study with 12 experienced professionals, who were asked to interpret and shadow short passages of scripted French prose into English at three different noise levels. Although Gerver's analytical techniques for assessing source–target correspondence are open to question, his findings clearly point to the detrimental effect of noise on the performance of simultaneous verbal tasks. More errors and omissions were recorded for both shadowing and SI in noisy vs no-noise conditions, and the quality of the renditions deteriorated more sharply in the interpreting task. Gerver (1974b: 165) concluded that difficulty in perceiving source language input had resulted in less 'channel capacity' being available for translation and output monitoring by the interpreter. Tommola and Lindholm (1995) obtained similar results in a study with eight professionals who were asked to interpret realistic conference presentations from English into Finnish with or without the addition of white noise at -5dB.

Interpretations were scored by two judges for propositional accuracy and reflected a significant impact of poorer sound quality on accurate performance in SI.

While technical standards for adequate transmission quality in conference interpreting were set in the early 1980s (» 11.1.1), the issue of noise, or signal quality, has re-emerged with a vengeance in connection with teleconferencing and remote interpreting (» 11.2). More so than sound quality, these developments impinge on the interpreter's **visual access** to the speaker and proceedings. Although conference interpreters have long insisted on the need for a direct view of the meeting room, research on the role of visual information in SI has yielded an ambiguous pattern of findings. Survey research has documented conference interpreters' demands to see the speaker as well as the rest of the participants so as to have access to the full range of nonverbal visual cues, including speaker **kinesics** (gestures, facial expressions), turn-taking signals and audience reactions (see Altman 1990; Bühler 1985; Cooper et al. 1982). However, several attempts at experimentally validating the need for visual access to ensure adequate performance have failed to produce clear-cut results. In an experiment with twelve final-year students who interpreted short extemporaneous or read speeches from either audio- or videotape, Balzani (1990) found significantly better performance (as assessed by two judges) in the video condition for extemporaneous texts but not for read speeches. In an earlier study by Anderson (1994), which involved twelve professional subjects who interpreted short authentic spontaneous speeches presented either with or without the video image, no such effect had been found. Similarly, Tommola and Lindholm (1995) reported no significant difference in propositional accuracy between SI with or without the video image.

6.4.2 Accent and Intonation

In interpreting from spoken languages, the aspect of message delivery that relates most closely to perception is the speaker's **pronunciation** and the resulting phonetic quality of the source-language input. Like any perceptual process, the recognition of speech sounds depends on prior knowledge, and any deviation from familiar acoustic-phonetic patterns is likely to make perception more difficult for the interpreter. In surveys on job stress among conference interpreters, 'unfamiliar accent' is cited by a majority of respondents as a frequent and serious problem (Cooper et al. 1982: 104; AIIC 2002: 25).

The detrimental effect of a strong accent on SI performance has been highlighted in several studies (e.g. Kurz 2008; Chang and Wu 2014). Such evidence of the difficulties posed by speakers with a non-native accent is in line with findings from second-language acquisition studies on "perceptual foreign accent" (McAllister 2000), which predict greater perceptual difficulties for users of an acquired language, particularly when the speech signal is masked by noise or an unfamiliar accent. This points to the possible advantage of interpreting from one's A into one's B language, at least in difficult perceptual conditions, and there is some evidence suggesting that a speech delivered with a non-native accent may be less difficult to interpret if the speaker's native language (i.e. the source of interference) is among the interpreter's working languages (Kurz and Basel 2009).

The input language that is most often subject to phonological, lexical and syntactic deviations is English, the world's dominant lingua franca and conference language. Most studies have therefore focused on the problems associated with non-native features of English used by speakers of other languages. Albl-Mikasa (2013) notes that **English as a lingua franca** (ELF) is likely to make additional demands on the interpreter's processing capacity and hamper strategies such as inferencing and anticipation. The frustration experienced by interpreters confronted with ELF is also discussed by Reithofer (2010).

In native and non-native speech alike, **intonation** and other components of **prosody**, such as tempo and rhythm, are particularly relevant to perception and understanding in the interpreting process. In an early experiment testing the impact of prosodically degraded input on the performance of simultaneous interpreters, Gerver (1971) had six professional interpreters render ten short texts from French into English. Half of the source texts had been read on tape (at 100 words per minute) with standard prosody, whereas the other half had been recorded with minimal intonation and stress and any pauses of 250 milliseconds or more eliminated. Gerver (1971) found that the monotonous (i.e. flat and inexpressive) passages had significantly lower accuracy scores, and concluded that prosodic cues like pauses, stress and intonation assist interpreters in segmenting and processing the source-language message. This was reaffirmed by Déjean le Féal (1982), who demonstrated the link between intonation patterns and the perception of input speed.

6.4.3 Speed and Mode of Delivery

While interrelated with prosodic cues like intonation and rhythm, the speed of message delivery, also referred to as **speech rate**, 'input rate,' 'presentation rate' or 'delivery rate,' stands out as a key input variable in its own right. Though the rate of input can be assumed to affect the interpreting process in any mode, attention has traditionally centered on source-text speed in SI. Whereas a rate of 60 words per minute had been suggested for speakers at the Nuremberg Trial (Gaiba 1998), 100 to 120 words per minute were considered comfortable for SI at an AIIC symposium on interpreter training in 1965. This was confirmed in an experimental study by Gerver (1969/2002) with ten professional interpreters working from French into English (their A language). At input rates above the range of 95 to 120 words per minute, subjects showed a decrease in the proportion of text correctly interpreted and an increase in ear–voice span and pausing. With reference to short-term-memory limitations, Gerver concluded that simultaneous interpreters can increase their output rate to cope with faster input only up to a point, at which they reach "a steady state of throughput at the expense of an increase in errors and omissions" (1969/2002: 66). As regards low-speed input, an explanation for its detrimental effect in SI was supplied by Shlesinger's (2000a, 2003) work on the decay of unrehearsed traces in working memory (« 5.2.3).

Notwithstanding the rather clear findings for the effect of input speed, measuring this variable is in fact a complex problem. Apart from the choice of unit (words vs syllables), delivery rates depend on the frequency and duration of pauses, and thus on the **pause criterion** used to net out the **articulation rate** from the composite of speech bursts and pauses. Given the use of word counts for morphologically dissimilar languages, and the use of pause criteria varying between 70 and 600 milliseconds, it is hard to make comparisons across different studies. But even assuming that this issue can be resolved, the analyst is faced with the discrepancy between the input speed measured and the input speed actually perceived. In her 1978 dissertation based on a corpus of six authentic speeches, Déjean le Féal (1982) showed that **prosodic patterns** influence interpreters' perception of the delivery rate: at the same objective rate, a source speech with monotonous intonation and short pauses was perceived as faster, and more difficult to interpret, than a speech with marked intonation contours. Contrasting impromptu speech with the reading of scripted material, Déjean le Féal suggested that the former was easier to understand because of a greater number of pauses (i.e. shorter speech segments), a distinct "acoustic relief" (i.e. hesitation pauses followed by stressed content words), and a higher degree of (accidental or deliberate) redundancy. Nevertheless, 'mode of delivery' must not be construed simply as a binary concept. As proposed by Kopczyński (1982) and developed in Pöchhacker's (1994c) "text delivery profile," there is a broad middle ground between improvised speech and reading, not to mention the combination of oral presentation and visual media.

6.4.4 Source-Text Complexity

One of the most difficult parameters of input load is the information content of the source message. Apart from Treisman's (1965) early attempt to calibrate her experimental input passages in terms of information per word (based on cloze testing 100 subjects on samples of ten words from each passage), few authors have systematically addressed this issue. At the **lexical** level, research might begin by considering such aspects as word frequency, lexical variability and specialized terminology (for which corpus-linguistic tools are increasingly available), move on to non-redundant items such as proper names and numbers (e.g. Gile 1984), and pay special attention to semantic phenomena like false cognates in a given language pair (e.g. Shlesinger 2000a), non-standard and culture-bound usage (e.g. Pöchhacker 2007), and 'creative' or humorous language use (e.g. Viaggio 1996). Notwithstanding the value of such research, the informational complexity of a text clearly could not be pegged to difficulties at the lexical level.

Nor has the use of readability measures (e.g. Flesch–Kincaid, Flesch Reading Ease), which are based on sentence length (lexical density) and word length, proved effective in predicting source-text difficulty in interpreting (Liu and Chiu 2009). With a view to auditory processing, Alexieva (1999) proposed a "listenability coefficient" based on the ratio of implicit (i.e. condensed, participial) to explicit **predications**. Similarly, Dillinger (1994), studying the effect of text structure on interpreters' comprehension, focused on propositions and related them to their syntactic environment in terms of clause density and embedding as well as textual macro-structures ("frames"). Dillinger's experiment, though criticized for some questionable choices of design, showed a clear negative effect of **propositional density** on accuracy of interpreting, with lower accuracy for propositions in embedded clauses. Tommola and Helevä (1998), in an experimental study with student interpreters working from English into Finnish, similarly found a significant effect of syntactic complexity on output accuracy as measured by propositional analysis. In contrast, **syntactic variables** as such (clause density and clause embedding) had only a weak overall effect on performance in Dillinger's English–French study. This would seem to agree with the conclusion drawn by Setton (1999) from his corpus-based analysis of professional Chinese–English and German–English SI that "syntactic structure ... does not of itself constitute an obstacle to SI" (1999: 270).

Finally, at the level of **text type**, the professional as well as untrained subjects in Dillinger's (1994) study performed significantly better on the narrative passage than on the text describing a procedure. Since the two texts were closely matched for the number of words, clauses, cohesive elements and propositions, Dillinger attributed his findings to the effect of the informational structure and concluded that the sequence of episodes making up the narrative text was more amenable to comprehension than the hierarchical structure of procedures and subprocedures.

6.5 Strategies

A goal-directed complex activity, interpreting has been conceptualized as an essentially 'strategic' process, particularly by researchers viewing it in terms of cognitive information-processing or text-processing skills (van Dijk and Kintsch 1983). A wide array of psycholinguistic processing steps has been discussed under the heading of 'strategy,' defined as a 'goal-oriented process under intentional control' (see Kalina 1998: 99). Interpreting-related strategies, variously referred to also as 'techniques' or 'tactics,' can be classified in different ways. With a view to the overall task, one can distinguish between **on-line** strategies (as considered here) and **off-line** strategies preceding or following translational cognitive processing as such (e.g. preparing glossaries or marking up documents). On-line strategies, in turn, may be specific to or typical of a given **mode** of interpreting. This applies for instance to note-taking in consecutive interpreting and lag adjustment in the simultaneous mode, even though notes may also be used in the booth and time lag may be significant in note-taking behavior (« 6.3.3). Though strategic behavior can be assumed to be vital also for discourse management in dialogue interpreting

(» 8.2.1), most work on the subject of strategies to date has focused on simultaneous conference interpreting, particularly in relation to the 'classic' issue of structural dissimilarity between the source and target languages.

6.5.1 Norms, Strategies, Constraints

The topic of processing strategies in interpreting has been closely linked with difficulties arising from the interpreter's input. In particular, high delivery speed (« 6.4.3) and structural complexity (« 6.4.4) have been cited as factors inducing high processing loads and thus requiring coping strategies, especially under the temporal and cognitive constraints of SI. And yet, as demonstrated by Shlesinger (1999, 2000a, 2000b), strategies cannot be accounted for purely in terms of input load. Rather, the interpreter's awareness of – and attempt to meet – certain expectations regarding his or her product and performance, which Chesterman (1993) refers to as translational "expectancy norms," may be as powerful as cognitive constraints in shaping the interpreter's strategic response. A performance standard such as fluent and smooth output, for instance, internalized in the course of an interpreter's training and professional experience, could be taken to license certain kinds of omissions or additions (see Shlesinger 1999). This suggests a distinction between **process-oriented** strategies for **coping** with high-load-inducing input (» 6.5.2) and **product-oriented** strategies for **communicating** effectively with the target-language audience (» 6.5.3). The line between the two would be hard to draw, however. Gile (1995b), for example, addressing the interplay between strategic and norm-guided behavior, suggests that an interpreter's choice of "coping tactics" may be guided by various "rules," such as "maximizing the communication impact of the speech" or "self-protection" (1995b: 201ff).

6.5.2 Coping with Structure: Timing, Restructuring and Anticipation

Ever since Glémet (1958: 120f) described output production in SI as involving "mortgaging your grammatical future," researchers have studied ways of coping with the challenge of dissimilar grammatical structures. Kade (1967), Kirchhoff (1976/2002) and others giving special consideration to German as a source language mentioned the strategy of **waiting**, if not 'for the verb,' as anecdotes would have it, at least for further disambiguating input. In line with Herbert's (1952: 65) injunction against any pauses in the interpreter's speech, waiting for further input can take the form of **stalling**, that is, slowing down delivery or using 'neutral padding expressions' or 'fillers' (e.g. Glémet 1958: 121; Kirchhoff 1976/2002: 116). However, the higher storage load resulting from such **lagging** strategies limits their application and suggests the need for more pre-emptive action such as segmentation, or **chunking**, also referred to as "salami technique" (Jones 1998: 101). As described by Kirchhoff (1976/2002), among others, this involves extracting and rendering independent input segments at phrase or clause level before the end of a complex input structure.

Seleskovitch and Lederer (1995: 125) refer to this widely taught strategy as "working with subunits of sense." Chunking and the reformulation strategies associated with it have been studied on the basis of experimental as well as fieldwork data. Meuleman and Van Besien (2009), for example, analyzed the strategies adopted by 15 professional interpreters in coping with a syntactically complex passage (French–Dutch). They observed that eight out of the ten interpreters who produced an acceptable rendering of the eight-layer-deep syntactic construction did so using segmentation, whereas the other two resorted to 'tailing', that is, using similarly complex syntax in the target language.

The most widely discussed strategy of SI, however, is **anticipation**. Aside from its fundamental role in comprehension in the broader sense of expectation-based ('top-down') processing (« 6.1.2), anticipation is defined specifically as the simultaneous interpreter's production of a sentence constituent before the corresponding constituent has appeared in the source-language input (see Setton 1999: 52). This mainly occurs in SI from languages with a subject–object–verb (SOV) sentence structure into SVO languages, in which the verb is needed earlier in the sentence. Authors such as Wilss (1978) and Lederer (1978/2002, 1981) have described and exemplified various subtypes of syntactic anticipation and made a basic distinction between 'linguistic anticipation' (i.e. 'word prediction' based on familiar lexico-grammatical patterns) and 'extra-linguistic anticipation' on the basis of 'sense expectation.' Linguistic antici-pation and the search for structural transfer regularities constituted a point of interest for interpreting scholars working in the tradition of the Leipzig School (« 2.3.1). This is best reflected in the large-scale experimental study of syntactic strategies in Russian–German SI carried out in the PhD research by Salevsky (1987). While most German authors, and not they alone, seem to have shared the belief that "any SI process is language-pair-specific" (Wilss 1978: 350), scholars in the IT tradition have played down the role of syntactic asymmetries. Aside from theoretical argument, the question has been investi-gated in various empirical studies, including Gile's (1992a) corpus analysis of the length and function of predictable sentence endings in Japanese; Alessandra Riccardi's (1996) experiment on German–Italian SI with students and pro-fessional subjects; and the study on verb anticipation in German–English SI by Udo Jörg (1997). Jörg's experiment, which involved both student subjects and professionals with either English or German as their A language, addressed the issue of directionality as well as expertise. Whereas his findings pointed to a slight superiority for anticipation from the interpreter's A language, the opposite result was found by Bartłomiejczyk (2006) in her study on directionality in Polish/English SI. More recent corpus-based analyses have suggested that stra-tegic anticipation in SI from SOV into SVO languages may occur as frequently as once every 1.5 minutes. Even so, Setton (1999) uses the findings from his German–English and Chinese–English corpus analysis to express skepticism about a "strategies-for-structure" approach, pointing out that "marked syntactic structure alone does not obstruct SI" (1999: 282), and foregrounding instead the cognitive-pragmatic processing of linguistic and contextual cues.

6.5.3 Communicating Content: Condensation and Adaptation

Strategies relating to various forms of adaptive processing of content evidently bear on the fundamental topic of performance standards and 'quality' (» 10.4). Nevertheless, some content-processing strategies, particularly of the 'reductive' kind, have been analyzed primarily as forms of coping with processing constraints. This applies especially to the strategy of **compression**, or 'abstracting,' in response to high input speed and/or information density in the simultaneous mode. As early as the 1960s, Chernov (1978, 1994) discussed lexical and syntactic compression and omission in response to excessive input speed, and the issue was taken up by several interpreting researchers in Eastern Europe. In a similar vein, Kirchhoff (1976/2002: 116) envisaged strategic "information reduction ... through selection (omission of irrelevant information)." An empirical demonstration of this is offered by Napier (2004), who used retrospective protocols to analyze the performances of ten professional interpreters working from English into Australian Sign Language and found that some of their omissions corresponded to conscious strategic decisions. In a similar study with 36 advanced interpreting students working between Polish and English, Bartłomiejczyk (2006) found compression to be one of the most frequently used strategies, particularly when interpreting into the B language.

The fact that compression can be viewed not only as a 'rescue technique' but also as a strategic orientation underlying the translational process is best illustrated with reference to consecutive interpreting. Herbert (1952: 67) stipulated that full consecutive interpretation should only take up 75% of the time taken by the speaker. Such a reduction was to be achieved by speaking at a faster pace and avoiding repetition, hesitation, and redundancy. From an experimental corpus of Spanish–Danish consecutive interpretations produced by ten students and two professional interpreters, Helle Dam (1993) concluded that "text condensing," achieved by various types of substitutions and omissions, was a necessary and usually good interpreting strategy. With reference to SI, UN chief interpreter Sergio Viaggio (1991: 51) argued that "saying it all" – that is, reproducing the sense of the message with all stylistic and semantic nuances – was not always necessary for the interpreter to "convey all of the sense." The latter explicitly relates to the sense-based vs verbal-transfer view of the interpreting process and to the basic distinction between a **form-based** and a **meaning-based** interpreting approach, as examined empirically by Dam (1998/2002, 2001).

The case for a 'synthetic' rather than a 'saying it all' approach rests on the basic strategy of 'condensation,' or **implicitation**. The latter term in particular points to the link between various techniques of compression and the language pair involved: what needs to be said or may remain unstated also depends on the language and culture in question. Conversely, and quite apart from its postulated status as a universal feature of Translation, **explicitation** may be needed as a strategy to circumvent linguistic and socio-cultural differences (e.g. Gumul 2006; Livingston et al. 1994). More generally, Kohn and Kalina

(1996: 127) posit the need for **adaptation** strategies with regard to target-discourse conventions, including "appropriate cultural adaptations." This issue has been touched on by many authors (e.g. Kondo and Tebble 1997) but has received very little systematic attention as a topic of empirical research. Exceptions include the fieldwork study by Chang and Wu (2009), who found that conference interpreters tended to render forms of address in line with target-cultural conventions, even though their communicative strategies in SI were also influenced by cognitive constraints.

Further Reading

Comprehension

See COMPREHENSION, INFERENCING and MENTAL REPRESENTATION in Pöchhacker (2015).

Production

See PAUSES and REPAIRS in Pöchhacker (2015).

Simultaneity

See COGNITIVE LOAD, EFFORT MODELS and TIME LAG in Pöchhacker (2015).

Input variables

See INPUT VARIABLES, NUMBERS, SPEECH RATE, TERMINOLOGY and VISUAL ACCESS in Pöchhacker (2015).

Strategies

See STRATEGIES, SEGMENTATION, ANTICIPATION, COMPRESSION and EXPLICITATION in Pöchhacker (2015).

7 Product and Effect

Research on the outcome of the interpreter's cognitive processing operations and on communicative aspects of translational behavior investigates interpreting as a process in the wider sense – as language use in social interaction. As has emerged from the evolution of linguistic theory toward the end of the twentieth century (e.g. van Dijk 1997a, 1997b), the examination of the textual product ('language as structure') is closely intertwined with the analysis of communicative performance ('language as social action'). The concept of 'discourse' is applied in either dimension but has become particularly important in relation to dialogic communication, as foregrounded in the notion of 'talk.' Where the focus is on the interpreter's product in terms of formal features, semantic structures and communicative effect, the term 'text' is predominant, despite its traditional bias toward written language. It should be clear, however, that 'text' and 'discourse' are closely related and are even used interchangeably, with either term serving to denote fundamental aspects of interpreting activity across modes, modalities and domains.

7.1 Talk as Text

Research focusing on the product of the interpreting process has often drawn on the process-oriented approach to text linguistics pioneered by Robert de Beaugrande (1980). As broadly introduced by Beaugrande and Dressler (1981), a text, whether orally produced or written, is defined as a 'communicative event' that meets seven standards of **textuality**. Two of these – cohesion and coherence – are characterized as 'text-centered,' the others as 'user-centered,' including intentionality, acceptability and informativity. Among the user-centered parameters, situationality points most clearly to the situatedness of interaction that is also captured in the concept of 'orality' (» 7.1.3), whereas intertextuality highlights the fact that texts do not exist in isolation but are usually linked in significant ways to texts encountered in the past or in the immediate context.

7.1.1 Texts in Context

The fact that interpreting is part of a process of communicative interaction in a given context was long taken for granted, and analytical work on the social and situational constellation of interaction in interpreting emerged relatively late. The text-linguistic view of language events in a communicative context, and of 'discourse' as a set of mutually relevant texts (Beaugrande and Dressler 1981), is easily applied to conference interpreting as a complex **discourse event**. Alexieva (1985: 196) spoke of "macro-text" to refer to "the whole aggregate of texts delivered at a conference," and Pöchhacker (1992) conceptualized the 'conference' as a communicative event with its own textuality. Labeling the conference as a **hypertext**, he distinguished different types of events in terms of their communicative purpose, internal structure, and target audiences. The significance of **intertextuality** at the conference level was explored further in particular by Alexieva (1994), who also suggested an event-level typology of **genres** of interpreter-mediated interaction (« 4.3.1).

Genres of discourse and the internal structure of speech events have also been a focus in research on dialogue interpreting. In the work of Wadensjö (1998), for instance, the basic unit of analysis is the "interpreter-mediated encounter" as an interaction event. Helen Tebble (1999), working within the systemic functional approach to discourse as championed by Halliday (e.g. 1985), proposes a typical **event structure** for medical consultations. Based on an authentic corpus of 13 interpreted consultations, Tebble identifies 11 "genre elements," such as "Introductions," "Stating/Eliciting Problem" or "Stating Resolution/Exposition," which represent the basic stages of the communicative event and can be broken down further into constituents such as "exchanges" and "moves" (see Tebble 1999: 184f). Similar analyses of the event structure of interpreted medical consultations have been carried out in the framework of 'functional pragmatics' at the University of Hamburg (e.g. Meyer 2002).

7.1.2 *Texture*

With a focus on text-centered aspects of textuality in translation and interpreting, Hatim and Mason (1997) use the term 'texture' as incorporating elements of **cohesion** and **coherence** as well as **theme–rheme** organization (thematic progression), which have been the subject of empirical analyses. Shlesinger (1995a) examined various types of **cohesive ties** (reference, substitution, conjunction, lexical cohesion) in an experimental English–Hebrew corpus produced by thirteen student interpreters and found ample evidence of SI-related **shifts**, mainly in the form of omissions of seemingly less important cohesive devices. Mizuno (1999) replicated Shlesinger's study with ten student interpreters working into Japanese and interpreted his findings with reference to language-pair-specific differences (e.g. regarding the use of pronouns and ellipsis). More recently, the fate of cohesive ties in interpreting has also been investigated in relation to interpreting mode and modality as well as level of expertise. McDermid (2014), for example, in a study with professional and novice sign language interpreters, identified the use of additional conjunctive devices as a reason for the higher fluency ratings given to the target texts of experienced professionals. This highlights the link between aspects of texture and features such as cohesion and fluency, which have long been regarded as important criteria for the evaluation of an interpreter's performance (» 10.4.1).

More fundamental than cohesion at the 'text surface,' and also more difficult to study, given its essentially cognitive nature, is textual coherence, viewed as the network of concepts and relations evoked by the verbal signals. In an approach from Rhetorical Structure Theory, Peng (2009) analyzed and compared the **coherence profiles** of English/Chinese consecutive interpretations performed by trainees and professionals. Aside from the directionality-related finding that interpretations into the A language tended to be more coherent, she observed that the professional interpreters' performances reflected better global coherence, whereas the renditions of novices showed only local coherence. This can be taken as evidence of more comprehensive **knowledge structures** available to experienced experts, whose top-down processing allows them to make better sense of the original speech, and render it more coherently in the target language (see also Pöchhacker 1993).

7.1.3 Orality

The concept of 'orality' refers to a significant distinction in the study of text and discourse. In a fundamental sense, orality points to the primordial form of language use in immediate ('face-to-face') interpersonal contact, prior to what Walter Ong (1982) called "the technologizing of the word" by the invention of secondary representations of language, that is, writing systems (see also Clark 1996: 8ff). Despite the apparent incongruity, 'orality' in the sense of primary or **natural language use** also includes communication in sign languages, as long as these are natural language systems rather than contrived manual codes or other secondary sign systems (see Ingram 1985: 92). Interpreting therefore implies 'orality' in the sense of natural language use for immediate communication – that is, 'talk' realized by speech sounds or signs in combination with a range of **nonverbal** signaling systems (see Clark 1996). And yet Ong (1982) and others have shown that written language has become so pervasive in modern societies as to make speech – such as the 'scripted speech' used in conferences or broadcasting – secondary to writing. This ambivalent nature of linguistic expression is captured in the analytical distinction of **orality vs literacy**, which is based not on the distinction between spoken/signed and written language use but on dimensions of discourse such as 'involvement vs detachment' and 'fragmentation vs integration.'

For dialogue interpreting in face-to-face communication, orality is generally assumed by default, and the issue of orality vs literacy has attracted little attention. Conference interpreting scholars in the IT paradigm have foregrounded the notion of 'orality,' using it in the common sense of extemporaneous speaking activity (e.g. Déjean le Féal 1982). Indeed, the evanescent, impromptu, and context-bound nature of discourse was a cornerstone in the sense-based approach of the Paris School, which posited 'orality' as the pre-requisite for 'true interpreting' and showed little interest in descriptive studies of the complex mix of spoken-like and written-like features in conference discourse.

A pioneering research effort in this regard was undertaken by Shlesinger (1989b), who examined an authentic English/Hebrew corpus of source texts and simultaneous interpretations for **shifts** in orality or literacy associated with the interpreting process. Based on a range of features indicative of factors such as degree of planning, contextual co-presence, and degree of involvement, Shlesinger found that SI reduced the range of the **oral–literate continuum** and consistently rendered a literate text more oral in either language direction. Similarly, SI tended to increase the literateness of oral-type Hebrew source texts and was thus found to have an "equalizing effect" on the position of source texts on the oral–literate continuum (see also Pym 2007).

A dimension of orality which is most immediately linked with the production process in interpreting (« 6.2) is the limited scope of planning and its reflection in the interpreter's product in the form of **hesitation** phenomena, or 'disfluencies.' The most general index of (dis)fluency is filled and unfilled **pauses**, as studied by Mead (2000, 2002) with regard to production skills at different levels of expertise (« 6.2.2). In his quantitative analysis of the 100,000-word English/German ICSB Corpus for voiced hesitations ('ums and ahs'), Pöchhacker (1994a, 1995b) found these phenomena to be significantly less frequent in the German interpretations than in the English source speeches. Bendazzoli et al. (2011), by contrast, analyzed the trilingual European Parliament Interpretation Corpus (EPIC) for two types of verbal **disfluencies** (mispronounced and truncated words) and found these to be more frequent in the interpretations (into English, Italian and Spanish), both in relation to the parallel corpus of corresponding originals (with some exceptions for English) and to the comparable corpus of original speeches delivered in these languages.

With the emergence of more accessible corpus-linguistic tools, inquiry into the relative orality of texts in interpreting can be expected to receive a significant boost. One example is Shlesinger's (2008) comparative corpus-based study of 'Interpretese,' which revealed salient differences between interpreted and translated versions of the same English source texts in terms of lexical variety and a range of linguistic features. Nevertheless, progress in corpus-based interpreting studies is hampered by the very orality of the interpreter's output (see Shlesinger 1998). Aside from the problem of segmenting the flow of speech into punctuation-delimited clauses and sentences, paralinguistic and nonverbal discourse features can be incorporated in machine-readable transcriptions only with great difficulty. Thus, until advances in speech signal detection and electronic text encoding (see Cencini and Aston 2002) make it easier to overcome the written-language bias of corpus linguistics, studies of the paralinguistic features of orality in interpreting will have to rely on the intensive 'manual' analysis of limited-scale corpora, albeit with ever more advanced technological support. An innovative example of such work is

Shlesinger's (1994) study on the **prosody** of interpreters' delivery. She examined ten random 90-second excerpts of authentic interpreted discourse (English/ Hebrew) for various prosodic features and identified non-standard pausing (i.e. within grammatical constituents), anomalous stress, low-rise nonfinal pitch movement and momentary alterations in tempo as the main features of what she called **interpretational intonation**. This was described on a larger scale by Ahrens (2005), who analyzed three German simultaneous interpretations of a 73-minute English speech and found the six professional interpreters in her study to use mainly rising, level and rise-level pitch contours, which indicate continuation rather than closure.

Even more challenging than acoustic analysis to describe paraverbal features is accounting for nonverbal visual components of 'oral' communication, also referred to as **kinesics**. These include a range of phenomena, such as gaze, facial expression, gesture and posture, which can have particular significance in face-to-face interaction (e.g. Davitti 2013). In the study of dialogic discourse, in particular, the distinction between verbal and nonverbal components has increasingly given way to a focus on **multimodality** – a holistic approach which foregrounds the interdependence of the verbal, vocal and kinesic modalities that together constitute orality (» 8.2.2).

7.2 Source–Target Correspondence

The central – and most theory-laden – issue in the examination of the interpreter's product is the nature of the relationship between the source text and its target-language rendition. Scholars of written translation have traditionally discussed this 'translational relation' in terms of 'equivalence' (see Munday 2001: Ch. 3). Interpreting scholars, in contrast, have sought to capture the 'ideal standard' for the interpreter's translational product with notions like accuracy, completeness, and fidelity.

7.2.1 Fidelity and Accuracy

The most widely acknowledged demand on an interpretation is that it should be **faithful** to the original. Aside from Glémet's (1958: 106) dictum that interpreters transfer speeches "with the same faithfulness as sound-amplification," most authors have echoed Herbert's (1952: 4) basic tenet that an interpretation "fully and faithfully" conveys the original speaker's ideas. Scholars in the IT paradigm have identified the object of fidelity as 'sense' (see Donovan-Cagigos 1990); with a more concrete focus on information processing, Gile (1992b: 189) demands fidelity to the "message and style" of the original, with priority given to the "informational content" rather than the linguistic "package" of the text (see Gile 1995b: 26); most generally, at the level of translational norms, Harris (1990: 118) refers to the norm of the "honest spokesperson," meaning that interpreters should "re-express the original speaker's ideas and the manner of expressing them as accurately as possible and without significant omissions." The conceptual linkage between **fidelity** and **accuracy** is also evident in Seleskovitch, whose original call for "fidelité absolue" (Seleskovitch 1968: 166) was translated into English as the demand for "total accuracy" (Seleskovitch 1978a: 102).

Fidelity and accuracy, with the implication of completeness, appear in the literature on interpreting as widely accepted standards of performance, and many researchers have sought to apply them in measuring and quantifying interpreters' output, even at the level of words (see Gerver 1969/2002). Given the obvious problems with word-for-word correspondence, attempts have been made to determine accuracy at a deeper, semantic level. For her experiment on message loss in relay interpreting, Mackintosh (1983) devised a scoring system based on the principle of "semantic equivalence," which involved an intuitive segmentation of the source text into (phrase or clause-level) units of meaning, each worth a predefined number of points depending on its informational constituents. Three judges were then asked to score the target texts for the number of correctly reproduced items in each unit, which yielded an overall number of points achieved out of the total score possible. (Average semantic accuracy scores were between 70% and 90% for both the direct and the relay interpreting condition.) Another approach to assessing the **informational correspondence** of source and target texts, proposed by linguist John Carroll for the evaluation of machine translation in the 1960s (see Carroll 1978: 120), has been applied by several interpreting researchers since the 1970s (e.g. Gerver 1974b; Anderson 1994; Tiselius 2009). In this transcript-based method, judges are asked to rate each sentence of the original for its informativeness compared to the target text, thus focusing on information not conveyed by the interpretation. Tiselius (2009) adapted Carroll's scales to spoken language, and reduced the number of steps, or grades, from nine to six, reformulating them to foreground the target-text assessment resulting from 'reading the original.' Using grader training for her two groups of judges (comprising six students and six professional interpreters each), she found acceptable **inter-rater reliability** for both groups, with a higher correlation ($r = 0.65$) among the professionals.

Efforts to develop stringent scoring systems have also been made on the basis of **propositional analysis** as developed in cognitive science for the study of text comprehension and recall. In essence, this calls for a decomposition of the 'natural-language' text into a set of structures ('propositions') made up of a head concept, or 'predicate,' and a number of related concepts, or 'arguments.' Lambert (1989), for one, used propositional analysis as proposed by Kintsch and van Dijk (1978) to score her experimental results, and Strong and Rudser (1985) developed a proposition-based assessment system for the output of sign language interpreters. Authors such as Dillinger (1994) and Tommola and Lindholm (1995) adopted variants of the cognitive-scientific approach to propositionalization, and Liu and Chiu (2009) used a proposition-based assessment by two raters to score students' consecutive interpretations. Notwithstanding the promise of methodological rigor, propositional analysis is not an all-purpose tool for measuring accuracy in interpreting (see Tommola and Lindholm 1995: 130f). Whatever the formalism used, the propositional decomposition of meaning remains language-bound and cannot resolve the fundamental issue of semantic comparability in Translation. Moreover, concept-based propositionalization usually sidelines expressions of attitude, modality and intentionality. Such 'procedural' elements of discourse call for a pragmatic approach, as implemented for SI by Setton (1998/2002, 1999).

7.2.2 Omissions, Additions and (Other) Errors

Ever since the first experimental studies of interpreting, researchers have sought to examine the interpreter's output for various types of lexico-semantic 'deviations' from the source text. Oléron and Nanpon (1965), though largely shying away from the issue of fidelity in their pioneering study, quantified the number of words omitted, added or rendered inaccurately in the target text. Gerver (1969/2002, 1974b) quantified what he called **errors** and **discontinuities** in the interpreters' output in terms of 'omissions,' 'substitutions' (or 'errors of commission') and 'corrections,' and distinguished various subforms according to the amount of linguistic material involved. Working at the same time, Barik (1972, 1975/2002) devised a comprehensive categorization of "translation departures" for the analysis of his experimentally generated corpus of interpretations. Under the three broad headings of **omissions, additions** and **substitutions** (or "errors of translation"), Barik distinguished a number of subtypes with reference to the extent or severity (e.g. "skipping omission," "mild" vs "gross semantic error") or the presumable cause of the departure (e.g. "comprehension omission"). Barik's elaborate analytical scheme has been challenged by various authors (e.g. Gerver 1976; Stenzl 1983) as too subjective and impossible to replicate. Nevertheless, error analyses along the lines of Barik's typology have been vital to the treatment of results in a large number of experimental studies. Since authors have usually devised their own variant of the scheme and its terminology, there are nearly as many error classification systems as there are empirical studies requiring an overall assessment of source–target correspondence. Some of the more innovative approaches include: Kopczyński's (1980) breakdown of the error category with regard to linguistic competence, linguistic performance, and communicative appropriateness; Balzani's (1990) criteria for message fidelity, or lack thereof, including such categories as omissions, meaning errors, unwarranted additions, and errors in rendering figures and proper names; Cokely's (1992a) typology of "miscues" in sign language interpreting, comprising omissions, additions, substitutions, intrusions (i.e. source-language interference) and anomalies; Wadensjö's (1993/2002) distinction between expanded, reduced and substituting renditions in dialogue interpreting; and Jemina Napier's (2004) classification of omission types in relation to sign language interpreters' linguistic coping strategies.

For all its usefulness to researchers faced with the need to analyze and quantify the (lack of) fidelity in an experimental or authentic corpus, the contrastive lexicosemantic approach to error analysis suffers fundamentally from its disregard for functional and pragmatic considerations. Indeed, notions of 'linguistic equivalence' have been rejected as a yardstick of source–target correspondence by interpreting scholars across various paradigms: Gile (1992b: 188f) points out that producing an acceptable target-language text "requires at least some 'deviation' from 'linguistic equivalence'," and that some "filtering" to enhance the communicative impact of the text will not necessarily detract from its "fidelity"; Sandra Hale (1997: 211) concludes that "linguistic omissions and additions are often required to ensure accuracy"; and Clare Donovan-Cagigos (1990: 400) stresses that fidelity is not a fixed quantity but relative to a concrete communicative situation – as emphasized more generally by scholars adopting a target-oriented (reception-oriented) approach to Translation.

7.2.3 *Textural and Pragmatic Shifts*

Mindful of the problems associated with a prescriptive assessment of 'deviations' from an ideal standard of accuracy, equivalence, or fidelity, some authors investigating the interpreter's product have adopted a more **descriptive** approach to source–target correspondence. Central to this line of research is the identification of shifts resulting from the interpreting process as such and/ or the interpreter's behavior in a given context of interaction. The notion of 'shifts' as used by Toury (1978/2000: 201) has been discussed by translation scholars and interpreting researchers with an emphasis on the domain of **texture**, that is, cohesion and coherence (« 7.1.2). Pending larger corpus-based studies, however, it is difficult to ascertain whether textural shifts in interpreting have more to do with idiosyncratic choices, constraint-induced strategies (« 6.5.2), task-related translational norms, or 'universals' of Translation such as the tendency toward **explicitation**.

A form of translational shifts in interpreting which has proved rather amenable to contrastive discourse-based study is changes in the **pragmatic force** of the interpreted text. Features of 'communicative style' such as **register, politeness** and **hedging** – and their translational fate – have been analyzed by drawing on linguistic pragmatics, in particular speech act theory and Grice's conversational maxims. Most work on pragmatic shifts in interpreting has concentrated on constellations of face-to-face communication, and the institutional setting which has attracted most research interest in this regard is the (adversarial) courtroom. Berk-Seligson (1990), in her seminal ethnography of *The Bilingual Courtroom*, studied such issues as politeness and register in a corpus of 114 hours of judicial proceedings involving interpreting between English and Spanish. In Jansen's (1995) case study of Spanish/Dutch court interpreting in a criminal trial, the academically trained interpreter was found to simplify, adapt and explain complicated speech for the defendant and to filter out hesitations, errors and ambiguities. On a larger scale, Hale (1997, 2004) reported findings on English/Spanish interpreters' handling of register and politeness forms in a fieldwork corpus of 13 Australian court cases. These studies yielded ample evidence of shifts in the pragmatic force of interpretations compared to the original utterances. Consequential shifts have also been demonstrated in the related domain of police interpreting (e.g. Krouglov 1999), with particular reference to hedges, polite forms and the implications of **footing** (» 8.1.2). Focusing their analysis on the issue of **face**, Mason and Stewart (2001) discuss court and police interpreters' failure to render devices like hedging, modality and register in such a way as to recreate their face-threatening or face-protecting illocutionary force. In the same vein, the complexity of facework is analyzed by Pöllabauer (2007) in asylum hearings and by Jacobsen (2008) in the courtroom setting. In studies such as these, the effect of feature shifts in the interpreter's rendition is gauged by a pragma-linguistic analysis of transcribed discourse, with due regard for the interlocutor's discursive response. An alternative approach involves the use of psychological methods to measure the cognitive and pragmatic effect of the interpreter's product on the addressees.

7.3 Effect

The translational principle of 'equivalent effect' has been invoked since the 1960s for translation and interpreting alike, both with regard to the cognitive end-result of the process – that is, comprehension by the target audience – and with regard to the emotive and pragmatic impact of the target text at the interpersonal level. In either dimension, though, the empirical research base is rather tenuous, with most work having been done in the field of signed language interpreting.

7.3.1 Listener Comprehension

The postulate of "faithfulness" as measured by "the extent to which people really comprehend the meaning" (Nida and Taber 1969: 173) is a crucial translational norm underlying the interpreter's production. In the words of Seleskovitch (1978a: 102), transmitting the message "with total accuracy" requires the interpreter "to have his listeners understand it as well as it was understood by those who heard it directly from the speaker himself" (see also Déjean le Féal 1990: 155). And yet few authors have attempted to measure comprehension in the interpreter's audience. Pioneering efforts were reported by Gerver (1976), who used post-task content questions to assess comprehension in experimental subjects who were listening to simultaneous vs consecutive interpreting. Gerver did not compare comprehension in interpreting vs direct listening; rather, he tried (and failed) to find differences in the **cognitive end-result** of interpreting under good vs noisy listening conditions, depending on the working mode.

More than two decades later, Shlesinger (1994) used a small-scale audience comprehension test in her study on prosodic patterns in SI. A total of 15 subjects listened to three passages either as interpretations recorded in authentic conditions or as transcriptions of the interpreted output read on tape by the interpreter. Comprehension scores based on three content questions on each passage were twice as high for the group receiving the read versions than for the group listening to authentic output with "interpretational intonation."

Shlesinger's (1994) groundbreaking work provided the inspiration for a larger project on the impact of paraverbal features – in the source speech and/or the interpreter's output – on audience comprehension. Whereas Holub (2010) measured the cognitive effect of a simultaneous interpretation with lively vs monotonous intonation, Reithofer (2013) compared audience understanding of a simultaneous interpretation into German to that of an English lecture on a business topic delivered with an Italian accent. Working with 58 English-proficient business students randomized into two groups, Reithofer (2013) found the comprehension scores of SI users, established with a thoroughly tested questionnaire, to be significantly higher than those of the group listening to the original speaker using English as a lingua franca.

7.3.2 Deaf User Comprehension

Experimental work on the comparative reception and **recall** of lectures interpreted into signed language dates back to the 1970s (see Frishberg 1990: 41f). In a study measuring comprehension by deaf subjects with reference also to hearing listeners, Peter Llewellyn-Jones (1981) focused more specifically on the effect of different types of interpreting performance. Using videotaped experimental interpretations into British Sign Language (BSL), Llewellyn-Jones found that deaf subjects' scores on multiple-choice questions (administered in BSL) were higher for passages interpreted by native signers, whose output reflected considerable restructuring and simplification. This finding also relates to the contrast between interpreting and transliterating, a uniquely significant issue in the field of signed language interpreting. A number of studies on the **comparative effectiveness** of interpretations into American Sign Language (ASL) vs Signed English were carried out, but experimental designs did not always control for confounding variables such as a preference for one or the other mode of transmission (e.g. ASL interpreting, 'manual coding,' or 'sim-com,' i.e. simultaneous lipspeaking and signing).

A particularly thorough and comprehensive study on the cognitive effectiveness of sign language interpreting vs transliterating was done by Livingston et al. (1994), who controlled for variables such as text type (narrative vs lecture) as well as subjects' educational background, sign preference, communicative competence, and knowledge of the subject matter. Their study involved a stratified sample of 43 deaf students mainstreamed in US colleges, who were asked to answer literal and inference-based comprehension questions after live renditions of two videotaped English presentations. The authors found significantly higher comprehension scores for interpretation into ASL than for transliteration, even in students who expressly preferred the latter kind of signing but had been randomized into a group receiving ASL.

Based on a critical appraisal of previous studies pointing to a superiority of interpreting over transliterating in the classroom, Marschark et al. (2004) not only measured comprehension by deaf college students receiving different modes of interpreting but also compared these comprehension scores to those of hearing students with unmediated access to a videotaped English presentation. Their carefully controlled study showed that the post-lecture test scores of deaf students were consistently lower, regardless of interpreting mode and test administration, than those of hearing students, and saw these findings as casting doubt on the effectiveness of mediated (i.e. interpreted) instruction.

No less critical than in the educational setting is the effectiveness of interpreter mediation in judicial proceedings. Napier and Spencer (2008) investigated this with regard to deaf jurors' communicative access to the proceedings. In their experiment, six deaf and six hearing would-be jurors were asked to respond to questions on two excerpts from a judge's summation. The authors found no significant difference between the comprehension test scores of hearing jurors, who had listened in English, and deaf jurors, who had received the information indirectly via an interpretation into Australian Sign Language. This evidence suggests that SI can be effective in offering equal communicative access to court proceedings, and that deaf persons should therefore be allowed to serve on juries.

Yet another important setting in which comprehension by deaf users of interpreting services has been investigated is television. Ben Steiner (1998) measured the differential cognitive effect of various forms of signed output on TV (interpreting into BSL, sight translation into BSL from autocue, reporting, and spontaneous talk in BSL) in a sample of 30 (BSL-dominant vs English-informed) deaf subjects and a hearing control group. Using 12 authentic sample passages and signed content questions, Steiner found a superior effect for BSL-dominant signing, consistently lower comprehension scores for interpreting compared to other modes of signed presentation, and lower overall scores for the BSL-dominant vs the English-informed group, both of which scored far below the control group of hearing subjects responding to the sample passages as broadcast in English (directly or as voice-over).

More recently, studies on the effectiveness of signed language interpreting in the media, which have great potential to inform public policy decisions regarding language access, have been carried out also in China and South Africa. The experimental study by Xiao et al. (2015) tested 49 deaf and 20 hearing viewers for their comprehension of 20 TV news clips in Mandarin Chinese with interpretation into Chinese Sign Language (framed in a lower corner of the screen). Even though deaf participants were allowed to watch each clip twice, the authors found an enormous comprehension gap between the deaf and hearing groups (with scores of 4.86 and 19.25, respectively) and attributed this to poor linguistic competence on the part of the interpreters. A similar lack of effectiveness, or acceptance, transpires from the survey by Wehrmeyer (2015) among 360 deaf viewers in South Africa's Gauteng province. Aside from questions about viewing preferences, respondents were asked to express their level of satisfaction with six evening news programs involving various interpreters. Though the demographic profile of her sample reflected potential literacy issues, the author found a distinct preference for subtitling rather than interpreting, and concluded that most interpreted news programs were not understood, for reasons including language variants, interpreter image size and visibility.

7.3.3 *Pragmatic Impact*

Features of the interpreter's verbal as well as nonverbal production are relevant not only for their cognitive effect but also for their impact on text receivers' evaluative and interpersonal response. In the domain of simultaneous conference interpreting, the experimental work of Collados Aís (1998/2002), who confronted a sample of 42 expert users of SI with intonationally manipulated Spanish renditions of a German presentation, highlighted that **nonverbal features** of the interpreter's product, in particular monotonous vs lively **intonation**, affect not only users' assessment of the target text as such but also the confidence they place in the interpreter's professionalism. Similar **attitudinal effects** surfaced in the study by Steiner (1998), whose deaf subjects reacted favorably to signers who gave an impression of "authority" in their demeanor and language production.

A setting in which the pragmatic impact of the interpreter's product on interpretation users is of critical importance is the courtroom. In an experiment using the so-called 'matched guise' technique, Berk-Seligson (1988/2002, 1990) presented a sample of over 500 subjects with two simulated audio recordings of a witness testifying in Spanish through an interpreter. The two versions were identical except for a single feature – the interpreter's consistent rendition or non-rendition of **politeness** markers. Asked to rate the convincingness, competence, intelligence, and trustworthiness of the witness on a seven-point scale, the mock jurors gave a significantly more favorable assessment of the Spanish witness when they had listened to the polite version of the English interpretation. A similar effect was observed with the same experimental design for interpretation in "hyperformal style," that is, an upward shift in **register** by the non-use of contracted forms in English. Using the experiment also to ascertain the effect of **hedging** ('well,' 'sort of') and the use of **passive vs active** voice in the English interpretation, Berk-Seligson (1990) found such discourse features to be associated with more negative evaluations of the witness. Moreover, lawyers who were interrupted by the interpreter (e.g. when asking for clarification) were given lower ratings for competence by the mock jurors in the experiment.

This line of work was continued in matched-guise experiments by Hale (2004), who used student raters to test the effect of stylistic deviations in the

English interpretations of Spanish witness statements. Asking two groups of law students to rate a witness for competence, credibility and intelligence on a five-point scale, she found that a stylistically polished interpretation (omitting features of powerless speech style) yielded significantly better ratings than a version that accurately reproduced the style as well as the content of the testimony. Thus, Hale (2004) demonstrates, through fieldwork data and experimental findings, that interpreters often introduce various alterations to courtroom participants' speech styles, which affect perceptions of competence and credibility and may thus have an effect on the evaluation of testimony in the adversarial courtroom.

Further Reading

Talk as Text

See COHESION, COHERENCE and ORALITY in Pöchhacker (2015).

Source–Target Correspondence

See ACCURACY, FIDELITY, ERROR ANALYSIS, OMISSIONS, EXPLICITATION, REGISTER and ASSESSMENT in Pöchhacker (2015).

Effect

See COMMUNICATIVE EFFECT in Pöchhacker (2015).

8 Discourse in Interaction

The term 'discourse' has an overwhelmingly broad range of application – from the philosophy of communicative processes in society at large to the empirical analysis of 'talk' in conversational interaction, in both spoken and signed languages. While it overlaps extensively with the notion of 'text' as covered in Chapter 7, the concept of discourse has been applied in particular – within a broadly 'socio-linguistic' perspective (« 3.1.3–5) – to the analysis of language use in (face-to-face) interaction. The point of departure is not a single speaker's intended message and communicative product, but a configuration, or constellation, of communicating parties from which the dynamics of interactive discourse will emerge. When interpreting is thus viewed as discourse-based interaction, the focus is on the status and role of the interpreter as a participant in the encounter and on the way s/he manages the discourse process – that is, acts to coordinate the flow of discourse in an interactive sequence that is jointly negotiated among the participants.

8.1 Participation

For most of the twentieth century, the way in which an interpreter participates in communicative interaction was largely taken for granted. Conceived of as an intermediary between two communicating parties (a speaker and a hearer), the (professional) interpreter was generally not considered a 'third party' in the interaction but as "a mere medium of transmission" (Knapp-Potthoff and Knapp 1986: 153). In combination with the axiomatic view of neutrality as a key principle of the interpreter's professional ethics (» 10.3.1), the status of the interpreter appeared as quite distinct from that of a participant. By contrast, untrained 'linguistic mediators' engaging in **non-professional interpreting** in informal settings were observed to become actively involved in the interaction, speaking on their own behalf and assuming **third-party status** (Knapp-Potthoff and Knapp 1986). It was mainly through the work of Cecilia Wadensjö (« 2.5.2) that the dichotomy between uninvolved professionals and untrained third-party mediators gave way to a more complex and differentiated understanding of the interpreter's status and role as a participant.

8.1.1 Participant Status

The analysis of the interpreter's role in interaction put forward by Wadensjö (1998) is largely informed by the sociology of Erving Goffman (e.g. 1981). One of Goffman's concepts is the role of **non-person**, which Wadensjö (1998, 2008) applies to the interpreter's 'social activity role,' arguing that in face-to-face communication the interpreter has a service function and is not treated as fully present (» 10.3.2). This expectation that the interpreter remain 'invisible' at the level of the communicative event is complemented by Wadensjö's analysis of the interpreter's participation as a listener and speaker in a given 'system of activity.' Going beyond constellation models of interpreting (« 4.3.1), Wadensjö (1998) describes the interpreter's involvement in communicative interaction in terms of Goffman's (1981) **participation framework** – an influential scheme that was taken up and adapted by various authors (e.g. Clark 1996). A hearer, in Goffman's terms, may be 'ratified' (as an addressed or unaddressed recipient or as a 'bystander') or 'unratified' (as in the case of an 'overhearer' or eavesdropper). The interpreter's participation status, though subject to interactively induced changes in the utterance-by-utterance development of the interaction, could be seen as corresponding to that of a ratified but unaddressed participant.

The interpreter's role as a speaker is analyzed by Wadensjö (1998) with reference to Goffman's **production format**, which posits three different stances (or combinations thereof) that a speaker can adopt with regard to his or her utterance: the speaker as 'animator' – or 'vocalizer' (Clark 1996) – is responsible only for the production of speech sounds; the speaker as 'author' is responsible for formulating the utterance (hence Clark's suggestion of 'formulator'); and the speaker as 'principal' bears ultimate responsibility for the meaning expressed.

Wadensjö complements Goffman's triple production format by an analogous breakdown of 'listenership.' With a view to the interpreter's multiple roles as a listener, Wadensjö (1998: 91f) proposes a threefold distinction under the heading of **reception format**: listening as a 'reporter' (expected only to repeat what has been uttered); listening as a 'recapitulator' (expected to give an authorized voice to a prior speaker); and listening as a 'responder' (addressed so as to make his or her own contribution to discourse).

The emphasis in Wadensjö's account is on the simultaneity of speakership and listenership. She argues that talk in face-to-face communication is always carried out simultaneously with listening, and that listening may include overt verbal activity (e.g. back-channeling). For the interpreter, as for other participants, the participation status at a given point in time during the interaction is partly a matter of individual choice and partly determined by the co-present participants. This is also evident in the scheme developed by Merlini and Favaron (2005), who extend Wadensjö's analysis by introducing additional categories of 'footing.'

8.1.2 Footing

The Goffmanian notion of footing relates to his analysis of the participation framework and production format and is defined by Wadensjö (1998: 87) as "a person's alignment (as speaker *and* hearer) to a particular utterance." For the interpreter in a mediated encounter, a basic distinction can be made between the stance taken when translating an utterance (speaking as an 'author') and that of speaking – as 'principal' – in relation to an utterance (to be) translated, as in the case of asking for clarification or offering an explanation. In addition, the interpreter's footing may be indicated by the personal pronouns used. The interpreter may maintain the speaker's use of the first person singular, as typically expected of professionals (Harris 1990), opt for reported speech by using third-person pronouns ('s/he says'), or even change a speaker's first person singular to plural, thus indicating **alignment** with the speaker as well as the utterance. All these footing-related choices have implications for the way interactive discourse evolves in an encounter.

Departures from the professional norm of carrying over the first person singular from the original to the interpretation were discussed with reference to the Demjanjuk trial by Shlesinger (1991), who observed that the use of third-person reference ('The witness says ...') indicates dissociation from the speaker and foregrounds the interpreter as "an independent persona" (1991: 152). Similarly, the case study by Metzger (1999) reveals subtle changes in footing as reflected in the rendering of pronominal reference. When addressed directly by either party, the (sign language) interpreter is seen as deliberately giving minimal responses, thereby limiting involvement as an active third party. Even so, interpreters appear in an intrinsically dual role as "both participants in the interaction and conveyors of discourse" (Metzger 1999: 175). A literally more visible example of this can be found in Straniero Sergio's (1999) case study of an interpreted talk show, in which the dialogue interpreter on the set is seen actively participating in meaning negotiation and topic management. Rosenberg (2002) confirms the interpreter's dual function and status in his quantitative discourse analysis of 11 audiotaped English/Spanish medical interviews in a pediatric primary care clinic, concluding that "the interpreter is a full-fledged participant in the discourse whose responsibilities lie in the *skopos* of the interpreted speech event and in the expectations that the primary parties bring with them" (2002: 222).

Footing shifts reflecting the interpreter's status as a full-fledged participant are not limited to face-to-face communication. As borne out by Diriker's (2004) case study of English/Turkish SI at a symposium on philosophy, the situated performance of simultaneous conference interpreters may include various forms of active involvement in the discourse. Examining the transcribed audio recording for what she calls "shifts in the speaking subject," that is, shifts from the speaker's first person (or "alien I") to the 'I' of the interpreter, Diriker (2004) shows that the experienced professional interpreters in her study tended not only to 'speak on behalf of the original speakers' but also

addressed their listeners directly, disclosed the source of problems and inter-
ruptions, blended explanatory or compensatory remarks into the speaker's
words, divulged their attitudes, voiced their comments and even criticism
towards the speakers or other aspects of the interaction, and responded in
self-defense to accusations of misinterpretation.

In the context of a corpus-based qualitative study, Merlini and Favaron
(2005) develop a typology of seven different footings that an interpreter may
take up in relation to the preceding utterance by a primary party. According
to this scheme, an interpreter rendering an utterance addressed to him or her
as a 'translator' is speaking as a direct or indirect 'recapitulator'; when not so
addressed, the interpreter may adopt the footings of 'reporter,' 'narrator' or
'pseudo-co-principal,' whereas the footings of 'principal' or 'responder' are
adopted when the interpreter speaks as a third party, either initiating an
utterance or responding to a previous utterance as an interlocutor. Identifying
these different footings in a corpus of three professionally interpreted speech
pathology sessions in Australia, Merlini and Favaron (2005) argue that the
flexible choice of footings allows the professionals observed in their study to
go beyond being 'just translators' and act as 'communicators' serving the
purpose of the encounter.

As the notion of footing is often linked, or limited, to the position chosen
by the speaker or interpreter, the concept of **positioning** has been proposed to
account more broadly for the way in which the stance of an individual participant is negotiated by those present in the interaction, with participants
positioning themselves as well as each other (e.g. Mason 2012). Positioning,
in this sense, is closely related to footing but also bears directly on the issue
of the interpreter's **role**, which is increasingly viewed as resulting from an
interactive, jointly negotiated process (» 10.3.2).

8.2 Discourse Management

As established through the discourse-analytical research by Wadensjö (1998)
and many other scholars working in the DI paradigm of interpreting studies
(« 3.4.4), interpreting in face-to-face interaction goes beyond strictly translational text production (i.e. renditions of previous utterances) and includes
various ways of managing the discourse process between the primary participants. Wadensjö (1998) describes this as the 'coordinating' function inherent
in dialogue interpreting, as investigated in particular with reference to turn-taking
processes.

8.2.1 Coordination

According to Wadensjö (1998), the dialogue interpreter organizes the flow of
discourse both implicitly and explicitly: **implicit** coordination is achieved
simply by the interpreter taking every second turn at talk, whereas **explicit**
coordination manifests itself in discursive 'moves' by the interpreter. With

regard to their status as texts, the latter can be classified as **non-renditions**, and they can take various verbal as well as nonverbal forms (» 8.2.2).

The need for explicit coordination may arise from translation issues or problems with the interaction order, hence the distinction between 'text-oriented' and 'interaction-oriented' coordinating moves. Examples of the former include requests for repetition or clarification, comments on translations, or moves by the interpreter to claim his or her 'speaking space' (Englund Dimitrova 1997). Such moves are similar to interaction-oriented coordinating moves, by which an interpreter may ask the primary parties to stop, start or continue talking, as in the case of overlapping talk (Wadensjö 1998).

Going beyond the distinction between implicit and explicit coordination achieved by renditions and non-renditions, Baraldi and Gavioli (2012a) suggest the notion of 'basic coordination' to refer to the intrinsic linkage of each discursive action to a previous action, in contrast with 'reflexive coordination' as a meta-communicative activity to resolve problems. Examples of such reflexive coordination are moves to clarify, expand or repair utterances, achieved in a complex interplay between renditions and non-renditions. In this respect, reflexive coordination is seen as closely related to the notion of (intercultural) **mediation**, as the interpreter co-creates cultural forms and gives access to features that are unfamiliar to the interlocutor(s) s/he is addressing.

The study of coordination in the interactional rather than intercultural sense centers on the notion of **turn-taking**, as developed in conversation analysis and applied to interpreting in particular by Roy (1996, 2000) and Davidson (2002). Unlike turn-taking in dyadic encounters, the interaction order in interpreter-mediated events is established among at least three participants, with each primary party exchanging turns with the interpreter in their own language. In theory, the interpreter thus takes every second turn at talk (Speaker 1 – Interpreter – Speaker 2 – Interpreter – Speaker 1, etc.), but the reality of triadic interaction is considerably more complex and may involve a variety of coordinating moves by the interpreter.

In her case study of an interpreter-mediated consultation between a professor and a deaf doctoral student, Roy (1996, 2000) observes different types of 'transitions' between turns. Aside from regular turn-taking ('smooth transitions'), she discusses various types of **overlap** (i.e. simultaneous talk). In the case of overlapping talk by the primary participants, the interpreter is challenged to manage the situation, by stopping one or both speakers, ignoring a part or all of the overlapping talk, or holding part of the talk in memory for subsequent production. In one example, the interpreter resolves the overlap by a gesture signaling the student to wait while finishing the ongoing rendition (Roy 1996: 57).

Overlap in interactive discourse also occurs between the interpreter and primary parties in the form of verbal or nonverbal 'minimal responses' (e.g. 'mhm'), signaling understanding and/or attention. Such 'back-channel' or **feedback** signals are discussed in a case study of Swedish–Spanish medical interpreting by Englund Dimitrova (1997), who points to the difficulty of reproducing interlocutor feedback in the interpretation due to the loss of temporal proximity. The interpreter's feedback, by contrast, is shown to have a coordinating function, encouraging the speaker to continue or indicating readiness to take the next turn.

Since most research on dialogue interpreting is based on encounters mediated in short consecutive mode, it is noteworthy that Roy's (1996, 2000) pioneering work on interactive discourse processes actually involved a sign language interpreter working in simultaneous mode. Her analysis of turn-taking therefore includes discourse phenomena such as pauses and lag, which have an impact on the interaction order. Thus, a primary party waiting for a response while the (simultaneous) interpreter is still rendering the question in the other language, perhaps with a lengthy lag, may start speaking again, thereby reclaiming the turn from the interlocutor. This is exacerbated by the involvement of two different language modalities, as the interpreter's signing for the deaf participant is perceived as a potentially awkward **silence** by the hearing participant. Such uncertainty regarding turn-taking signals also applies to the other language direction, and highlights the importance of accounting for the complex interplay of auditory and visual perception in interactive discourse.

Coordination problems are by no means limited to encounters involving two different language modalities; rather, the multi-semiotic nature of discourse as a combination of verbal, paralinguistic and kinesic sign systems (Poyatos 1987/2002) must be regarded as fundamental to the analysis of interpreter-mediated interaction, regardless of mode or modality. This applies all the more to modes of mediation in which the repertoire of nonverbal sign systems produced and perceived by the participants is constrained by the use of technology. Telephone interpreting (audio only) is an obvious case in point (» 11.2.1), and there is substantial evidence that the lack of visual cues strongly impacts the nature of triadic interaction. In his analysis of more than 1,800 telephone interpreting assignments, Rosenberg (2007) finds that the lack of visual contact favors the use of reported speech, by the primary parties as well as by the interpreter; utterances addressed to the interpreter result in "dyadic-triadic shifts" (Rosenberg 2007: 71), and poor audio quality necessitates non-renditions by the interpreter asking for repetition or clarification. Likewise, Wadensjö (1999) concludes from her case-based comparison of face-to-face versus over-the-phone interpreting in a police interview that the lack of visual cues hampers the smooth coordination of participants' talk.

The spread of video telephony and videoconference-based interpreting has resolved some of the coordination needs resulting from the lack of visual cues but at the same created new, additional challenges (» 11.2.2). This has heightened awareness of the role of nonverbal visual signals in interactive discourse, as studied more recently under the heading of 'multimodality.'

8.2.2 Multimodality

Interactive discourse and its coordination by an interpreter can be assumed to involve the full range of verbal to nonverbal sign systems, which is also implied in the concept of **orality** (« 7.1.3) and which Poyatos (1987/2002) models as a combination of acoustic and visual sign-conveying systems perceived by participants in various constellations of auditory and/or visual co-presence. In research on dialogue interpreting, most attention so far has been given to kinesic and proxemic phenomena such as **gesture, gaze** and physical positioning. In one of the earliest contributions on the subject, Lang (1978) performed a micro-analysis of a five-minute extract from filmed court proceedings in Papua New Guinea and found the interpreter avoiding eye contact so as to position himself as detached and neutral, which potentially conflicts with the need for constant visual monitoring of his clients. In line with the view that the interpreter's role, or positioning, is co-constructed by the participants in interaction, Lang concluded that the interpreter "depends on the active co-operation of his clients and the extent to which they wish to include him as an active participant not only linguistically but also gesturally, posturally, and gaze-wise" (1978: 241).

The use of gesture, which is of obvious relevance in consecutive interpreting, has attracted surprisingly little research interest in the study of dialogue interpreting. As highlighted by Roy's (1996) example of an interpreter gesturing to stop a speaker talking out of turn, gestures and other kinesic resources can be assumed to be highly effective in the interpreter's control of turn-taking. The same applies to gaze, which has been the subject of several detailed studies. The interdependence of gaze and the interpreter's spatial position(ing) was analyzed in interpreter-mediated psychotherapy sessions by Wadensjö (2001), who stresses the need for the interpreter to be included in the 'shared communicative radius' of the participants. This is achieved by a triangular seating position, which allows unobstructed eye contact (mutual gaze) between patient, therapist and interpreter.

In an effort to treat verbal and nonverbal resources as an integrated system, Davitti (2013) uses software-based transcriptions annotated for gaze in her micro-analysis of three videotaped parent–teacher meetings, each involving a mother, two teachers and an interpreter working in consecutive mode between Italian and English. Though her study centers on interpreters' 'upgrading' of evaluative assessments, Davitti's innovative approach demonstrates that qualitative conversation-analytical techniques can accommodate multimodal analyses to explore how gaze may complement or substitute verbal elements of discourse.

With a specific focus on gaze, Mason (2012) presents a fine-grained analysis of immigration hearings filmed in Germany for a documentary. In all five hearings (involving Russian-speaking asylum seekers), the seating of the three participants roughly approximates a triangular configuration. While acknowledging the problem of incomplete ('impoverished') video data, Mason finds fairly regular patterns of gaze behavior by the immigration officers conducting the hearings as well as by the interpreters. When speaking, the officers are seen to direct their gaze to the asylum seeker most of the time but to deflect it to the interpreter at or just before the end of their turns, signaling the transition to the interpreter's rendering. Similar glances are directed at the interpreter when the officer has been in listening mode, reaffirming the importance of gaze shift in the management of turn-taking. The interpreters, by contrast, mainly direct their gaze at the asylum seekers when listening, signaling understanding and/or attention, but limit eye contact with the officers during their renditions. Beyond the role of gaze in showing attention and regulating turn allocation, Mason (2012) also finds evidence in his data of gaze being used as a resource in interactive positioning, which involves the combined (mutually reinforcing) effect of departures from the unmarked pattern of gaze behavior by two of the participants. He concludes that gaze and other multimodal resources should be examined in research on dialogue interpreting, not only for their function in the coordination of talk but also for the way in which they express attitudes and alignments in co-constructed discourse.

Further Reading

Participation

See PARTICIPATION FRAMEWORK and FOOTING in Pöchhacker (2015).

Discourse Management

See DIALOGUE INTERPRETING, DISCOURSE MANAGEMENT, MEDIATION, NON-RENDITION, TURN-TAKING and GAZE in Pöchhacker (2015).

9   History

For as long as academic interest in interpreting was dominated by professional conference interpreting, very little scholarly work was done on the practice of interpreting in history. Until the 1990s, the knowledge base appeared to be limited to a few dozen publications. Since then, a number of substantial contributions to the history (and historiography) of interpreting have been made, by members of the interpreting community as well as by historians, and interpreting studies could be said to have taken a 'historical turn.' Against this background, the aim of the present chapter is to review the state of the art in the historiography of interpreting and discuss some highlights and focal points of research to date.

9.1 Historiography

The historiography of interpreting is encumbered by some fundamental problems. Chief among them are the ephemeral nature of an activity which left no tangible trace through the ages, and the frequent tendency to regard it, in many historical settings, as a commonplace support activity deserving no special attention in its own right. With few exceptions, available sources are only marginally concerned with interpreting, making it an arduous task for the historian to locate references to the topic in chronicles, letters, autobiographies and literary works spanning a range of languages and cultures. It is from these disparate sources that a range of themes in historical research on interpreting have emerged.

9.1.1 Themes

In a review of the state of the art, Jesús Baigorri-Jalón (2006) notes the lack of a comprehensive 'handbook' that could claim to cover all types of interpreting in all periods of history. Summary accounts aiming at broad coverage include book chapters by Bowen (2012) and Baigorri-Jalón (2015a), and an encyclopedia entry by Andres (2013). Most, if not all other publications have a more specific thematic orientation, in many cases based on a combination of two or more chronological, geographical and typological parameters.

Historical research can be expected, first and foremost, to cover various **periods** in the development of human civilization, but the balance in this respect is extremely uneven. Aside from a handful of works on interpreting in antiquity (» 9.2.1), and fewer still on the Middle Ages, most historical research reaches back no further than the twentieth century, when interpreting gradually emerged as a worldwide profession (» 9.3.1). The resulting gap is now slowly being filled by studies on interpreting through what is usually referred to as the early modern period, between the late fifteenth and late eighteenth centuries (» 9.2.2).

The picture is no less uneven in terms of geographical **regions**, given the predominantly Western perspective on the history of interpreting, which centers on the Greco-Roman world and modern European powers, such as Spain, as they pursued and consolidated their imperial expansion. This imbalance is gradually being redressed by studies on interpreters in Asia, most notably China, Japan and Korea, as well as in Africa (e.g. Lawrance et al. 2006).

Most typically, and realistically perhaps, research on interpreting and interpreters in history covers particular **events** in a given socio-political context. Examples include wars, expeditions, negotiations and tribunals. In a similar vein, the object of study may be a specific national or international **institution**, either as an example of reliance on the services of interpreters (as in the case of multilingual parliaments or international organizations) or as a body representing the interpreting profession within a given domain (» 9.3.1–2).

The narrowest thematic focus for the history of interpreting is on a given **individual**, as in biographies of interpreters. This line of work, in particular, is constrained by the scarcity – or absence – of documentary sources, so that any such studies focusing on interpreters further back in history than the twentieth century are few and far between. Noteworthy exceptions include Doña Marina, or 'La Malinche' (Valdeón 2013), and Sacajawea (Karttunen 1994).

9.1.2 Sources and Methods

Though would-be historians of interpreting frequently lament the dearth of documentary evidence as a basis for factual reconstruction, work done in recent decades reflects an impressive range of sources that afford varying degrees of insight into interpreting practices through the ages. Some of these sources are fairly accessible even to less experienced researchers, while others require specialized knowledge and considerable scholarly expertise. Among the more challenging sources are **archeological artifacts** such as depictions and inscriptions (e.g. Kurz 1985), often in extinct languages, and written records left by ancient civilizations, not only in the so-called **classical languages** of the Greco-Roman world (Gehman 1914; Thieme et al. 1956) but also through the medium of Chinese, Arabic and Sanskrit texts from many different eras. Indeed, a thorough knowledge of language(s) and cultural traditions such as these is an important prerequisite for much historical research on interpreting. Researchers must be well versed not only in the associated fields of learning, but also in linguistic and historical reconstruction based on primary sources which are often difficult to identify, locate, access and contextualize.

Many different types of **archives** are central to the historian's work, ranging from ancient chronicles, annals and government records (e.g. Lung 2011) to the official documentation of public and other institutions (e.g. Baigorri-Jalón 2014) or, from an individual viewpoint, private collections of correspondence and other papers. Indeed, historiographers traditionally rely on a wide range of **written documents**. Examples of particular relevance to the study of interpreting include legislation (e.g. Giambruno 2008), judicial records and transcripts (e.g. Takeda 2010), but also published memoirs (e.g. Schmidt 1949) as well as letters, diaries and other such items.

Increasingly, visual records (**images**) have also been examined for historical insights. Aside from depictions of interpreters in chronicles and paintings from periods of colonial expansion, visual evidence includes photographs (e.g. Fernández-Ocampo and Wolf 2014) and films. As part of audiovisual records, but also as items of interest in their own right, **oral sources** play a key role in historical research on interpreting in the last century. Thus, life-story interviews have been used in an oral-history approach designed to elicit the recollections of pioneering twentieth-century interpreters with experience of tribunals, media events and diplomatic relations (e.g. Torikai 2009).

9.2 From Ancient to Modern Times

Considering the frequency of interpreting activities that must be assumed to have taken place in cross-cultural contacts for thousands of years, historical records are scant. In sources from antiquity, interpreters are generally conspicuous by their absence. Even where there is evidence of their activity, it has proved difficult to fully construe and contextualize its relevance.

9.2.1 Ancient Egypt and Rome

In the first known piece of research on interpreters completed in the twentieth century, Henry Gehman (1914), a student of classical languages, examined Greek and Latin sources for references to interpreters. Relying, among others, on the accounts of Herodotus and Xenophon, he recounts interpreter-related information about the Egyptians, Persians and Carthaginians: one example is the tale of how King Psammetichus (663–610 BCE) entrusted Egyptian boys to the care of Hellenic settlers so they would learn Greek and later serve as interpreters, while another interesting reference is to the use of interpreters in the multilingual armies of Alexander the Great and Hannibal. On the whole, however, Gehman concludes that historians were generally "not troubled by the difference of language" and were interested in events rather than "the incidental matter of the interpreters or the linguistic difficulties" (1914: 61).

Further research efforts along these lines were not made until the mid-1950s, when Thieme et al. (1956) published three 'Contributions to the History of Interpreting.' One of these, by Egyptologist Alfred Hermann (1956/2002), proved particularly influential. His references to Ancient Egypt, Greece and Rome were followed up and elaborated on by authors such as Kurz (e.g. 1985) and Vermeer (1992). Most notably, the volume by Thieme et al. (1956) also includes a picture and explanation of the **interpreter relief** from the Memphite tomb of General Horemheb (c. 1340 BCE). Though a most fascinating piece of pictorial evidence, the interpretation of this relief scene is uncertain. Another point of doubt concerns the honorific title translated as "overseer of dragomans" (e.g. Kurz 1985). It has been argued that the hieroglyph in question, traced back to the third millennium BCE, may refer not only to interpreters but to speakers of foreign languages in general (Hermann 1956/2002: 16).

More solid documentary evidence, however patchy, is available for interpreters in the Roman Empire. Aside from Gehman (1914) and Hermann (1956/2002), there is recent work by historians on the status of interpreters in the **Roman army** and administration as well as in distant regions of the Empire. Mairs (2015) identifies over a hundred references to interpreters and interpreting in Roman Egypt and the Greek papyrological record, and distinguishes broadly between commercial middlemen and army officers bearing *interpres* as a professional title, when their status was acknowledged at all.

9.2.2 China and Korea

Research on interpreters and interpreting in early China and Korea has become prominent only in the new millennium, and the great potential for further studies to become available to a worldwide readership in English is obvious. A major point of reference is the monograph by Lung (2011), which brings together a series of studies on the functions of interpreters in the multi-ethnic Chinese context over the course of some 1000 years. Aside from enriching the discussion on the concept and lexicalization of interpreting (and translation), Lung presents case studies of interpreting on the frontier and in tributary visits by the Empire's vassal states, of different translation officials in the central government of the Tang dynasty (618–907), and of interpreters' involvement not only in diplomatic encounters as such but also in creating the historical record of such events.

Along similar lines, Kim (2015) investigates the titles, functions, education and social status of interpreting officials in Korea's Goryeo (Koryŏ) period (918–1392) and Joseon (Chosŏn) dynasty (1392–1910). As in the case of China, the function of interpreting in Silla, one of Korea's Three Kingdoms, is found to be closely intertwined with **diplomatic affairs**, not least with nearby China itself. Kim (2015) mentions early 'training' efforts, consisting in sending high-ranking officials to Tang China to learn the language and later serve as messengers and, presumably, interpreters. More importantly, she also describes the creation, in the late fourteenth century, of an institution in charge of both training and service provision: the *Sayeogwon* (*Sayŏgwŏn*), located in the capital city of Seoul, with branch offices near the Chinese border, offered some three years of language instruction in Chinese, Japanese, Jurchen or Mongolian to young middle-class men. At the same time, the institution also served as the office providing interpreters for diplomatic affairs, with some 600 interpreting officials.

These historical relations, as well as the fact that Kim's (2015) study relies on annals written in classical Chinese, point to considerable potential synergies for future research on interpreting in the history of China and Korea.

9.2.3 Early Modern Empires

For historians of interpreting in early modern Europe, two regional focal points, which are also linked to key dates marking the beginning of this era, are Spain and the Ottoman Empire. From the year 1492 and the Fall of Constantinople in 1453, respectively, the rise of these two powers was associated with significant developments in the history of interpreting.

While the situation in Spain around 1500 is also interesting from the perspective of inter-ethnic domestic and regional dynamics (see Baigorri-Jalón 2015b), it is the Spanish 'discovery,' conquest and colonization of Central and South America that gave special significance to interpreting, with important repercussions to this day. Aside from efforts by Christopher Columbus to forcefully conscript local interpreters, the role of **Doña Marina** ('La Malinche'), interpreting for Hernán Cortés and thus contributing to the downfall of the Aztec Empire, has inspired a number of studies (e.g. Karttunen 1994; Valdeón 2013). Thanks to the chronicle of the expedition written after the event by one of Cortés' soldiers (Bernal Díaz del Castillo), the involvement of Malinche and other interpreters in the Aztec conquest is exceptionally well documented. Another noteworthy figure is **Felipillo**, who served as interpreter in the Spanish conquest of Peru and was brutally killed for purposely misinterpreting Pizarro's message to the Inca king Atahualpa.

No less significant than their service to the conquistadors was the role of interpreters, on a much broader scale, in the administration of Spain's colonial empire. A total of 14 **interpreter laws** were enacted by the Spanish Crown between 1529 and 1630 to regulate the activity of interpreters in civil (e.g. tributary) and criminal matters before the *Audiencias* (tribunals), and protect their indigenous clients from abuse (Giambruno 2008).

In Europe, the sixteenth and seventeenth centuries were marked by the impressive rise of the **Ottoman Empire**. Since the Turkish rulers of this multi-national and multilingual conglomerate preferred to conduct diplomatic affairs in their own language rather than a lingua franca, such as French or Latin, European powers were forced to avail themselves of interpreters, or **dragomans** (Rothman 2015a). In order to avoid reliance on local recruits, efforts were made to train trusted nationals by sending teenage boys to Constantinople for language training and subsequent service as interpreters. The institution of the so-called *jeunes de langues* (Rothman 2015b) was originally a Venetian practice, later adopted in particular by France and the Habsburg Monarchy (see Wolf 2015: 104ff).

In contrast with the emergence of shared practices for the training of interpreters in Europe, where rulers from the House of Habsburg were involved in the spread and consolidation of interpreter-related arrangements from the Eastern Mediterranean to the Americas, contemporary practices in Japan's Edo period (1603–1867) developed in isolation. After Portuguese interpreters had assisted foreign trade for a period of about thirty years, the Tokugawa shogunate limited contact with the outside world to trade with China and Korea, allowing only a tightly controlled group of Dutch interpreters to remain active in the port of Nagasaki. These *Oranda tsuji* were officials with hereditary titles, who worked with Dutch traders and also apprised the central government of world affairs. Such information became increasingly important as Western science and technology took center stage in Japan's era of modernization, coinciding with the historical period up to World War I (Takeda 2015).

9.3 Professionalization

Throughout history, there are examples of places and periods in which interpreting was exercised as a professional function. Nevertheless, it is fair to say that the decisive political, technological, economic and social developments that turned the millennial practice of interpreting into a profession recognized worldwide occurred in the twentieth century (« 2.1.1–2). Research on the emergence of the interpreting profession(s) therefore covers three (partly overlapping) phases: the emergence of conference interpreting, in two major waves following World Wars I and II; the professionalization of signed language interpreting, beginning in the US in the 1960s, and considerably later elsewhere; and the emergence of community interpreting in the final decades of the century.

9.3.1 Twentieth-Century Milestones

Most research on twentieth-century professionalization centers on conference interpreting, and much of it was done in the late 1990s by Jesús Baigorri Jalón, a UN staff interpreter with an academic background in history. His monograph on the origins of the profession (Baigorri-Jalón 2014) gives a detailed description of interpreting and interpreters (such as Paul Mantoux) at the **Paris Peace Conference** after World War I. Based on administrative and personnel records in the Archives of the **League of Nations** and the **ILO** in Geneva, he also reconstructs the development of simultaneous interpreting from Edward Filene's initial idea for a 'telephonic translation system' to its successful testing in the late 1920s. The crucial event for the coming of age of simultaneous interpreting, the **Nuremberg Trial**, is the topic of an in-depth study by Francesca Gaiba (1998), who used both judicial records and interviews with interpreters for a comprehensive account of the trials with a focus on interpreting arrangements and their effect on the proceedings. A detailed account of interpreting at the **United Nations**, the international organization in which simultaneous interpreting was first institutionalized, is provided by Baigorri-Jalón (2004).

Aside from these studies, parts of which are also included in the special issue of *Interpreting* (4:1, 1999) on *The History of Interpreting in the 20th Century*, few scholars have conducted similarly detailed historical research based on archival records and interviews. Wilss (1999), for one, offers a review of German translation and interpreting in the twentieth century, with particular emphasis on training programs. On a more sociological level, the study by Tseng (1992) describes the professionalization of conference interpreting in Taiwan, and has served as a model for similar accounts of (spoken-language) community interpreting and signed language interpreting in various countries (e.g. Mikkelson 1999).

Training as a cornerstone in the professionalization of interpreting has commanded particular attention among history-minded scholars, although only conference interpreter training in Europe goes back more than fifty years (e.g. Mackintosh 1999; Seleskovitch 1999). Biographical research has been done, for instance, on Antoine **Velleman**, the founder of the interpreter school in Geneva and later director of the school founded by Paul Schmidt in Munich. Developments in interpreter education in other professional domains and regions are relatively recent. Signed language interpreting, for instance, is covered by Roy and Napier (2015: Ch. 6), and an account of interpreter education in China is provided by Bao (2015).

9.3.2 Getting Organized

A significant aspect of professionalization is the founding of professional organizations of interpreters, some of which date back to the early twentieth century. Paradigm cases in this regard are **AIIC** (see Keiser 1999) and the US Registry of Interpreters for the Deaf (**RID**), which is the subject of a doctoral thesis (Vidrine 1979) as well as a personal account by Lou Fant (1990). Furthermore, descriptions of the interplay between such aspects of professionalization as legal provisions, professional bodies, training programs, and certification in a given national context and/or domain of interpreting are also part of the overall historical picture, reflecting the highly fragmented nature of the interpreting profession as it has emerged in various contexts and settings (» 10.1).

Further Reading

Historiography

See HISTORY in Pöchhacker (2015).

Ancient to Modern Times

See EGYPT, ROME, CHINA, KOREA, SPAIN, DRAGOMANS, JEUNES DE LANGUES, HABSBURG MONARCHY and JAPAN in Pöchhacker (2015).

Professionalization

See MANTOUX, NUREMBERG TRIAL and VELLEMAN in Pöchhacker (2015).

10 Profession

In a historical, and even more so a contemporary, perspective interpreting studies is fundamentally concerned with those who practice interpreting as a profession, commonly defined as an occupation that requires special knowledge and skills acquired through education, and consequently enjoys recognition and a certain status in society. This focus on the interpreting profession(s) derives from the deep roots of the academic field of study in the professional field of practice (« 2.1.1–2). Topics of research broadly range from sociological issues of professional identity and status to the nature of a professional's competence and ethical behavior, and the quality of his or her professional service delivered under a given set of working conditions.

10.1 Sociology

As a more or less clearly defined professional group in society, interpreters can be studied at different levels of sociological inquiry: at the macro level, interest centers on the status and power of interpreters as an occupational community in society at large (» 10.1.2); at an intermediate or meso level, interpreting is viewed in the context of particular social settings and institutional domains (» 10.1.1); and on the micro level, the focus is on the nature and function of professionally mediated interaction (» 10.3.2), as also discussed in Chapter 8.

10.1.1 Domains and Settings

Professional interpreting is situated in a particular social context, which places certain constraints on the activity. It is the dialectic between institutional requirements and expectations on the one hand, and interpreters' performance standards on the other, that gives rise to the level of professionalism prevailing in a given institutional setting. By definition, interpreting in international settings is less constrained by socio-institutional factors than community-based interpreting, which is invariably set within a specific national, legal, political, economic, and cultural framework.

With its origins in the **multilateral conferences** of international organizations, and thanks to the worldwide efforts of professional bodies like AIIC,
international conference interpreting is based on widely accepted standards of
practice for consecutive and simultaneous interpreting in what remains
loosely defined as **conference-like settings**. Indeed, it is these generic standards
rather than the requirements of particular institutional settings that came to
define the profession of conference interpreting. Work in such diverse settings
as international tribunals, private talks between heads of state, or television
broadcasts is therefore commonly seen as part of the professional territory of
conference interpreters.

This broad approach may explain why the role of institutional constraints
in international settings has received very little systematic attention. Among
the few exceptions is an effort by Carlo Marzocchi (1998) to highlight the
specifics of interpreting in the **European Parliament** (see also Vuorikoski
2004). A major milestone in this regard is the ethnographic study by Duflou
(2016) of EU interpreters as a 'community of practice.' On the basis of
documents, in-depth interviews and extended observation, Duflou describes
the trajectory from 'beginnerdom' to situated professional competence, as
manifested, among other things, in smooth turn-taking arrangements among
team members.

Setting-related constraints are also evident from studies on user expectations
(» 10.4.2), particularly for interpreting in the **media** (see Kurz and Pöchhacker
1995). Media interpreting, however, while typically involving 'international'
input, is essentially set within the institutional context of a specific socio-cultural
community and is therefore community-based as well as international. Apart
from media interpreting in a transnational institutional setting (e.g. the
Franco-German channel ARTE), socio-cultural specifics play a prominent
role. Examples include delayed-broadcast news interpreting in Japan (e.g.
Tsuruta 2011) and TV interpreting practices in various European countries
(e.g. Castillo 2015; Mack 2002). Most clearly a matter of language transfer in
an intra-social context is the rendition of TV broadcasts for deaf viewers,
which has been investigated in various countries, such as the UK (Steiner
1998), China (Xiao et al. 2015) and South Africa (Wehrmeyer 2015).

The most explicitly constrained community setting in which interpreters
have played a significant role for centuries is the **courtroom**. Legal provisions
establishing standards of practice for court interpreting in Spain's colonial
empire were enacted as early as the sixteenth century (« 9.2.3), and there is a
long, if problematic, tradition of interpreter use in English courts (see Morris
1995). The existence of legal provisions governing the use of interpreters, such
as the US *Court Interpreters Act* or *Directive 2010/64/EU on the Right to
Interpretation and Translation in Criminal Proceedings*, favors the emergence
of a distinct professional identity for this domain. Nevertheless, as highlighted
by Morris and other authors (e.g. Laster and Taylor 1994; Mikkelson 1998;
Brennan 1999), the constraints placed on interpreters in the legal system are
often at odds with the standards promoted by the interpreting profession,

leaving a gap between unrealistic institutional demands for 'verbatim translation' by 'invisible' interpreters on the one hand and a widespread lack of specific training and commonly accepted performance standards for judicial interpreting on the other. Moreover, **legal settings** are highly diverse and range from police interviews and asylum hearings (e.g. Pöllabauer 2015) to various types of civil and criminal proceedings (e.g. J. Lee 2015) and even prison settings (Martínez-Gómez 2014), each with their specific institutional constraints. Interpreting in cases involving gender violence, as studied in the Spanish-led SOS-VICS project, is another case in point. Given this diversity, and the different national legal traditions and great variety of languages involved, the goal of consistent professional standards comparable to those prevailing for international settings is not likely to be achieved in the near future. To what extent this can be accelerated by newly adopted international standards, such as ISO 13611 ("Interpreting – Guidelines for community interpreting") and ISO 18841 ("Interpreting – General requirements and recommendations"), remains to be seen. At any rate, there is a need for systematic empirical research in this field along the lines of Berk-Seligson's (1990) pioneering ethnography of interpreting in US courtrooms, the British project on *Deaf People's Access to Justice* (see Brennan 1999) and Hale's (2011) more recent work in Australia (see also Hale 2006).

A comparable picture emerges for interpreting in **healthcare settings**, the second major domain of spoken-language interpreting in the community (Hale 2007). Though not as tightly constrained by legal precepts and traditions as judicial interpreters, medical interpreters have similarly faced a powerful and highly structured institution in their efforts to promote professional standards. In fact, with few exceptions (see Puebla Fortier 1997), there are no specific legal provisions for an enforceable right to an interpreter in medical settings, nor is there a strong interest on the part of healthcare institutions to provide – and pay for – professional interpreting services. This lack of a well-defined 'market' has made it difficult for a profession to emerge even in the face of well-documented needs, and has favored *ad hoc* models of service provision relying on untrained or minimally trained bilinguals. Under these circumstances, professionalization has largely been "institution-driven" (Ozolins 2000), and research since the 1960s on interpreting in healthcare strongly reflects the medical-institutional rather than the professional-translational perspective (see Pöchhacker 2006a). A number of studies by Hsieh (e.g. 2007) have addressed role-related conflicts between the interpreter and service-provider perspectives and highlighted the latter's 'utilitarian approach.' Aside from broader public health issues and consultations in general medicine, special attention has been given to interpreting in **mental health** settings (e.g. Bot 2003, 2005, 2015). On the whole, discourse-based as well as ethnographic studies (e.g. Angelelli 2004a; Bolden 2000; Davidson 2002) have highlighted the extent to which the diverse constraints of the healthcare setting impact on the practices of more or less professional interpreters in this field.

While work in legal, medical and social service settings is as common for sign language interpreters as for spoken-language interpreters, there are additional community-based settings which are uniquely important to the practice of signed language interpreting. In countries with legislation providing for the 'mainstreaming' of deaf students (as adopted in the US in the 1970s), **educational interpreting** is one of the chief professional domains of sign language interpreters. In the US, where schools, colleges and universities are the most important users of sign language interpreters, educational interpreting has been the subject of an impressive body of literature (Smith 2015). There and elsewhere, researchers have investigated the cognitive effectiveness of interpreted lectures (e.g. Livingston et al. 1994; Marschark et al. 2004) and discussed the dynamics of mediated classroom interaction as well as the broader ideological challenges of using interpreters to provide equal access to education. The latter also apply to spoken-language interpreters in higher education, as used in some South African universities (Verhoef and du Plessis 2008).

Among the diverse institutional contexts in which sign language interpreters may be expected to work, special challenges have been described for the **theater** and for **religious settings** (see Frishberg 1990). Church interpreting, in particular, has recently come to the fore as an area of practice and research also in spoken-language interpreting (e.g. Hokkanen 2012; Karlik 2010), albeit mainly under the heading of non-professional interpreting.

10.1.2 Identity and Status

Before a distinct professional identity for interpreters emerged, their social position was mainly characterized by their dual (and hence often dubious) **cultural identity**. Historically, it was immersion in more than one cultural community that qualified individuals to assume the role of interpreter, and this hybrid cultural status raised issues of loyalty. Empires and dominant groups therefore sought to assure themselves of 'their own' trusted interpreters by what Cronin (2002) calls 'autonomous' (rather than 'heteronomous') provision, avoiding reliance on the cultural Other (« 9.2.3). Nowadays, issues of cultural identity and allegiance arise particularly in signed language interpreting, where **Deaf interpreters** as members of the Deaf cultural community can cover only part of deaf users' communication and interpreting needs. As discussed by Cokely (2000), sign language interpreters, who now gain access to the profession mainly via the academic route rather than through cultural immersion, are seen by deaf people as members of the majority culture responsible for their marginalization. In spoken-language community interpreting, on the other hand, interpreters belonging to the ethnic minority or migrant culture of the individual client are likely to be subject to reigning attitudes to the cultural Other in mainstream society, with profound implications for the recognition and professional status afforded them. The only professional domain for which the (high) status of interpreters seems to be beyond doubt – and only tenuously linked to cultural identity – is international conference interpreting.

In his comprehensive review of the conference interpreting profession in Germany, Feldweg (1996) touches on such issues as recognition and the public **image** of conference interpreters as reflected by **fictional interpreters** in literary works (e.g. Kurz 2007) and in the mass media. On a strictly empirical basis, conference interpreters' **occupational status** has been investigated by Dam and Zethsen (2013), who surveyed some two dozen Danish staff interpreters at the EU and found them highly trained, highly skilled, and also highly paid in the eyes of non-interpreters. Even so, conference interpreters did not see their profession at the top of the **prestige** scale. This may be related to empirical findings from surveys such as the AIIC Workload Study (AIIC 2002), in which respondents felt that the **prestige** of their profession has declined over the years. Some authors have linked this to the **feminization** of the profession, in which women generally outnumber men by a ratio of 3:1 or 4:1. At the international level at least, these perceptions of prestige and status appear not to detract from the generally high level of **job satisfaction** among conference interpreters. In the Workload Study, 88% of the 607 respondents expressed their satisfaction with the profession. The situation varies, however, in different national contexts. Kondo (1988), for instance, described the status of the profession in Japan as rather modest. This has generally been found also in survey research among community interpreters (see Hale 2007), often in the face of high expectations among service providers regarding practitioners' professional competence.

10.2 Competence

For a practice or occupation to be acknowledged as a profession, it must be perceived to rest on a body of knowledge and skills, mastery of which can only be acquired by specialized training. Competence in interpreting can thus be defined as the congruence between task demands and qualifications. An understanding of the latter is crucial to professionalization in general and interpreter education in particular, and key to regulating access to the profession by way of certification (» 10.2.3). Chiefly informed by approaches from psychology, there is a growing body of research into the abilities and expertise which make up an interpreter's professional competence.

10.2.1 Personal Qualities and Abilities

Interpreters and psychologists have long pointed to a number of psychological prerequisites for those who would exercise the profession of interpreter. Based on interviews with twenty conference interpreters, whose performance he observed at the League of Nations and the ILO, Sanz (1930) listed a dozen qualities, including **cognitive** abilities (e.g. intelligence, intuition, memory) as well as **moral** and **affective** qualities (e.g. tact, discretion, alertness, poise). The original RID Code of Ethics, adopted in 1965, similarly required interpreters to be "of high moral character, honest, conscientious, trustworthy, and of emotional maturity" (Cokely 2000: 35), and comparable requirements are often found in legal provisions for court interpreters. The list of personal prerequisites given by van Hoof (1962: 59ff) for court, military, liaison as well as conference interpreters includes **physical** qualities such as stamina and strong nerves, **intellectual** qualities, in particular language proficiency and wide general knowledge, and **mental** qualities such as memory skills, judgment, concentration and divided attention. With reference to conference interpreting, Keiser (1978: 17) emphasizes 'knowledge' (mastery of languages and general background knowledge) and 'personal qualities' including "the ability to intuit meaning," adaptability, concentration, memory skills, a gift for public speaking and a pleasant voice. A more recent summary of 'ideal interpreter profiles' is provided by Russo (2011: 10). For liaison interpreting, Gentile et al. (1996: 65ff) suggest language skills, cultural competence, interpreting techniques, memory skills and professional ethics as the main components of an interpreter's competence. For sign language interpreters, Frishberg (1990: 25ff) places particular emphasis on interpersonal and cross-cultural skills.

Several attempts to draw up a **personality profile** of interpreters with the help of standard psychological instruments have yielded little conclusive evidence: examples of psychometric tests used include the neuroticism scale of the Eysenck Personality Inventory (Gerver 1976); the questionnaire for determining Type A (coronary-prone) behavior (Cooper et al. 1982); the Wechsler Adult Intelligence Scale and the California Personality Inventory (Strong and Rudser 1992); the State-Trait Anxiety Inventory (Kurz 1996); and the Myers-Briggs Type Inventory (Schweda Nicholson 2005). In a more specific line of investigation, psychological tests have been applied to discriminate between typical translator and interpreter personalities. Kurz et al. (1996) discussed previous studies as well as results from a student survey with reference to the model of communication value orientation by Casse. Whereas the dominant orientation for translators was toward 'process' and 'people,' the typical interpreter was found to be 'people-oriented' and 'action-oriented', that is, focusing on social interaction and 'getting things done.' Feldweg (1996), in an interview-based survey of 39 German AIIC members, reaffirmed the consensus among professionals regarding the cognitive skills and affective disposition characteristic of a good interpreter. And yet the chief intellectual abilities required of interpreters – broad general education and knowledge, proficiency in working languages, cultural competence, analytic and memory skills – are difficult to establish as distinctive of interpreting. Researchers have therefore focused on the way this set of abilities evolves into the specific skills which make up an interpreter's expertise.

10.2.2 Special Skills and Expertise

The crucial starting point for the development of interpreting proficiency is bilingual skills (« 5.1.1), which, according to the theory of natural translation (Harris and Sherwood 1978), imply a rudimentary ability to translate. Just how this and other baseline abilities give rise to professional performance has been studied in the framework of expertise research – an area of cognitive psychology which has grown out of work on information processing and artificial intelligence since the 1970s (see Hoffman 1997). As has been established for a diverse range of domains, experts rely on richly integrated knowledge representations and elaborate **mental models**, and use advanced reasoning processes in perceptual and problem-solving tasks. Progressing beyond declarative ('rule-based') knowledge, experts have at their disposal flexible, context-sensitive **strategies** which have become automatic to the point of being regarded as intuition and tacit (procedural) knowledge. While this makes knowledge elicitation from expert interpreters a considerable challenge, a number of methodological approaches, including structured interviews, task analysis and contrastive performance analysis, have been suggested – and fit in well with previous studies on interpreting. The task analysis for consecutive interpreting described by Hoffman (1997: 205), for instance, is reminiscent of the pioneering study by Seleskovitch (1975), and there is a long tradition of experimental research comparing the performance of professional subjects ('experts') with that of beginning students or bilingual controls ('novices'). Examples include Barik (1973, 1975/2002) on pauses and errors, Lambert (1989) on recall and recognition, Dillinger (1994) on comprehension, Padilla et al. (1995) on working memory capacity, Kurz (1996) on simultaneous listening and speaking, Andres (2002) on note-taking, and Mead (2002) on disfluencies in consecutive renditions.

   In an experimental study set explicitly in the so-called **expert–novice paradigm**, Moser-Mercer et al. (2000) investigated various language processing skills assumed to be part of expert proficiency in interpreting. However, while professionals were better able than students to avoid attentional disturbance in the 'delayed auditory feedback' task, neither the shadowing task nor a series of verbal fluency tasks yielded evidence discriminating between expert and novice performance. More surprisingly still, the only significant group effects found by Köpke and Nespoulous (2006), who used various working memory tasks, showed superior performance by the novice interpreters rather than the experts. Along these lines, the work of Liu et al. (2004) suggests that expertise in simultaneous interpreting is not a function of discrete cognitive abilities (such as working memory capacity) but of task-specific skills (selective processing, efficient output monitoring and allocation of working memory resources in SI) which are acquired through extensive time-on-task, as in training and, in particular, real-life experience. Beyond cognitive processing and task performance as such, expertise in interpreting also includes assignment-related interactional skills (e.g. the negotiation of working conditions) and strategies for knowledge acquisition.

10.2.3 Certification

An interpreter's demonstrated skills in performing the task are a fundamental prerequisite for access to the profession, at least where the necessary regulations are in place. For court interpreters, some jurisdictions require no more than the swearing of an **oath**. As stated by Berk-Seligson (1990: 204), however, "No amount of oath-swearing can guarantee high quality interpreting from an interpreter who does not have the necessary competency." In domains for which professional training is either lacking or not well established, recourse is therefore made to certification procedures involving some form of **testing** or performance assessment. An early model was the RID certification system launched in the early 1970s. The RID system and its assessment methods have been the subject of several studies addressing issues of validity and reliability (e.g. Strong and Rudser 1985, 1992). Other examples, and no less worth investigating in this regard, are the skills-based examinations conducted by NAATI, Australia's National Accreditation Authority for Translators and Interpreters; certification programs for US legal interpreters, in particular the Federal Court Interpreter Certification Examination (FCICE); the Diploma of Public Service Interpreting in the UK; and two national certification schemes for healthcare interpreters in the US.

Certification systems for interpreters range from state-controlled schemes, such as the China Accreditation Test for Translators and Interpreters (CATTI), to programs operated by professional bodies (see Hlavac 2013), and may be based on testing, evidence of completed training or relevant prior experience, and **peer evaluation**. The strict membership policy of AIIC, for instance, relies on on-the-job performance assessment by peers as well as prior professional experience. The AIIC admission system has thus served the purpose of a certification system for conference interpreters, and the organization's directory of members has been regarded as a register of qualified professionals. In most cases, however, interpreter certification implies some form of test-based assessment, and this has become an important field of research. The study by Clifford (2005), which investigates the psychometric properties of an existing interpreter certification test in comparison with a newly constructed one, is an early case in point. More recently, Liu (2013) offers a data-based critical appraisal of Taiwan's government-sponsored T/I competency examinations and formulates a number of recommendations for good practice, including rater training, clear descriptors for analytical as well as holistic scoring, and fidelity rating based on smaller source-text subdivisions differentiated for primary and secondary meaning units.

10.3 Ethics and Role

An occupation takes shape as a profession as the values and principles underlying expected and accepted behavior are codified and reaffirmed collectively by its practitioners. While some professional codes also specify performance levels, for example in terms of 'fidelity,' 'accuracy' and 'completeness' (« 7.2.1), their main concern is with practitioners' ethical conduct as members of the interpreting profession and as incumbents of a particular role. Indeed, the notion of role – a relational concept defined by sociologists as a set of more or less normative behavioral expectations associated with a 'social position' – has become one of the most prominent topics in interpreting studies, linked in particular to interpreting in community-based settings.

10.3.1 Codes and Conduct

Written standards of conduct for interpreters can be traced back at least to sixteenth-century Spanish colonial laws (« 9.2.3). In contrast to such rules imposed on practitioners by higher authority, international conference interpreters forging their profession some four hundred years later acted autonomously when they adopted the **AIIC Code of Professional Ethics** in early 1957. At the heart of this code of professional conduct and practice is a 'Code of Honor' which consists of five articles, chief among them the principle of professional secrecy. The remainder contains detailed provisions concerning working conditions, and these interrelate with the more specific 'Professional Standards' formulated by AIIC to regulate the exercise of the profession. Thus settled, questions of ethics and standards of practice received little attention in the literature on conference interpreting until the 1990s, when an anti-trust case brought against AIIC in the US led to some deregulation. At any rate, the AIIC Code remains silent about issues of role and performance quality (aside from the impact of working conditions) which have loomed large in other domains of the profession.

A trailblazing achievement in the professionalization of interpreting beyond international conferences and organizations was the adoption of the **RID Code of Ethics** in early 1965. Even though RID members at the time were less concerned with building a profession than with promoting the availability of competent interpreters (see Fant 1990), their Code of Ethics proved fundamental to the professional identity of sign language interpreters in North America. Indeed, the RID Code, revised and updated in the late 1970s and more recently turned into the NAD-RID **Code of Professional Conduct**, served as a model in moves to establish professional standards in other countries and domains of interpreting.

Since the RID Code of Ethics also addressed such principles as 'impartiality' and 'faithfulness,' the approach to ethics in community-based domains inevitably intersects with the complex issue of the interpreter's role (see Hale 2007). Particularly in the field of signed language interpreting, problems of ethics (and role) have thus generated considerable debate and research. A number of authors have expressed dissatisfaction with the strictures of the Code. Tate and Turner (1997/2002), for instance, who surveyed some 100 British sign language interpreters about ethically challenging scenarios, proposed that the Code should be complemented by a kind of "case law" providing guidance on particularly complex situations. A more fundamental reorientation is advocated by Cokely (2000), who faults the RID Code of Ethics for its deontological approach – that is, its focus on rigid limitations and prescriptions. Instead, Cokely proposes a "rights-based approach," giving interpreters more freedom for professional decision-making in a given situation or case.

Efforts to codify professional practice in spoken-language community interpreting have been made particularly for legal and healthcare settings (see Mikkelson 2000). Whereas some codes – and authors – oriented towards court interpreting typically exhibit a more conservative, mechanistic attitude (e.g. Schweda Nicholson 1994), authors like Niska (1995) and Mikkelson (1998) have advocated the **emancipation**, if not 'empowerment,' of the (court) interpreter as a responsible professional rather than an unobtrusive message converter. Similarly, the descriptive research by Wadensjö (1998) has pointed to the inadequacy of the Swedish Guide to Good Practice (*God tolksed*) in regulating the real-life dynamics of interpreter-mediated encounters. By the same token, standards of practice for healthcare interpreters in the US and Canada have been reviewed critically by Kaufert and Putsch (1997). Using case examples, these authors show how principles such as confidentiality, accuracy and completeness, and client self-determination are difficult to maintain in certain constellations of interaction. An effort to address these concerns through empirical research while building on established traditions of codification was made by the California Healthcare Interpreting Association (CHIA). The CHIA *Standards* comprise six ethical principles as well as guidance on issues of intervention and advocacy. Their application has been investigated by Angelelli (2006) in a focus group study which points to the difficulties of scrupulously respecting codified principles under real-life working conditions, and highlights the challenge of defining the interpreter's role.

10.3.2 Role Descriptions

The role of interpreter, which bilinguals have assumed in various contexts throughout history, has been closely linked with such **intermediary** functions as messenger, guide, and negotiator. It was only with the professionalization of interpreting in the course of the twentieth century that the interpreter's role became codified in more specific terms. The more narrowly construed professional role generally prescribes faithful, accurate and complete rendition (« 7.2.1), and proscribes any discourse initiative on the part of the interpreter, who is conceptualized as a 'non-person' in a **neutral** position between the interlocutors. Hence the widespread assumption that in professional and institutional settings, "the interpreter's function in general is comparable to that of a machine, giving a more or less literal translation of what is said in language A in language B" (Knapp-Potthoff and Knapp 1986: 152). This **mechanistic** conception has engendered metaphors such as 'faithful echo,' 'channel,' 'conduit,' 'switching device,' 'transmission belt,' 'modem' or 'input–output robot' to describe the nature of the interpreter's role (see Roy 1993/2002). This view of the interpreter as an **invisible** translating machine would appear to be inspired by the technology-based mode of simultaneous conference interpreting. In fact, however, it is deeply rooted particularly in the field of court interpreting, where the legal profession has traditionally denied court interpreters any latitude in dealing with meaning (i.e. 'interpreting') and limited their role to "verbatim translation" (see Morris 1995). As described by Laster and Taylor (1994: 112f), the standard of "literalism" associated with the **conduit model** of interpreting is a legal fiction necessitated by the inadmissibility of hearsay evidence (i.e. information reported by someone other than the witness) in the common-law courtroom. Pointing to the linguistic, socio-cultural and interactional complexity of the interpreter-mediated encounter, these authors challenge the prescriptive standard of literalism on principal grounds and argue instead for a redefinition of the (legal) interpreter as a more visible and accountable **communication facilitator**. This role description had gained currency in the field of signed language interpreting by the 1980s. It is one of four role constructs identified by Witter-Merithew (1986/2015) and subsequently discussed by Roy (1993/2002), namely: helper, mechanistic conduit, communication facilitator, and bilingual, bicultural specialist.

In other domains, too, normative discussions have emphasized a more broadly construed role for the interpreter. In the literature on interpreters in healthcare, Joseph Kaufert and associates (e.g. Kaufert and Koolage 1984), studying native Canadian interpreters from the perspective of medical anthropology, are frequently cited as representing the view of interpreters as **culture brokers** and patients' **advocates** working to redress power imbalances in cross-cultural clinical encounters. For the legal setting, particularly beyond the adversarial courtroom as such, authors such as Laster and Taylor (1994) and Mikkelson (1998) have highlighted the need for the interpreter to further the interests of the individual client in an unfamiliar institutional environment, and Barsky (1996) concluded from interviews with 56 applicants for refugee status in Canada that interpreters needed to empower the disadvantaged claimant by serving as **intercultural agents**. As summarized by Kondo and Tebble (1997), the need for the interpreter to make adjustments so as to 'smooth over cultural differences,' if not 'bridge a wide cultural gap,' has been discussed for virtually all domains of interpreting, essentially suggesting that "the ideal role of the interpreter is to serve not only as a linguistic but also as a cultural mediator" (1997: 158).

These diverse labels and normative claims for the interpreter's role bear out Bruce Anderson's early assumption that "the interpreter's role is always partially undefined – that is, the role prescriptions are objectively inadequate" (1976/ 2002: 211). The inherent risk of **role conflict** has been demonstrated in a number of case studies of interpreting in institutional settings. In her analysis of the Demjanjuk trial in Jerusalem, which involved an unprecedented complexity of interpreting arrangements, Shlesinger (1991) drew attention to the 'fluidity' of the interpreter's role. Based on an examination of the trial record and on participant observation, she found that the professional interpreters working between English and Hebrew were responsible for certain omissions and stylistic shifts which reflected a significant degree of **intrusiveness** (as perceived by the participants) or **latitude** (as perceived by the interpreters themselves). Davidson (2002) studied communication and interpreting practices in a Californian outpatient clinic and found the Spanish/English interpreters employed by the hospital to keep the medical interviews 'on track' by asking their own follow-up questions and suppressing 'irrelevant' complaints, clearly in response to overriding institutional constraints. Similarly, Bolden's (2000) analysis of two history-taking interviews in a large US hospital in the Midwest shows the Russian/English interpreter, a 25-year-old man with some training in community interpreting, acting as a **'pre-diagnostic agent'** who actively probes for medically relevant information while excluding the patient's narrative experiential accounts from his summary renditions. Similar evidence of what Anderson (1976/2002) referred to as **role overload** exists for asylum settings. Pöllabauer (2004) found the three interpreters in her study of 20 German/English hearings to assume discrepant roles mainly determined by the officers' expectations. They shortened and paraphrased statements, provided explanations and intervened to resolve face-threatening situations, often verbally allying with the officers. These findings were corroborated in an analysis of 14 appeal hearings by Kolb and Pöchhacker (2008), who highlighted the interpreters' active involvement in formulating the written record of the proceedings, in line with adjudicating officials' expectations.

Given the interdependence between role performance more or less in line with 'professional norms,' on the one hand, and client expectations, or 'expectancy norms' (Chesterman 1993), on the other, attempts at defining the interpreter's role have also relied on survey research – among professionals using interpreters as well as among interpreters themselves. In a questionnaire-based survey of more than 600 healthcare and social service providers in Vienna, Pöchhacker (2000) found different expectation profiles among doctors, nurses, therapists and social workers with regard to such tasks as 'explaining technical terms for the client' and 'explaining foreign cultural references.' In a similar survey by Mesa (2000) among community service providers in Canada, the expectation that the "cultural interpreter" should 'explain cultural values' ranked rather low, and even fewer respondents considered it very important to receive cultural explanations from the interpreter after the mediated exchange. In contrast, most of the 12 interpreters in Mesa's study considered it very important to be able to provide such explanations. This readiness among healthcare interpreters to adopt a more 'visible' role in the interaction is clearly reflected in the work of Angelelli (2004a, 2004b), who used survey methods as well as extensive fieldwork to ascertain interpreters' role perceptions and role performance. Based on data from hundreds of questionnaires and interpreted interactions as well as eleven interviews, Angelelli concluded that interpreters perceived, enacted, and described their role as **visible agents** in the interaction.

In the legal sphere, Kadrić (2001) conducted a survey among some 200 local court judges in Vienna and found respondents rather accepting of tasks such as 'simplifying the judge's utterances' and 'explaining legal language' for the clients. In contrast to the study by Kelly (2000), most of whose 53 respondents were against a **cultural mediation** role for the interpreter, as many as 85% of the judges surveyed by Kadrić (2001) expected the interpreter to explain cultural references for the court. A survey by Lee (2009), contrasting the perspectives of over 200 legal professionals and three dozen interpreters in the Australian context, revealed a significant gap between the perceptions of the two groups. Whereas two-thirds of the judges and lawyers, with some ambivalence, viewed the interpreter as a 'translation machine,' most practitioners described their role as 'facilitator of communication.' On the other hand, interpreters were less ready to accept cultural intervention as part of their role than were the legal professionals.

While the issue of cultural differences has been less prominent in the literature on conference interpreting (see e.g. Kondo 1990; Pöchhacker 1994b), role expectations have also been investigated for this professional domain. In a survey of users of conference interpreting in Poland, Kopczyński (1994) questioned a total of 57 professionals with different academic backgrounds (humanities, science and technology, diplomacy) on their expectations regarding the interpreter's 'visibility' or intrusiveness. Respondents generally preferred what Kopczyński calls the **ghost role** of the interpreter over the "intruder role," but would at the same time give interpreters licence to "correct the speaker" and "add his own explanations." Zwischenberger (2011), in an online survey of AIIC members, elicited conference interpreters' self-perceptions of their role. The role constructs most widely embraced by the 704 respondents were **communication facilitator** and 'mediator,' whereas only a minority used more mechanistic labels such as 'conveyor,' 'vehicle' or 'link' to describe their professional role. Adopting parts of the role inventory developed by Angelelli (2004b), whose respondents also included some 100 conference interpreters in North America, Zwischenberger found high levels of acceptance for an active role comprising various kinds of 'intervention in the original,' such as improving comprehensibility and explaining cultural references. At the same time, her respondents strongly agreed with normative precepts regarding loyalty toward the speaker and the original message, in particular the need to reflect the speaker's tone and achieve the same **communicative effect**.

On the whole, discourse-based case studies as well as survey research on the interpreter's role has revealed varying, ambivalent and sometimes even contradictory views and behaviors, prompting some authors to move away from attempts at definition and foreground instead the need for **flexibility**. On the assumption that interpreting is first and foremost a situated social practice, Llewellyn-Jones and Lee (2014), approaching the topic from the field of signed language interpreting, propose a 'three-dimensional' **role-space**. Along the axes of variable alignment with the interlocutors, interaction management, and 'presentation of self,' they account for ways in which interpreters adapt their role(s) to contextual demands in a given setting and in the course of a particular interaction.

10.4 Quality

While quality in interpreting has been a basic concern underlying the process of professionalization, its emergence as a topic of research dates back only to the 1980s. In conference interpreting, more and more attention has been paid to product-oriented analyses, whereas the issue of interpreters' abilities and qualifications (« 10.2.1) remains dominant for community-based domains, where the quest for consistent professional standards is still under way. Whether the focus is on the 'product' or on those providing the service, however, quality is acknowledged as an essentially relative and multi-dimensional concept which can and must be approached with different evaluation methods from a variety of perspectives. Indeed, quality is a complex, overarching theme which relates to many of the topics covered in this book. Aside from interpreter education as a key prerequisite for achieving professional qualifications (Chapter 12), quality has to do with such features of the interpreter's product as texture (« 7.1.2), source–target correspondence (« 7.2) and communicative effect (« 7.3), and with behavioral aspects such as special skills and expertise (« 10.2.2) and role performance (« 10.3.2). Its coverage here is therefore limited to explicit notions such as quality criteria and users' quality expectations, as well as the measurement and judgment of quality in interpreting.

10.4.1 Quality Criteria

As conference interpreting scholars went beyond the tradition of equating quality with the professional status afforded by university-level training and/ or membership of AIIC or similar associations, there was a need for explicit criteria for assessing the quality of interpreting and interpreters. An initial step in that direction was taken by Hildegund Bühler (1986) in a survey of AIIC members. Using a list of 16 criteria to be rated on a four-point scale, Bühler asked her 47 respondents to indicate the relative importance of inter-preter-related qualities (such as thorough preparation, reliability, endurance, poise, pleasant voice, pleasant appearance, etc.) and eight features of the interpreter's output (native accent, fluency of delivery, logical cohesion, sense consistency with original message, completeness, correct grammar, correct terminology, appropriate style). Bühler found **sense consistency with the original message** to be the top-ranking criterion of quality, rated as 'highly important' by 96% of her respondents. Three other criteria (**logical cohesion, reliability** and **thorough preparation**) were given this rating by 73% to 83%, and five others (**correct terminology, fluency of delivery, correct grammar, completeness, teamwork**) by nearly half the respondents.

The fact that all but a few of the 16 criteria in Bühler's (1986) study were considered 'important' by a large majority of her respondents motivated Chiaro and Nocella (2004) to design a follow-up study that would better discriminate between the criteria in terms of their relative weight. In a pioneering online survey, they recruited 286 interpreters worldwide to rank two sets of criteria largely based on Bühler's list. For the set of output-related criteria, Chiaro and Nocella (2004) found identical items at the top ('sense consistency') and bottom ('native accent') of their list, whereas 'completeness' ranked second, and 'correct terminology' only sixth. Since access to their survey was not limited to conference interpreters and the sample may have included practitioners working in legal or other institutional settings, the significance of this discrepant pattern of findings is unclear.

In a better controlled large-scale replication of Bühler's (1986) study, Zwischenberger (2010) conducted a full-population survey of AIIC members, who were asked to rate (on a four-point scale) an amended list of Bühler's output-related criteria. Zwischenberger's (2010) results from 704 respondents closely matched the pattern in the original study, with only 'fluency of delivery' and 'correct terminology' exchanging places in the order of importance.

10.4.2 User Expectations

Bühler (1986) had suggested that the expectations of conference interpreters regarding the quality of professional output corresponded to the needs of those using their services. Putting this assumption to the test, Kurz (1993/2002) administered a questionnaire with Bühler's output-related criteria to a total of 124 participants in three different conferences with SI (in the fields of medicine, engineering and education). Her findings matched Bühler's only for **sense consistency, logical cohesion**, and **correct terminology**, whereas delivery-related aspects received consistently lower ratings, with users' expectation profiles differing according to their professional background. This was confirmed by a subsequent survey of 19 'users,' if not end-users, of SI in media settings, who put considerably less emphasis on completeness while giving special importance to such criteria as **pleasant voice, native accent**, and **fluency of delivery** (Kurz and Pöchhacker 1995).

The variability of quality-related expectations among users of conference interpreting has been investigated and confirmed in a number of small-scale studies (as reviewed by Kurz 2001) and in a major international survey commissioned by AIIC. On the basis of 201 interviews conducted by 94 interpreters at 84 different meetings, Peter Moser (1996) reported **faithfulness** to the original as the most common expectation expressed spontaneously by the interviewees, followed by **content, synchronicity, rhetorical skills** and **voice quality**. Although the survey findings generally confirmed the importance given by users to criteria such as completeness, clarity of expression, and terminological precision, expectations tended to vary considerably, depending on meeting type (large vs small, general vs technical), age, gender and previous experience with SI.

Variability of quality-related expectations is even more pronounced in community-based domains, given the diversity of institutional settings and role descriptions (« 10.3.2). With much less product orientation than in simultaneous conference interpreting, the emphasis tends to be on criteria for a 'good interpreter' and desirable interpreter behavior. With few exceptions, such as the qualitative study by Edwards et al. (2005) on **trust** as a critically important element of individual clients' expectations, most studies have elicited the perceptions of professional service providers. As part of a multi-perspective survey, Mesa (2000) asked 288 service providers from 30 different institutions in the Montreal region to rate the importance of over thirty interpreter qualities and behaviors on a three-point scale. The items which received the highest ratings ('very important') from most of the respondents included proficiency in the client's language (96%) and pointing out a client's lack of understanding' (92%). However, such user or client expectations are likely to vary depending on the institutional and even socio-cultural context. Kadrić (2001), in her survey of judges in Vienna, also inquired about expectations regarding interpreters' qualifications and found that her 133 respondents rated 'interpreting skills' and 'linguistic and cultural competence' as more important in a good courtroom interpreter than 'basic legal knowledge' and 'knowledge of court organization and procedure.' Since the judges surveyed by Kadrić were directly in charge of hiring interpreters when needed, the study also addressed the perspective of the 'client' in the broader sense of 'employer,' which has received very little attention to date. Kadrić highlights the specifics of this perspective by pointing to 're-hiring criteria' such as 'smooth facilitation of communication' and costs. For the employer's perspective in conference interpreting, Moser-Mercer (1996) suggests that criteria such as team discipline, adaptability, flexible scheduling and availability form part of the expectations regarding an interpreter's quality of service.

10.4.3 Measurement and Judgment

The need for measuring quality-related features of interpreting performance such as 'accuracy' and 'completeness' first arose in early experimental research on SI, and various ways of scoring and assessing source–target correspondence were proposed (« 7.2.2). Such measures of quality are equally required in certification testing (« 10.2.3) and are also applied in educational assessment, but mostly in conjunction with expert judgment. Indeed, the purely **inter-textual** perspective on quality has been relativized by functional considerations. If, as maintained by Donovan-Cagigos (1990), fidelity cannot be quantified but is relative to the communicative situation, then user expectations – such as a preference for essentials rather than a complete rendition (Vuorikoski 1993; Moser 1996) – serve as higher-order principles which qualify accuracy and omission scores. In this 'client-centered' (or target-oriented) perspective, the focus shifts from scoring accuracy to judging **acceptability** and user satisfaction.

There have been some fieldwork studies in which users were asked directly to judge the quality of the interpretation received. Gile (1990b) used a short bilingual questionnaire to elicit judgments from 23 participants in a medical conference with English/French SI. Asked to assess the interpretation received with regard to "general quality," "linguistic output quality," "terminological usage," "fidelity" and "quality of voice and delivery," respondents gave rather consistent – and favorable – overall ratings. Nevertheless, responses revealed differences between the two language groups (i.e. more critical ratings by French listeners) as well as a differential assessment of the two interpreters working into French with regard to voice and delivery.

For dialogue interpreting in various community settings, fieldwork on interpreting quality was done in Canada by Garber and Mauffette-Leenders (1997), who developed a cumulative case-based survey method to elicit evaluative feedback from service providers and non-English-speaking clients. Question items related to the interpreter's intelligibility, accuracy, confidentiality and impartiality, and responses from a total of 34 clients in three language groups (Vietnamese, Polish, Portuguese) indicated a high level of satisfaction with the seventeen interpreters involved. A similar evaluation was carried out by Mesa (2000), who asked 66 clients of eleven different language backgrounds to express their agreement (or disagreement) with ten evaluative statements on features of the interpreter's performance.

In an effort to relate text-bound measurements to subjective performance assessment, Strong and Rudser (1992) asked 12 deaf and hearing raters to assess the (videotaped) performance of 25 interpreters on a rating form which included a general assessment ("dislike – OK – like") as well as three criteria to be rated on a five-point scale ("low/high sign language ability," "hard/easy to follow," "unpleasant/pleasant to watch"). The authors found inter-rater correlation coefficients between 0.52 and 0.86 and concluded that the reliability of subjective ratings was considerably lower than that of accuracy scores obtained with a proposition-based assessment instrument (Strong and Rudser 1985). Indeed, the fact that user ratings are not very sensitive to such important components of quality as fidelity and linguistic correctness has been stressed by Gile (2003) on the basis of several studies, which clearly suggests a need for multiple approaches to quality-oriented investigations.

10.4.4 Multiple Approaches

An initiative combining several perspectives on quality was taken by Anna-Riitta Vuorikoski (1993), who used fieldwork as well as survey techniques to investigate interpreting quality in five seminars with English–Finnish SI involving some 500 participants. With the help of a questionnaire and follow-up telephone interviews, Vuorikoski elicited both expectations and case-based quality judgments from a total of 177 respondents. Her findings included insights on **user motivation** and attitudes as well as a clear preference for a focus on essentials. Respondents had generally experienced the interpretation provided as "informed" and "coherent, or easy to follow" but felt more ambiguous about fluency and the interpreter's rhythm of speech. A similar combination of **expectations** and **judgments** was part of the study by Mesa (2000), who asked service providers in community settings to express their generic expectations and to state whether these had been met by the interpreter under evaluation.

As suggested by Kurz (2001: 405), the evaluative relationship between 'quality perceived' and 'quality expected' could be cast in the formula "Quality = Actual Service – Expected Service." However, several authors have pointed out that "user expectations are often unrealistic" (Bühler 1986: 233) and called for a shift from the concern with 'ideal quality' to "quality under the circumstances" (Pöchhacker 1994c: 242). In line with the assertion by Moser-Mercer (1996: 45) that "quality will always have to be evaluated against the background of the working conditions that prevail in the particular situation under observation," Pöchhacker's (1994a) conference-level case study addressed the issue of quality in an authentic setting by documenting preparatory, situational and text-delivery variables in addition to source- and target-text transcriptions. More recently, Kalina (2002) presented a contrastive analysis of two interpreted conferences in terms of the numerous factors described as relevant to interpreting quality in the literature.

An alternative and more focused methodological option for combining different dimensions of quality is to relate specific features of performance to expectations and judgments in controlled experiments. Pioneering work in this regard was done by Collados Aís (1998/2002), who contrasted the expectations elicited from forty-two specialist interpretation users as well as fifteen professional interpreters with the actual assessment given by these subjects to a simulated interpreting performance delivered with either monotonous or lively intonation, with or without factual errors. She found that subjects who, in line with previous findings, had given less importance to delivery features in the expectation survey, were nevertheless distinctly affected by monotonous intonation, as reflected in lower ratings for overall quality and several other criteria. In contrast, content errors in the 'melodic' interpretation did not result in lower scores, thus confirming that the criterion valued most highly by the users ('fidelity') is the one that they, by definition, fail to appreciate and are likely to judge by such 'secondary' criteria as fluency and lively delivery. While a subsequent replication study failed to reproduce these findings for intonation, Collados Aís et al. (2007) applied their research design to the entire range of output-related quality criteria (« 10.4.1) and found ample evidence of the gap between the relative importance given to certain (formal and delivery-related) parameters in expectation surveys and their impact on actual judgments of performance.

Adopting a similar approach, Garzone (2003) collected expectation ratings for four of Bühler's (1986) output criteria from 16 professional subjects (doctors, engineers) before asking them to judge a SI performance delivered with or without hesitation and erratic prosody. Again, poor delivery had a marked impact on quality assessments, not only for the criterion of delivery but for voice quality, fidelity and coherence as well. This interdependence of quality criteria was confirmed also in an experiment by Cheung (2003), who asked 120 student subjects to rate the quality of a simultaneous interpretation (into Mandarin Chinese and Cantonese) delivered with either a native or a non-native accent. Although the experimental material differed only with regard to accent, subjects, especially in the Cantonese group, gave lower ratings to the non-native version for criteria like clarity, pacing, completeness, interference ('code-mixing'), fluency, and coherence.

Experimental evidence of the **interrelations** between various components of quality as perceived by users adds yet another layer of complexity to a topic that is unique for its multiple dimensions. These can be conceptualized in an 'onion' model of superimposed quality standards situated between a product-oriented perspective, on the one hand, and the view of interpreting as a professional service, on the other (Pöchhacker 2002). In this model, 'accuracy' of source-text rendition appears as a core, enveloped by the need for 'adequacy' of target-language expression and, more broadly, by the goal of achieving 'equivalent effect' as well as the ultimate purpose of enabling 'successful communicative interaction.' Against this theoretical background, the evaluation of interpreting quality in the field requires a multi-method **case-study** approach which includes a thorough description of situational and interactional variables (i.e. institutional constraints and working conditions), inter- as well as intra-textual discourse-based analysis, subjective assessment by users, and insight into the attitudes and expectations of the various 'stakeholders,' with particular regard for the perspectives of interpreters and their clients.

10.5 Occupational Issues

Interpreters are subject to a variety of constraints arising from the communicative situation and the environment in which they perform their work. Interpreters' working conditions have given rise to concerns about occupational health, some of which have been the subject of empirical research.

10.5.1 Working Conditions

In the broader sense of 'employment conditions,' investigations of professional practice focus on such **industrial issues** as level of compensation, treatment by employers, and amount of work – both in the sense of excessive workload and underemployment. In conference interpreting, such issues have been addressed rather effectively by AIIC, which was after all conceived as a hybrid between a professional body and a trade union (see Keiser 1999). Through collective agreements negotiated every five years with the major institutional employers (UN, EU, etc.), AIIC shapes the working conditions, remuneration and pension provisions for freelance interpreters (including non-members) employed by these organizations. Community-based interpreters have sought to follow a similar course, through professional associations or trade unions, but effective action is obviously hampered by the multitude and diversity of institutional employers (with lower budgets and prestige than international organizations) and, with few exceptions beyond legal interpreting, by the lack of an assured level of professional qualifications. Moreover, public service authorities often contract with large commercial

agencies rather than individual professionals, subjecting the latter to conditions set by the former (see García-Beyaert 2015).

In a more specific sense, interpreters' working conditions in a given assignment are shaped by the physical environment, including time, place and facilities; by task-related factors such as preparation, cognitive workload and a range of input variables (« 6.4); and by inter-personal factors (e.g. relations with team members, client feedback). For spoken-language simultaneous conference interpreters, the booth is a well-defined physical workspace. An international standard for **permanent booths** (ISO 2603) was first adopted in 1974 (Jumpelt 1985). Together with a comparable standard for **mobile booths** (ISO 4043), it was updated in 1998 and then again in 2016, when the requirements for **equipment** (sound system, console, microphone, headsets) were formulated in a separate standard (ISO 20109), along with a new standard (ISO 20108) defining requirements for the quality and transmission of **sound and image input** which also covers remote interpreting arrangements (» 11.2.2).

Other factors assumed to have a direct impact on conference interpreters' performance have been identified in several studies. Altman's (1990) early survey among Brussels-based staff interpreters and freelance AIIC members pointed to the availability of documents and the density and delivery of the source speech as critical input variables. This was reaffirmed in the mail-survey component of the **Workload Study** commissioned by AIIC (2002), in which the 607 respondents confirmed fast speakers and speakers reading from a script as well as lack of material or time for preparation as the most frequent potential difficulties in their work. The Workload Study also included on-site measurements of such physical factors as air quality, temperature and humidity in the booth in an effort to measure the impact of various aspects of working conditions on perceived levels of occupational stress.

10.5.2 Stress and Health

The AIIC Workload Study (AIIC 2002), which examined **physical** as well as **physiological** and **psychological** parameters in the professional practice of conference interpreting, is the most comprehensive investigation to date of sources of job stress in interpreting and their impact on professional performance. A previous AIIC-supported study (Cooper et al. 1982) involved 33 interviews in Strasbourg, Brussels and Geneva as well as a worldwide postal survey, in which a total of 826 AIIC members responded to a 14-page questionnaire on issues such as job satisfaction, sources of stress, mental health status, and cardiovascular risk factors (Type A behavior). In the Workload Study, the 607 respondents reported high levels of work-related fatigue, exhaustion and mental stress, associated with poor booth conditions and source-speech-related stress factors. Interpreters' perception that theirs is a highly stressful occupation was matched by objective measures such as hormone levels (cortisol) and cardiovascular activity (blood pressure and heart rate). However, the feeling, expressed by 40–60% of respondents, that work-related stress causes a drop in performance quality was not substantiated by an assessment of interpretation samples for meaning correspondence, linguistic correctness, and delivery. There is, however, experimental evidence that the fatigue resulting from excessively long turns in SI (up to 60 minutes) has a significant detrimental effect on performance (see Moser-Mercer et al. 1998).

The types and levels of stress experienced by interpreters on the job are clearly subject to a variety of **situational** and **personal** factors. Whereas the Workload Study was geared to on-site interpreting in conference settings, its survey component also touched on videoconference/remote interpreting (» 11.2.2), of which nearly two-thirds of respondents had at least some experience. More than 80% felt that videoconferencing resulted in higher stress levels, but the assumption that this is linked to lower performance quality, held also by the interpreters participating in the UN remote interpreting trial (UN 2001), has not been substantiated (see Roziner and Shlesinger 2010). Higher stress levels compared to conventional conference interpreting have also been reported for media interpreting. Kurz (2002a) used cardiovascular indicators as well as sweat gland activation, measured by reduced galvanic skin resistance, to demonstrate differences in physiological stress responses when working during a technical conference and a live-broadcast interpreting assignment.

While most stress research has focused on spoken-language SI in conference settings, signed language interpreting has been shown to involve high levels of task-related stress as well. Peper and Gibney (1999) traced respiration rates, skin conductance, and upper extremity electromyographic activity in nine experimental subjects and found elevated levels of physiological arousal which they concluded were conducive to a deleterious cycle of pain. This relates in particular to educational settings, where turns may be as long as an entire class period, with little recovery time, and where thorough preparation of the subject matter is hardly feasible. Several authors have shown educational interpreters to be particularly at risk from repetitive strain injury, or 'upper extremity cumulative trauma disorders' like tendinitis and carpal tunnel syndrome. Feuerstein et al. (1997) surveyed some 1400 sign language interpreters and found the prevalence of upper extremity disorders (up to 32%) to be associated with a combination of work demands, psychosocial stressors, and workstyle (e.g. excessive hand/wrist deviations from the neutral position as the sign equivalent of shouting).

Occupational **health hazards** for interpreters in the community also include the risk of infection in medical settings and threats to personal safety, as in police settings and legal cases. Most importantly, though, various authors have discussed psychologically troubling experiences as risk factors and sources of job stress in community-based interpreting. Post-traumatic stress has been described for interpreting in the hearings of the South African Truth and Reconciliation Commission (see Wiegand 2000) and in war crimes tribunals (Ndongo-Keller 2015), and the risk of **vicarious trauma** is felt to be high in therapeutic settings where interpreters work with survivors of torture or other traumatic experiences (e.g. Bontempo and Malcolm 2012). Such health risks, together with low levels of compensation and certain personality traits, have been cited as reasons for interpreter **burnout** in the field of signed language interpreting (Schwenke et al. 2014). This topic was also addressed in the AIIC Workload Study (2002), and burnout levels among conference interpreters were found to be as high or higher than for comparable stressful professions.

Further Reading

Sociology

See PROFESSION, SETTINGS, PARLIAMENTARY SETTINGS, POLICE SETTINGS, PRISON SETTINGS, ASYLUM SETTINGS, PEDIATRIC SETTINGS, MENTAL HEALTH SETTINGS, RELIGIOUS SETTINGS, STATUS and FICTIONAL INTERPRETERS as well as CONFERENCE INTERPRETING, COMMUNITY INTERPRETING, LEGAL INTERPRETING, HEALTHCARE INTERPRETING and SIGNED LANGUAGE INTERPRETING in Pöchhacker (2015).

Competence

See COMPETENCE, EXPERTISE, PERSONALITY and CERTIFICATION in Pöchhacker (2015).

Ethics and Role

See ETHICS, NEUTRALITY, ROLE and MEDIATION in Pöchhacker (2015).

Quality

See QUALITY, QUALITY CRITERIA, USER EXPECTATIONS and ASSESSMENT in Pöchhacker (2015).

Occupational Issues

See WORKING CONDITIONS, AGENCIES, STRESS, VICARIOUS TRAUMA and BURNOUT in Pöchhacker (2015).

11 Technology

Technological advances since the early twentieth century have fueled the emergence of new forms of interpreting and extended the reach of interpreters' services. Since the 1990s, the confluence of telecommunications and digital data processing systems has had a major impact on professional practice. A range of digital equipment and tools have become available to aid interpreters in their work, deliver their services in distance mode, and ultimately replace (some of) their human skills. All of this generates enormous research needs and indicates that technology looks set to take on an increasingly central role in interpreting studies.

11.1 Equipment

Decades before the most recent leaps in the Digital Revolution, simultaneous conference interpreting was highly dependent on modern communication technology. Over and above the use of electro-acoustic transmission systems, the principle of which has undergone little change since their development in the late 1920s, conference interpreters have availed themselves of digital tools – mainly for documentation and preparation – since the final decades of the twentieth century.

11.1.1 Electro-acoustic Transmission

Spoken-language interpreting in multilingual conference settings was revolutionized by the application of electrotechnical systems for carrying speech streams simultaneously and over a distance, but essentially 'on site,' to those listening. As described by Baigorri-Jalón (2014), Edward Filene's idea for a system of 'telephonic interpreting,' developed in collaboration with Gordon Finlay, initially met with great skepticism. Though tested at the ILO as early as 1925, the Filene–Finlay system, later adopted by IBM, gained widespread attention and acceptance only two decades later through its use at the Nuremberg Trial. Its subsequent introduction at the United Nations gave the technique a major boost, though again not without stiff opposition from interpreters used to working in consecutive mode (Baigorri-Jalón 2004). Whereas the electric circuitry involved in SI was still a novelty worth detailed description in the early 1960s (see van Hoof 1962: 119ff), it drew little further attention in subsequent decades.

Since the 1970s, the spread of digital audio systems has raised new challenges for the quality of sound transmission. Beyond the consensus that the sound system used for SI must correctly reproduce frequencies between at least 50 Hz and 15000 Hz, recent standards require a sampling rate of 32 kHz or better, with a depth of 16 bits. Moreover, source microphone input must be processed by an automatic mixer ensuring a Speech Transmission Index of at least 0.6 according to digital signal processing standard IEC 60268–16 (2011).

11.1.2 Tools

Aside from spoken-language SI from a booth, most forms of interpreting can be performed without the use of special tools. Whispered interpreting using mobile equipment known as the *bidule* system is a hybrid form in this respect. Another variant of the simultaneous mode was described by Paneth (1990) as "projected interpretation," involving the real-time conversion of source-language speech into a written target-language summary, originally on an overhead projector. Paneth herself had envisioned projection from a PC as a major asset for this technique, but could obviously not have anticipated what automatic speech recognition (ASR) (» 11.3.1) would be able to do only two decades later.

For consecutive interpreters, the use of 'tools' has been limited since the heyday of the technique in the 1920s to a notepad and a pen, and even these are often dispensed with in short-consecutive dialogue interpreting. A radical innovation for this mode, pioneered by SCIC interpreter Michele Ferrari (Gomes 2002), involves the use of digital recording technology to replace note-taking. In what has become known as 'simultaneous consecutive,' or **SimConsec**, interpreters use a digital device to record the source speech and then, replaying it into a headset, render it for the audience in simultaneous mode. Using a digital pen, or **smartpen**, recording and note-taking can be done with a single device (Orlando 2010). Regardless of the digital recording device employed, however, the potential and limitations of SimConsec remain to be fully explored. Several experimental studies (e.g. Hamidi and Pöch-hacker 2007) have vindicated Ferrari's claim of superior accuracy compared to note-based consecutive, but pointed to a lack of rapport with the audience during the interpreter's replay-based simultaneous delivery. In an experiment with seven participants using a smartpen for recording and note-taking, Hiebl (2011) gave interpreters a choice between SimConsec and note-based con-secutive in rendering three short speeches with different levels of information density. Despite limited practice with the technique and poor recording quality, participants clearly preferred SimConsec for source speeches with lower redundancy.

Speech and text processing technologies with a potential to benefit simultaneous as well as consecutive interpreters include ASR-based applications, examples being term extraction from the source speech as well as real-time transcription, often used in legal depositions. Systematic research on the use of such tools and their impact on interpreters' performance has yet to be done.

The same applies to another digital function that can aid 'on-mike' processing – a buffer memory incorporated into the SI console. A 'repeat original' button allows the interpreter to replay the previous seconds of the source speech and then catch up with the speaker's real-time delivery.

More than digital speech processing, though, it is computer-based text processing and document management which have brought change to the working environment and techniques of simultaneous conference interpreters. Leaving aside standard communication and office tools that are now common in any profession, interpreters rely on digital technology in particular to prepare for assignments, with special attention to documenting and managing specialized **terminology**. While glossary management practices among experienced professionals still appear rather traditional (Jiang 2013), specialized software tailored to the requirements of the simultaneous interpreter's workflow has been developed, essentially from within the profession. Programs such as Interplex and InterpretBank (Fantinuoli 2013) are geared to flexible documentation ('off-line') and quick 'on-line' consultation in the booth. Originating in database tools, these systems now include 'workbench' functions offering interpreters more comprehensive support with their **knowledge management** needs.

11.2 Remote Interpreting

Technological progress means that co-presence, with all participants sharing a perceptual space in a given location, need no longer be seen as a defining feature of an interpreter-mediated communicative event. The earliest and simplest form of communication mediated at a distance ('in remote mode') is interpreting over the phone; the most recent relies on web-based videoconferencing technology. Both permit various configurations – from three-way teleconferences to dialogic or multiparty encounters mediated by a distant interpreter. These remote interpreting scenarios are generally distinguished from interactions in which one party is 'remote' and communicates via audio/video link, with the interpreter present in the same location as either of the communicating parties. The use of videoconferencing technology for this form of mediated distance communication is termed videoconference interpreting. It shares some features of remote interpreting, however, and is therefore included under the present heading.

11.2.1 Telephone-Based Interpreting

Telephone interpreting (audio only) was proposed as early as the 1950s (see Paneth 1957/2002) and is now widely used to enable cross-language dialogic communication. Its systematic implementation began in the 1970s, most notably in Australia, where an Emergency Telephone Interpreter Service was set up in 1973. In the US, telephone interpreting became popular in the early 1980s and enjoyed rapid growth and commercialization. Judged against its global (billion-dollar) business volume, systematic research into telephone interpreting has been very scarce and mostly centers on the (dis)advantages of telephone-based vs other arrangements.

In a case study comparing face-to-face and over-the-phone interpreting in two Swedish/Russian police interviews with the same participants, Wadensjö (1999) found the tele-interpreted encounter lacking in fluency and smoothness of coordination. The participants' audiovisual co-presence in on-site interpreting facilitated a shared conversational rhythm, permitting more talk and interaction in less time. Rosenberg (2007) examined the interactive dynamics of telephone interpreting in relation to the technical set-up used, that is, **three-way conversations** (with three speakers on the phone in different locations), face-to-face conversations interpreted via a **speakerphone**, and 'telephone passing.' In his analysis of more than 1,800 telephone interpreting assignments handled over two years, he found speakerphone-based remote interpreting to be most susceptible to problems with sound quality and intelligibility. The author also highlights the impact of the interactive configuration on the interpreter's choice of footing: the fact that clients mostly address each other indirectly, using the third person, means that the interpreter is more likely to deviate from the professional norm of first-person interpreting (« 8.1.2).

One of the fundamental concerns in telephone interpreting is the lack of visual cues. In a comparative study involving some 240 Spanish postpartum patients and two dozen healthcare providers using seven different interpreters, Locatis et al. (2010) elicited encounter quality ratings and comments for in-person and telephone interpreting and also video interpreting (80 cases each). Their findings showed a preference for on-site (face-to-face) over remote interpreting, whether in audio-only or video mode; telephone interpreting was the least-liked option. This was confirmed in a survey of some 50 healthcare interpreters, who rated the adequacy of the three options (in person, over the phone, video remote) for different clinical scenarios (Price et al. 2012). While all three arrangements were considered satisfactory for information exchange, respondents favored in-person over telephone interpreting for interactions requiring **rapport** and intercultural understanding.

The extent to which a video image can compensate for the lack of physical co-presence is crucial to the debate about remote interpreting in general. For telephone interpreting, this is in part decided by technological and economic developments. Given the uncertain fate of landline telephony and the increasing accessibility of videoconferencing over the internet, interpreting in audio-only mode may be on its way out. Video telephony and web-based videoconference calls have been the standard for some time in tele-communication with deaf users. In what is known as **video relay service**, deaf persons can communicate with hearing persons over the phone through a 'video interpreter' who is connected with the latter in audio mode, and with the former via some digital device (e.g. smartphone) incorporating video communication capabilities. Since two different language modalities are involved, video relay interpreting can be done in simultaneous mode, whereas spoken-language telephone interpreters are limited to consecutive, due to technological constraints.

11.2.2 Videoconference-Based Interpreting

The first experiments with sound-and-picture teleconference interpreting were carried out by UN bodies in the late 1970s, using costly satellite links. When ISDN-based videoconferencing generated renewed interest in the 1990s, transmission capacity was still a major limitation (see Mouzourakis 1996). This was echoed in several further experiments conducted by international organizations (see Mouzourakis 2006), as well as in a pioneering study by Braun (2007) on simultaneous dialogue interpreting in ISDN-based videoconferencing.

Subsequent developments took two different orientations: further testing of **remote SI** in supranational organizations with regard to its impact on quality as well as physiological and psychological parameters, and the large-scale introduction of videoconference-based dialogue interpreting in consecutive mode in community-based settings. In one of the most comprehensive studies, conducted in late 2004 in the European Parliament, little evidence was found that remote SI from a booth with high-quality video screens had a detrimental impact on performance quality (Roziner and Shlesinger 2010). Nevertheless, aside from eye strain and drowsiness, interpreters working in remote mode mainly showed significantly higher levels of burnout in terms of mental and physical exhaustion, cognitive fatigue and mental stress. Roziner and Shlesinger (2010) conclude that their findings concerning differences in environmental conditions cannot account for the interpreters' sense of discomfort and **alienation**. This is consistent with earlier findings (e.g. UN 2001) and suggests that the impact on interpreters of remote interpreting in conference settings is mainly psychological.

While the conference interpreting profession has been wary and critical of tele-interpreting, or 'distance interpreting,' possibly slowing down its more widespread introduction, remote interpreting arrangements have spread in many national institutional contexts. Rather than lack of space for booths or better utilization of available interpreting staff, as in the case of international organizations, the motivation in public service settings has mainly been to make qualified interpreters available where and when it is difficult, or uneconomical, to have them on site. Thus, in their rationale as well as other respects, these developments are similar to early efforts at introducing tele-phone interpreting services. Many initiatives are geared to the **healthcare** context, particularly in the US and Canada; as in the case of telephone interpreting, research into the new practice has not kept pace with its increasing use.

In several studies, healthcare interpreters have expressed a preference for video-link interpreting over telephone interpreting while still viewing on-site interpreting as preferable (e.g. Locatis et al. 2010). The impact of the technological set-up on interactional dynamics remains unclear, except for the fact that commercially established systems only accommodate interpreting in **consecutive mode** when two spoken languages are involved. In the field of signed language interpreting, where videoconference-based remote interpreting is usually referred to as **video remote interpreting**, work in simultaneous mode is equally feasible. To achieve this for spoken-language dialogue interpreting, an additional audio channel, or videoconference link, is required. A feasibility test of remote simultaneous dialogue interpreting in a healthcare setting is reported by Pöchhacker (2014), and technological progress (i.e. increased transmission capacity) is likely to eliminate current constraints on using remote interpreting in simultaneous mode for spoken-language interpreting in face-to-face interaction.

Whereas videoconference-based interpreting in healthcare settings typically involves direct patient–provider encounters mediated by an interpreter from a remote site, the use of videoconferencing in **legal settings** is more diverse. Indeed, practices there often take the form of **videoconference interpreting** rather than remote interpreting as such. For reasons of efficiency and security concerns, audiovisual links between courtrooms, police stations, detention centers and prisons are used to support distance communication in legal proceedings, with or without interpreters (see Braun 2015: 357ff). The implications of such technologically mediated forms of interaction for interpreting have been thoroughly investigated in the EU-funded AVIDICUS projects (Braun and Taylor 2012, 2015). Several experimental studies were conducted to explore the feasibility and reliability of videoconference and remote interpreting, using 'traditional' on-site interpreting as a control condition. In the study focusing on Polish/English videoconference interpreting, transcript-based scores in combination with expert assessment yielded comparable assessments for the on-site and the two videoconference conditions (A – interpreter next to the legal professional; B – interpreter next to the 'remote' witness). In the study of 16 simulated police interviews (Dutch/Hungarian), which also included a remote interpreting condition, product-based assessment and participant feedback again showed high levels of feasibility and acceptance for the various arrangements, despite a general preference for face-to-face interpreting and discomfort with the video-link condition when the interpreter was in the other location. The potential problems involved in video-link interpreting have been investigated, on the basis of observations and interviews, in a separate project on prison settings by Fowler (2013).

In the AVIDICUS study comparing on-site and remote interpreting in English/French police interviews, which involved 16 simulations based on two different scripts, the remote condition was found to magnify known problems in legal interpreting (with more **errors** occurring) and appeared to be associated with an earlier onset of **fatigue** in the interpreter (Braun 2013). The study also showed a significantly higher number of **turn-taking** problems, such as overlapping speech, in the remote interpreting condition, and found these to co-occur with omissions more frequently than in face-to-face interpreting. These findings are complemented by a qualitative investigation of video remote interpreting and video-link scenarios involving Australian Sign Language: Napier (2012) found that hearing participants found video-mediated arrangements equally effective, whereas deaf participants expressed concerns relating to image quality, camera angles and screen positions as well as constraints on feedback and interaction.

Some of the problems identified for remote interpreting in AVIDICUS 1 (2008–11) were subsequently addressed on the basis of recommendations derived from the experimental studies. These included training measures (for legal staff as well as interpreters) and improvements to the videoconference equipment used. As summarized by Braun (2015), the replication studies conducted in AVIDICUS 2 (2011–13) yielded a complex pattern of findings, tempering the claim that training and better equipment clearly lead to enhanced performance.

11.3 Automation

The idea of fully automatic speech-to-speech translation has long held special fascination for engineers as well as science fiction writers, but it was only several decades after initial progress with machine translation that the complexity of speech began to yield to computer-based analysis. The automatic recognition of acoustic speech signals as verbal text is the fundamental prerequisite for subsequent machine-based translation. However, speech recognition also supports other interpreting-related functions, with considerable potential for changing the way interpreting is practiced.

11.3.1 Speech Recognition

As a result of limited data storage and processing capacity, early speech recognition systems could perform with reasonable accuracy only when geared to a certain 'domain' (i.e. subject matter or field of application) or to a given speaker's vocal characteristics (voice quality and diction). The increasing availability of massive computing power has largely eliminated these constraints, and automatic speech recognition, which is typically based on so-called Hidden Markov Models, has made enormous progress in the twenty-first century. The recognition process involves the extraction of acoustic features from the speech stream and the matching of the resulting 'feature vectors' to sound forms, which are in turn identified with entries in the lexicon, followed by a check against syntactic constraints. In relation to interpreting, the coexistence of acoustic models and language models (lexicon, syntax) for different languages in a single system remains a challenge, but ongoing advances in **deep learning** and 'big data' hold great promise.

One obvious application of speech-to-text technology is transcription, or captioning, as used in **speech-to-text interpreting** for the deaf. Here, instead of using speed-writing or stenographic systems, interpreters (like court reporters) can speak their (written) target text. This technique, known as **respeaking**, is at present used mainly for intralingual live subtitling and text interpreting in educational settings for the deaf and hard of hearing. Its interlingual application seems quite feasible, though, and human skills in producing a more concise and readable target version (see Romero-Fresco 2012) may remain superior to what machines can do for some time.

Instant transcription based on speech recognition also aids court interpreters in legal depositions, allowing them to check their rendering against the textual record of the source utterance 'at sight.' With improved accuracy rates in speech recognition, speech-to-text output may also become available for source speeches in other interpreting settings, including additional functions such as term extraction. At that point, however, the process might also be continued as machine interpreting rather than a skilled human performance.

11.3.2 Machine Interpreting

Automatic **speech-to-speech translation**, or machine interpreting, is crucially dependent on machine translation (MT) as the core component, between speech recognition supplying the verbal input and speech synthesis converting the MT output into speech. Whereas early MT systems relied on a transfer approach (i.e. source–target correspondence rules) or an 'interlingua,' current systems are mainly statistics-based, relying on large parallel corpora.

Early projects, particularly in Japan, placed the emphasis on interpreting telephone conversations (see Kitano 1993; LuperFoy 1996). The large-scale German *Verbmobil* project, a multi-center undertaking which received nearly €60 million in public funding between 1993 and 2000, was aimed at building a portable machine interpreting system for face-to-face dialogue (see Wahlster 2000). Aside from achievements in the area of speech recognition and language processing, research in the *Verbmobil* project yielded insights into 'dialogue acts' which are highly germane to the study of human interpreting. Jekat and Klein (1996), for instance, highlighted the inadequacy of a close ('semantic') rendition of spontaneous speech and argued for a translational approach based on the 'intended interpretation,' as determined with reference to the dialogic context and the communicative purpose of a given speech act in that setting.

To what extent aspects of pragmatics and features of orality (« 7.1.3) can be harnessed to enhance the power of machine interpreting systems remains to be seen. The current focus on corpus-based MT using massive computing resources has certainly given machine interpreting a major boost, and the results of this process are being brought to consumers in various forms, including smartphone apps (e.g. SayHi Translate) and cloud-based teleconference support systems such as the 'Translator' feature of Microsoft's Skype.

Further Reading

Equipment

See TECHNOLOGY, SIMULTANEOUS CONSECUTIVE and TERMINOLOGY in Pöchhacker (2015).

Remote Interpreting

See TELEPHONE INTERPRETING, VIDEO RELAY SERVICE, REMOTE INTERPRETING, VIDEO REMOTE INTERPRETING and VIDEOCONFERENCE INTERPRETING in Pöchhacker (2015).

Automation

See MACHINE INTERPRETING in Pöchhacker (2015).

12 Education

From the earliest writings on interpreting in the 1950s, imparting the requisite knowledge and skills to the next generation of professionals has stood out as an overriding concern in the literature. Assuming that teaching presupposes a thorough understanding of what is to be taught, much research on interpreting, as presented in previous chapters, has been carried out in the context and, more or less directly, in the service of interpreter training. Most authors in interpreting studies are involved in interpreter education, and many studies have been carried out on student subjects. Increasingly, the large body of experiential descriptions of educational practices has been complemented with systematic empirical investigations. Aside from basic curricular issues, prominent themes in the literature on interpreter training include student selection and performance assessment as well as teaching methods for developing the skills that make up the interpreter's core competence (« 10.2.2).

12.1 Curriculum

While courses for the development of interpreting-specific skills date back to the early twentieth century, systematic reflection on curricular issues remained very limited until the 1980s and 1990s, when the strongly profession-based tradition of conference interpreter training was complemented by a scientific, process-oriented approach, and new training needs for interpreting in community-based settings highlighted the role of the curriculum as an organizational structure framing and guiding teaching and assessment practices.

12.1.1 Approaches

For most of the twentieth century, nearly all training programs and institutions were geared to spoken-language interpreting in multilingual international settings. With the clear goal of developing professional skills in consecutive and simultaneous interpreting, first-generation teachers of interpreting, themselves accomplished professionals, established a lasting tradition of training by **apprenticeship** – that is, transfer of know-how and professional knowledge from master to student, mainly by exercises modeled on real-life tasks. In the face of expansive growth in interpreter training in Europe in the 1950s and 1960s, and the growing influence of foreign-language pedagogy on training, the conference interpreting profession as represented by AIIC reaffirmed the apprenticeship approach in a series of meetings and asserted its influence on university-level interpreter training by a **school policy** (see Seleskovitch 1999: 58). The single most important force shaping what Mackintosh (1995) described as the "training paradigm" for conference interpreting was the strongly profession-based program at ESIT, Paris. Underpinned by Seleskovitch's holistic theory (« 3.4.2, « 4.4.1), the Paris School's pedagogy was laid down in a comprehensive training manual (Seleskovitch and Lederer 1989). Co-published and endorsed by the European institutions, the *Pédagogie raisonnée* appeared in an expanded second edition in 2002 as well as in an English translation published by the RID (Seleskovitch and Lederer 1995).

As the certainties of the Paris School paradigm came to be questioned in the 1980s (« 2.4.1), calls for a more **scientific approach** were also made for interpreter training (see Gran and Dodds 1989). Representatives of the cognitive process-oriented paradigm have applied their models to skill training for interpreters, highlighting aspects such as component skills (e.g. Moser-Mercer et al. 1997), strategies (e.g. Kalina 1998; Riccardi 1996), processing capacity management (Gile 1995b) and the development of expertise (Moser-Mercer et al. 2000). As an early advocate of a more scientific, theory-driven training paradigm, Arjona (1978, 1984) was among the few interpreter educators who not only turned to fields like psycholinguistics and cognitive psychology for insights into the interpreting process, but also drew on the theory of education as such to address issues of curriculum. In her 1990 PhD thesis on curriculum policy-making, Arjona-Tseng demonstrated, on the basis of an ethnographic case study in Taiwan, how socio-cultural, political and institutional constraints impact on curriculum design and implementation. With a more specific focus, Sawyer (2004) similarly leveraged advances in curriculum theory for a case study of curriculum and assessment at a T/I school in the US. Sawyer shows how, alongside a scientific approach centered on processing-skill components and stages of expertise, a **humanistic** approach to curriculum foregrounds the personal and social aspects of instructional interaction and the process of socializing students into a "community of professional practice" (see 2004: 75). Thus concepts such as 'situated cognition,' 'reflective practice' and 'cognitive apprenticeship' can be used to underpin a more student-oriented and interaction-oriented refinement of established interpreter training practices.

12.1.2 Levels and Formats

Rather than philosophical foundations, most of the literature on training, particularly in less well-established domains, is devoted to **organizational issues** like the level, duration and intensity of training programs. In conference interpreting, curricular formats range from six-month postgraduate courses, such as the in-house training formerly offered by the European Commission or the course at the former Polytechnic of Central London (Longley 1978), to four- or five-year BA/MA university degree courses for comprehensive T/I training. Of the various models described in the literature (e.g. Arjona 1984; Mackintosh 1999; Sawyer 2004), trends in the organization of higher education have favored conference interpreter training in graduate (master's level) degree programs of one or two years' duration. In Europe, the core curriculum of the EMCI (European Master's in Conference Interpreting) has become a major benchmark. Its counterpart in China is the government-approved MTI (Master of Translation and Interpretation) (Bao 2015). Major differences exist in the relative weight given to **professional vs academic** course content and the requirements for a graduation thesis. The academic component remains as controversial as the role of translation in the curriculum, and the study by Sawyer (2004) is exceptional in addressing this issue on the basis of quantitative empirical data.

The master's degree courses that have emerged as the rule in conference interpreter education have rather been the exception for signed language interpreting. Given the variety and heterogeneity of the courses offered, the Conference of Interpreter Trainers (CIT), a professional body founded in 1979, developed "Interpreter Education Standards" as a basis for accreditation in the US. The field of sign language interpreter training has traditionally been associated with sign language studies rather than T/I education. Nevertheless, signed languages have come to be accepted among the working languages offered in CIUTI-type T/I programs, and the second edition of Seleskovitch and Lederer's *Pédagogie raisonnée*, published in 2002, features a section devoted to the pedagogy of interpreting with sign languages.

With few exceptions, spoken-language community interpreters do not (yet) have the option of dedicated master's or even bachelor's degree programs. According to Roberts (2002: 169f), "Much, if not most, community interpreter training is provided by organizations which hire community interpreters." With little involvement of higher-education institutions, training courses offered by interpreting agencies or user organizations like hospitals are usually limited in duration (from one-day orientation workshops to anywhere between 40 and 100 hours of basic-level training) and geared to specific settings. Research in this context, often unpublished, primarily relates to needs assessment and program evaluation, but also to the general issue of selecting candidates for training (» 12.2).

12.1.3 Content and Structure

Most interpreter training courses established since the 1940s have featured roughly similar curricular **components**: basic concepts of language and communication, language enhancement (e.g. specialized terminology), 'area studies' (i.e. sociocultural background knowledge), skill training in consecutive and simultaneous interpreting, and professional ethics (see Arjona 1984). In the EMCI core curriculum, the five components are summarized as theory of interpreting, practice of interpreting, consecutive interpreting, simultaneous interpreting, and EU and international organizations. In addition to a focus on international institutions and their terminology, conference interpreter training has also involved specialized subjects like law, economics, science and technology, either explicitly or indirectly through the choice of source texts (see Kurz 2002b). In curricula for community-based interpreters, the orientation toward particular **settings** is much more prominent. More often than not, training is geared to specific domains, such as legal interpreting or medical interpreting, either in the program as a whole or in a specialization following basic-level training (e.g. Corsellis 1999).

While there is considerable consensus regarding the various contents of a curriculum for interpreter training, the sequence in which they are to be taught is more controversial. Whereas there is agreement that simultaneous is more complex than consecutive, it is moot whether students should be allowed to acquire both modes at the same time, or work in both directions (into B as well as into A). One of the basic tenets of the Paris School approach is to require considerable mastery in consecutive before students are allowed to progress to training in SI. This **progression** also informs the structure of the *Complete Course* described by Setton and Dawrant (2016), who propose that consecutive as well as sight translation should be practiced prior to and in preparation for SI. From a process-oriented perspective, Viezzi (1990) questioned the similarity of cognitive demands assumed for simultaneous processing tasks, leading some to view sight translation as a task *sui generis* – a case that can arguably be made for the two basic modes, consecutive and simultaneous, as well.

The relative effectiveness of various curricular arrangements is difficult to assess, since many aspects of implementation are not manifested in the 'official curriculum.' As emphasized by Sawyer (2004), researchers need access to the **hidden curriculum**, that is, the curriculum as experienced by the individual student and teacher. This suggests an important role for classroom 'fieldwork' and **action research** in the investigation of curricular and didactic practices, as demonstrated for the Marius project at the University of Granada by Boéri and de Manuel Jerez (2011).

12.2 Selection

The selection of suitable candidates for training has been a prime concern to interpreter educators across the different professional domains. While there is considerable consensus regarding the nature and extent of the abilities to be demonstrated on entry into a training program, there is little certainty regarding objective ways of testing candidates for the requisite knowledge and skills.

12.2.1 Entry Requirements

In line with the widely accepted **competence** profile of professional interpreters (« 10.2.1), knowledge (of languages and of the world), cognitive skills (relating to analysis, attention and memory) and personality traits (including stress tolerance and intellectual curiosity) are expected of candidates for interpreter training to varying degrees, depending on the level and duration of a given training program. For conference interpreting, the basic tenet is that language acquisition must precede training in interpreting (e.g. Arjona 1984), which makes the would-be interpreter's degree of bilingual or multilingual competence a fundamental criterion for admission. Although given less explicit attention, cultural knowledge and competence are generally considered equally indispensable, and indeed viewed as closely interrelated with high-level language proficiency (e.g. Arjona 1978). More so than in international conference interpreting, where the focus tends to be on cognitive-linguistic skills, issues of socio-cultural identity and attitude may come to the fore in community-based interpreting and require special consideration (e.g. Cokely 2000; Bot 2005).

There is some uncertainty regarding the level of **written language skills** as an entry requirement in interpreter training. Translation tests, in particular, have been rejected outright by some, defended by others, or questioned in hindsight (e.g. Lotriet 2002). In an overview of 18 T/I programs, Timarová and Ungoed-Thomas (2008) reported that eight schools used translation, while nearly all admission tests involved short-consecutive interpreting to test for language, communication and analytical skills. In many university-level programs, the acquisition of translation skills prior to interpreter training remains built into the curriculum, suggesting a need for studies along the lines of Sawyer (2004) on the relationship between modality-specific translational skills.

12.2.2 Aptitude Testing

Subject to legal provisions governing access to higher education in particular countries, a variety of procedures have been adopted by different institutions to test candidates for the knowledge, skills and personal qualities considered necessary to successfully acquire professional competence in interpreting. As reviewed by Keiser (1978), Moser-Mercer (1994b) and Russo (2011) for conference interpreting, traditional examination methods include holistic **communicative tasks** such as bilingual or multilingual interviews, impromptu speech production, and oral summary rendition in another language. Notwithstanding their validity for ascertaining a candidate's general knowledge and communicative language use (i.e. comprehension and expressive skills), such aptitude tests have been criticized for their strong subjective component and, hence, lack of reliability (e.g. Dodds 1990). On the other hand, the use of **translational tasks** such as written translation, sight translation and written summary in another language have been challenged for lack of validity as well as poor reliability (see Dodds 1990; Gringiani 1990).

Despite their appeal as efficient screening procedures, standardized test instruments for **personality traits** (« 10.2.1) have proved of limited use in predicting interpreting proficiency (see Longley 1989: 106). Some recent studies have investigated **soft skills** such as learning styles, motivation and stress tolerance (anxiety) in interpreting students and found some evidence of their contribution to overall aptitude (see Pöchhacker and Liu 2014). Most attention, however, has been devoted to aspects of cognitive and linguistic aptitude. Carroll (1978) had proposed a number of **psychometric tools**, especially for "verbal intelligence" and "verbal fluency," some of which were later put to the test. In a seminal study carried out at the Polytechnic of Central London in the late 1970s (see Longley 1989), Gerver et al. (1989) explored the value of various tests assumed to address the ability to quickly grasp and convey meaning. Recall, cloze and error detection tests as well as "subskill-based" tests of verbal fluency and comprehension (see Carroll 1978) and a generic speed-stress test were administered to a total of 30 students enrolled for six-month post-graduate training in conference interpreting. When related to students' final examination ratings, seven out of the 12 tests, mainly of the text-based type, showed significantly higher scores for students who had passed the course compared to the 12 who had failed.

More recent proposals for tasks tapping interpreting-related skills include simultaneous paraphrasing (Pippa and Russo 2002; Russo 2014) and the SynCloze test (Pöchhacker 2011b). Using versions of cloze as well as other tasks, such as 'cognitive shadowing' (Kurz 1992), Chabasse and Kader (2014) describe the development and testing of a comprehensive admissions test battery, pointing out that an assessment of usefulness must balance the predictive value of a given test against issues of feasibility when large numbers of students need to be tested.

A different approach was taken by Moser-Mercer (1985), who developed a ten-week monolingual **screening course** on the basis of her process model of SI (« 4.4.3). Students were given exercises in shadowing, dual-tasking (speech comprehension while counting aloud), paraphrasing and number processing, and received a positive, conditional or negative recommendation for further training based on their performance in the course as well as additional criteria (e.g. English language skills, coping with stress, assertiveness). A significant relationship was found between the type of recommendation given and students' pass/fail rates in the mid-term and final (second-year) examinations.

With particular emphasis on shadowing exercises and recall tests for evaluating interpreting-related skills, Lambert (1991) described a battery of selection instruments which combines cognitive processing skills with sight translation and interviews. This approach also informed the oral screening of candidates for an intensive two-week training course in SI for community interpreters in South Africa (see Lotriet 2002). More comprehensively, Arjona-Tseng (1994) developed and implemented a **two-day screening** procedure for admission to a two-year graduate program. Following a five-part written test for language proficiency and general knowledge, final selection was based on a series of oral tests, including written recall of a recorded passage, error detection, and sight translation. Out of a total of 565 applicants over three years, 11 candidates were selected as 'trainable' in conference interpreting between English and Mandarin Chinese.

Similarly elaborate and rigorous screening procedures are difficult to find in the literature on community-based interpreting, not least because most training courses are less formally structured and less institutionalized. Some of the languages required in candidates for community interpreter training are not taught and tested in the local education system. Thus, Carr and Steyn (2000) find that "bilingual pre-screening procedures, written and oral, are time-consuming and costly to prepare and administer." Though standardized **language grades**, such as the Common European Framework of Reference for Languages, may facilitate screening for linguistic aptitude, interpreting-related entry requirements of a cognitive and affective nature remain difficult to address. Skaaden (2013) describes the design and implementation of an admission test in Norway taken by more than a thousand undergraduate students in some 50 languages between 2007 and 2011. Centered on a short consecutive rendition in the other language, the test is found to offer high validity but to present multiple challenges with regard to reliability. Thus, despite some recent progress in research on aptitude for interpreting (see Pöchhacker and Liu 2014), it is generally acknowledged that the complex set of personal qualities and cognitive abilities assumed to underlie successful skill acquisition and course completion may well elude any one-time selection procedure.

12.3 Teaching

With the overall teaching and learning goal of developing task-specific expert skills, most of the literature on interpreter training falls into three prototypical subdivisions: consecutive interpreting with note-taking; simultaneous interpreting of monologic speeches as delivered at international events; and dialogue interpreting in community settings. Contributions to the didactic literature often take the form of reports by teachers willing to share their particular approach, and range from the descriptive ('How I do it') to the prescriptive ('How it should be done'). The latter orientation is inherent to textbooks on interpreter (and translator) training (e.g. Seleskovitch and Lederer 1989, 1995; Gile 1995b; Kautz 2000; Setton and Dawrant 2016; for an overview of Chinese textbooks, see Wang and Mu 2009: 275f). Increasingly, didactic issues are being investigated through systematic empirical research, particularly in China, where interpreter training has experienced enormous growth.

12.3.1 *Didactic Issues*

Beyond the focus on specific interpreting techniques, a number of broader didactic issues have been raised, if not systematically addressed. One of these is the extent to which theoretical **models** should inform teaching or be explicitly taught (e.g. Seleskovitch and Lederer 1989; Gile 1995b; Pöchhacker 1992). Another concerns the choice of overall didactic approach – based on **subskills vs holistic**. Setton and Dawrant (2016) adopt a holistic, 'real-life' orientation which they characterize as 'incremental realism.' Nevertheless, like many other authors, they leave room for **preliminary** and **ancillary skills** for interpreting in general, such as analytical comprehension and 'public speaking' skills (e.g. Seleskovitch and Lederer 1989; Kalina 1992; Weber 1990; Winston and Monikowski 2000). Other 'pre-interpreting skills' are mostly discussed in relation to the two major working modes, that is, as preparatory exercises for either consecutive or simultaneous interpreting.

In connection with either mode, the management of **stress** and **anxiety** in interpreting students has been a topic of concern (e.g. Kellett 1995; Russo 1995; Chiang 2010). On a broader level, linking curriculum and actual teaching, is the issue of **ethics.** Most authors view this in terms of behavior to be learned by would-be professionals (e.g. Donovan 2011; Setton and Dawrant 2016); Boéri and de Manuel Jerez (2011) go beyond this view and advocate a 'socio-critical pedagogy' that exposes students to 'resistant discourses' and aims to educate 'reflective citizens.' They propose doing this with the help of advanced technologies – as widely used for interpreter training in general.

12.3.2 *Computer-Assisted Training*

The use of technology in interpreter education has become a cross-cutting theme with many different manifestations. Early initiatives had relied on videotapes for source-speech presentation and for performance assessment in consecutive (e.g. Kurz 1989); current practices commonly include access to web-based **speech repositories** and the use of e-learning platforms and other virtual learning resources. All of this goes far beyond the dedicated computer software for student practice that originally gave rise to the notion of 'computer-assisted interpreter training' (see Gran et al. 2002). One of the most striking examples in this regard is the European project IVY (Interpreting in Virtual Reality), in which students can (inter)act as avatars in a virtual institutional setting created in Second Life (Braun and Slater 2014). At similar remove from the traditional focus on on-site instruction is interpreter training in distance mode. Ko (2008) reports an experiment, in which two groups of seven students participated in a 13-week dialogue interpreting course taught either face to face or over the phone. While administering the course in distance mode was found to place a considerably higher workload on the teacher, Ko (2008) concludes that teaching interpreting via sound-only teleconference is technologically and pedagogically feasible, permitting students taught in distance mode to achieve a level of interpreting skills comparable to that of on-campus students. More typically, though, information and communication technologies are applied to interpreter training in 'blended' formats of **e-learning**, and various authors have described the use and implications of digital interpreter training facilities. Gorm Hansen and Shlesinger (2007), for instance, found higher student success rates after the introduction of a digital lab allowing students to practice 'self-paced' consecutive and video-based dialogue interpreting. Going even further, videoconferencing can be used to bring speakers, teachers and students in different locations and institutions together in a **virtual classroom**. Describing an online teaching experiment along these lines, Ko and Chen (2011) suggest that synchronous teaching and learning is feasible, but acknowledge the didactic constraints arising from limited visual interaction.

12.3.3 Consecutive Interpreting

While no hard and fast line can be drawn between short consecutive (as used in dialogue interpreting) and the 'classic' form of consecutive implying the rendition of some five to ten minutes of uninterrupted discourse (« 1.4.2), consecutive interpreting skills are usually taken to be synonymous with the latter and thus closely linked to **note-taking** skills. Indeed, most publications on the teaching of consecutive interpreting – as reviewed by Ilg and Lambert (1996) – are mainly concerned with note-taking. Nevertheless, authors describing their teaching approaches (e.g. Seleskovitch and Lederer 1989, 1995; Kalina 1998; Dingfelder Stone 2015) usually stress the need for preliminary exercises to enhance 'active listening,' message analysis, and recall, including such techniques as 'clozing,' 'chunking' and visualization.

Though few systematic studies on the pedagogy of consecutive interpreting have been carried out, the interaction between memory and note-taking stands out as a focus of investigation. The experimental study by Andres (2002) has supplied particularly detailed evidence of **processing overload** in student interpreters during the listening and note-taking phase. On the whole, though, descriptive data on note-taking techniques are scarce, and little is known about the practical application of the approaches put forward by various authors – from the seminal proposal by Rozan (1956) to the elaborate symbol-based system developed by Matyssek (1989). Exceptions include a line of experimental research on the language of interpreters' notes (Dam 2004; Szabó 2006) and the data on student interpreters' notes in the corpus compiled by Andres (2002). A tool with great promise in this regard is the **smartpen**, which allows simultaneous source-speech recording and note-image capture on micro-chipped paper, and subsequent synchronized replay and visualization on a computer screen (Orlando 2010, 2015). This permits posterior analysis of the note-taking process 'in real time,' with respect to both the type of notes taken and temporal aspects of their production.

Comparatively less emphasis has been given to the production phase of consecutive interpreting, though the role of **public speaking** skills has often been stressed. Didactic suggestions include sight translation exercises (e.g. Weber 1990; Ilg and Lambert 1996) and the use of video recording for feedback on students' performance (e.g. Kellett 1995; Kurz 2002b).

12.3.4 Simultaneous Interpreting

Much more than training in the complex skill of simultaneous interpreting as such, it is **preliminary exercises** that have commanded most attention in the pedagogical literature. Most authors have suggested introducing students to the crucial task demand of simultaneity, perceived as the skill of listening and speaking at the same time, by way of 'dual-task' exercises. These involve a listening task in combination with a second, different task, such as simultaneously counting backwards or reading aloud (see Moser 1978: 363; Seleskovitch and Lederer 1989: 168). However, the usefulness of dual-tasking as an introductory exercise has been questioned on the grounds that the performance of cognitively unrelated tasks does not approximate the processing demands of SI (e.g. Déjean le Féal 1997; Kalina 1998; Andres et al. 2015).

A specific exercise in simultaneous verbal processing is **shadowing**, which is the immediate repetition of auditory input in the same language with either minimal delay ('phoneme shadowing') or at greater latencies ('phrase shadowing'). As one of the most contentious issues in interpreter pedagogy to date, the shadowing task has both fervent advocates (e.g. Lambert 1991) and staunch opponents (e.g. Seleskovitch and Lederer 1989: 168), and exemplifies the division between the holistic training approach championed by ESIT and the 'cognitive approach' based on the identification and separate practice of component skills (« 12.1.1). Unlike most other didactic issues, the case for or against shadowing has been made not only by statements of faith but also with reference to research. Kurz (1992), citing neuropsychological findings, characterizes monolingual repetitive speech production as a poor approximation to simultaneous interpreting, pointing out that "a crucial element is missing in those exercises: the *active analysis of the speech input*" (1992: 248). In a longitudinal study, Kurz (1992, 1996) tested five first-year students on a shadowing task and two simultaneous question and answer tasks at the beginning and at the end of one semester of regular training in simultaneous interpreting. While test results were significantly better on all three tasks, Kurz found the most pronounced improvements for the more demanding task (i.e. answering a why-question while listening to the next question). This is in line with the results of the pioneering study by Moser (1978), who found that a program of introductory exercises (including abstraction of ideas, message prediction, dual-tasking and shadowing) resulted in the least significant difference between the test performance of course participants and a control group for the shadowing task, whereas the most pronounced difference was found for the *'décalage'* or extended lag test, which required subjects to repeat or translate input sentences while staying one or two sentences behind. Moser's (1978) conclusion that shadowing requires less processing for meaning was confirmed in a subsequent expert–novice study: Moser-Mercer et al. (2000) found that their five student subjects were more efficient shadowers than the five professional interpreters, who presumably brought their acquired content-processing strategies to bear on the task.

A closer approximation to SI, and less controversial, are preliminary exercises with a focus on content processing, such as simultaneous **paraphrasing** and shadowing tasks combined with **cloze** exercises (see Kalina 1992, 1998). Russo

(1995), who developed and tested paraphrasing as an aptitude test (« 12.2.2), used a questionnaire to elicit students' perception of difficulties and found that the paraphrasing task was experienced as particularly taxing. Within the Paris School, Déjean le Féal (1997) proposed taking the route via consecutive interpreting when introducing students to SI, but admitted that it is difficult, if not impossible, to measure the comparative effectiveness of any one method of initiation to SI, including her own approach.

Beyond the first stage of training designed to familiarize students with the technique of SI, didactic proposals have emphasized the need to focus on the **process** rather than the product (e.g. Gile 1995b); to teach **strategies**, particularly for coping with lexical and structural difficulties (e.g. Kirchhoff 1976/2002; Riccardi 1996; Kalina 1998); and to create a training environment that is as close to **real-life conditions** as possible (e.g. Kurz 2002b; Setton and Dawrant 2016). Apart from what is described by various authors, however, little is known about actual teaching practices adopted by individual instructors or institutions. Dodds and Katan (1997), for instance, expressed serious doubts regarding the impact of the literature on interpreting and interpreter training on instructional practices. This was confirmed in a questionnaire-based classroom survey by Pöchhacker (1999), who found highly varied approaches to input text presentation, media use, and correction in a total of 25 SI courses given by 22 teachers within the same institution.

The teaching of **sight translation** as a special form of interpreting in the simultaneous mode has received very little attention. With few exceptions (e.g. Weber 1990), most authors have discussed interpreting at sight as a preliminary exercise, or even an aptitude test, rather than a curricular component in its own right. Although the implications of input processing by reading rather than listening remain unclear, there is no doubt that sight translation is an integral part of an interpreter's translational competence. Aside from its use in various institutional settings, simultaneous conference interpreters frequently rely on it when a speaker reads from a text that is available in the booth. Interpreting at sight while working from auditory input, known as **SI with text**, involves a high degree of complexity that has yet to be addressed in detail from a didactic perspective. The same holds true for spoken-language interpreting practiced in the simultaneous whispering and the relay mode (see Seleskovitch and Lederer 1989) as well as in remote conferencing, for which special training needs have been identified and, to some extent, addressed (see Kurz 2002b; Braun and Taylor 2012).

Since sign language interpreters are trained mainly to work in the simultaneous mode, much of the didactic literature on spoken-language conference interpreting also has a bearing on interpreting with signed languages, especially on voice-to-sign interpreting in educational settings or in the media. However, training for sign language interpreters needs to give special attention to dialogic settings, where, as in the case of spoken-language community interpreting, the focus is less on processing skills for high information loads than on interactive skills in interpersonal dialogue.

12.3.5 Dialogue Interpreting

The skills required for dialogue interpreting, or 'liaison interpreting,' which may be practiced in the short consecutive or simultaneous (signed or whispered) modes, have more to do with the dynamics of **interpersonal interaction** than with 'content processing' as such (see Roy 2000b). Therefore, the teaching methods developed for consecutive and simultaneous interpreting apply only to a certain extent, in areas of shared ground such as note-taking (e.g. González et al. 2012; Schweda Nicholson 1990) and whispered simultaneous. A more specific didactic focus has been the management of interactive discourse, with particular regard to turn-taking and role performance. On the theoretical foundation provided by discourse-analytical concepts and descriptions (e.g. Englund Dimitrova 1997; Metzger 1999; Roy 2000a; Wadensjö 1998), **role plays** and simulations of interpreting scenarios have emerged as the key method for developing interpreting and discourse management skills which are sensitive to the purpose of the interaction and the constraints of a particular communicative context (e.g. Zimman 1994; Metzger 2000; Rudvin and Tomassini 2011; Kadrić 2014). A technology-based approach to fostering students' situated interactional skills has been developed in the IVY project (« 12.3.2), which creates an immersive **3D world** (Braun and Slater 2014). The pedagogical focus on contextualized decision-making is particularly important because most training in dialogue interpreting is geared to specific institutional settings and interactional genres (e. g. Tebble 2014). Ultimately, then, the pedagogy of dialogue interpreting in the community shares with the – distinctly mode-oriented – teaching approach to conference interpreter training an appreciation for expertise-building on tasks which approximate real-life conditions.

12.4 Assessment

Assessment in interpreter training is a highly complex subject, since it is not only linked to curricular and didactic issues but also closely interdependent with topics such as 'competence' (« 10.2) and the multi-dimensional theme of 'quality' (« 10.4). Within the pedagogical context, assessment covers a range of approaches for evaluating student performance and educational attainment, few of which have been thoroughly treated in the literature.

12.4.1 Types and Levels

In one of the most substantial contributions to the topic of assessment in interpreter education, Sawyer (2004) discusses the scant literature on the subject within a systematic framework of concepts and principles derived from the fields of language testing and educational assessment. Including entry-level assessment (aptitude testing) in his purview, he highlights the distinction between intermediate and final assessment in a given curriculum, and between **formative** assessment by the instructor as part of the teaching and learning process and **summative** assessment by one or more examiners at the end of a program. For in-training evaluation, some authors (e.g. Kellett 1995; Schjoldager 1996; Riccardi 2002) have proposed checklists and evaluation sheets with regard to mode-specific components. As a complement to 'traditional' interpreter testing, some authors (e.g. Humphrey 2000; Sawyer 2004) have suggested the use of **portfolio** assessment (i.e. the systematic collection and evaluation of student products to document progress and learning outcomes), which allows for self-assessment, peer review and extensive instructor feedback.

Final examinations at the end of a program not only test students' educational attainment – and the effectiveness of training – but also serve as a gateway to the professional interpreting market; hence the special significance of the methodology used for such **professional-level** testing, which bears a crucial relation to the testing done by certification authorities (« 10.2.3) and by institutions hiring staff interpreters. The examination practices described in the literature (e.g. Seleskovitch and Lederer 1989; Lotriet 2002; Setton and Dawrant 2016) involve **realistic** consecutive and simultaneous interpreting tasks and **holistic** assessment by a panel of instructors and, where admissible, external examiners (e.g. from employer organizations). From his detailed examination of assessment practices, Sawyer (2004) concludes that **professional judgment** clearly prevails over systematic approaches to test design and evaluation. Acknowledging professional judgment as necessary but not sufficient, he calls for a standardization of test parameters, or 'test method facets,' and more transparent assessment criteria and procedures so as to ensure maximum validity and reliability.

12.4.2 *Parameters and Criteria*

The key issues in final testing (and, by the same token, in competence testing by employers or certifying bodies) are the **tasks** on which candidates are to be examined, and the criteria by which their performance is to be evaluated. Would-be conference interpreters are generally expected to give a consecutive rendition with notes of a speech lasting some five to ten minutes, working both into their A and their B language, and to perform SI in the booth for up to 20 minutes, working into their A language (and sometimes *retour*). Setton and Dawrant (2016) stress the importance of also testing SI with text. The status of interpreting at sight ('sight translation') and dialogue interpreting remains unclear in programs geared to conference interpreting, whereas sight translation and dialogue interpreting are seen as principal components of examinations for community-based interpreters (e.g. Roberts 2000).

Even for prototypical components in tests for interpreting skills, there is little systematic information on parameters such as the mode and context of source-text delivery, text type, authenticity, level of technicality, or the time and resources allowed for preparation. It is largely left to the professional judgment of the examiner(s) to gauge the combined impact of these input variables (« 6.4) on the level of difficulty and to make appropriate allowance for it in assessing a candidate's performance.

Considerably more published information than on the methods of test administration is available on performance targets and assessment **criteria**, not least because these link up with the more extensive literature on professional standards and quality assessment (see Riccardi 2002). There is widespread agreement that performance must be assessed for both **content** (i.e. source–target correspondence) and target-language **presentation** (i.e. expression and delivery), but little consensus on how these notions can be operationalized in a transparent assessment procedure. The use of **error counts** is notoriously problematic even in transcript-based descriptive research, and impractical in on-the-spot judgments on several grounds, including the lexical variability of interpreters' output (e.g. Lamberger-Felber 2003), the variable information value of individual text components, the variability of error ratings between different assessors (Gile 1999c), and the impact of norms and expectations (Shlesinger 2000b). Similarly, output features such as clarity, style, fluency, rhythm, intonation, and so on largely elude an itemized assessment, notwithstanding the various lists of relevant features that have been proposed for use in student assessment (e.g. Kellett 1995; Schjoldager 1996; Riccardi 2002). Several authors have expressed their disappointment with detailed scoring systems (e.g. Longley 1978; Roberts 2000) and have reaffirmed the more holistic approach relying on the professional judgment of experienced interpreters. The latter is no doubt vital for evaluating the **overall impression** made by an interpreter in terms of professionalism, credibility, poise, technical skill, and so on, particularly in consecutive and in dialogue interpreting. Efforts have nevertheless been made to explore the (in)consistency of examiners' judgments. A noteworthy example is the study by Wu (2013) on the assessment behavior of eight examiners in evaluating five simulated SI exam performances. The findings, based on quantitative data (student ranking and overall marks) and a qualitative analysis of verbal comments, demonstrated considerable variation in examiners' judgments, partly as a result of the relative weight attached to individual assessment criteria. The crucial issue of criteria and their **relative weight** is addressed in a study by Sang-Bin Lee (2015), who developed and tested an analytic rating scale for students' consecutive interpreting performances. A statistical analysis of two interpreter trainers' ratings of 33 interpretations indicated a ratio of 2:1:1 for the three main categories of 'content,' 'form' and 'delivery,' under which the 22 assessment criteria had been grouped.

12.5 Further Education

In addition to 'primary' interpreter training as reviewed in the previous sections of this chapter, educational efforts which go beyond the focus on would-be interpreters' professional skills have emerged as important complementary pathways toward the goal of professionalization and improved professional standards. These include continuing professional development for practicing interpreters, training for teachers of interpreting, user education, and training in research skills, and are variously connected with the primary level of interpreter pedagogy.

12.5.1 *Continuing Professional Development*

Although not often reflected in the pedagogical literature, continuing education for practicing interpreters has become increasingly significant even in the most highly professionalized domains of interpreting. Courses offered for conference interpreters within or outside AIIC focus on particular working languages or subject areas (e.g. medicine, law) and aspects of technological support, particularly for documentation and terminology. As one of the first professional bodies, the RID institutionalized continuing professional development (CPD) by making it a basic tenet of its code of professional conduct (« 10.3.1) and a requirement for maintaining certification. In spoken-language community interpreter training, CPD needs are particularly acute, and many training initiatives are geared to the professionalization of working (and even 'natural') interpreters rather than novice students. Given the diversity of community-based institutional settings, topics for add-on training are numerous. Recent examples include UNHCR-sponsored courses for interpreters working in asylum hearings and the training measures developed in the EU-funded SOS-VICS project on interpreting for victims of gender violence.

12.5.2 *Training of Trainers*

As early as the mid-1960s, AIIC stipulated that courses in consecutive and simultaneous interpreting should be "designed and taught by practicing conference interpreters, preferably AIIC members" (Mackintosh 1995: 124). It was only a quarter of a century later that the profession began actively to address the need for training of trainers. The symposia on the teaching of interpreting convened in the late 1980s at Trieste (Gran and Dodds 1989) and Monterey set clear signals for a more systematic approach to interpreter pedagogy. AIIC went on to offer a series of **workshops**, on topics such as instruction methods and testing, which met with a highly favorable response (see Mackintosh 1995, 1999). In 2003, the first two-day 'training of trainers' seminar was held in Porto, and AIIC has since offered such **seminars** on a regular basis, in Rome and other locations. Among the university institutions for (conference) interpreter training that are joined together in CIUTI, few have been as committed to pedagogical skill development as the Faculty of Translation and Interpreting (formerly 'ETI') at the University of Geneva. Under the leadership of Barbara Moser-Mercer, a biennial **certificate course** for interpreter trainers was launched in 1996 and was subsequently transformed into an accredited Master of Advanced Studies course, most of which is offered in a virtual environment (Moser-Mercer et al. 2005). Experiences with this blended-learning course in interpreter training are discussed by

Moser-Mercer (2007) with regard to principles of collaborative learning and characteristics of adult learners in a distinctly multicultural community.

Similar initiatives have been taken by educators of American Sign Language interpreters in the framework of the **CIT**, which organizes regular conferences and publishes proceedings reflecting the exchange and development of pedagogical expertise among its members. An early example is the proceedings volume of the Fourth CIT Convention, held at Monterey in 1984 with the involvement of spoken-language interpreter trainers (e.g. McIntire 1984); more recently, a collaborative event on the topic of aptitude gave rise to an international workshop and subsequent publications (e.g. Pöchhacker and Liu 2014). For spoken-language community interpreters, the **Critical Link** conference series (« 2.5.2) has yielded a wealth of literature relevant to training, pointing to the obvious role of academic conferences in the continuing education of those involved in university-level interpreter training.

12.5.3 User Education

The professional literature on interpreting is rife with complaints about the lack of appreciation and understanding of the interpreter's job on the part of clients. With the possible exception of conference interpreters working for international organizations, informing users and clients about the nature and constraints of the interpreter's work is therefore considered a vital task of individual practitioners as well as their professional associations. And yet, while **advice for conference organizers** and **guidelines for conference speakers** are readily available, little is known about the delivery and effectiveness of this type of user-oriented material. The best documented initiatives to date have addressed client education needs in community-based domains. Ann Corsellis (1997: 78) formulated training needs for public service personnel, emphasizing "understanding and practice in the communicative processes required to work through, and with, interpreters." Based on data from a survey of officers, interpreters and clients of a British probation service, Corsellis (2000) developed detailed recommendations for a **modular training course**. Tebble (1998), drawing on her research on the discourse structure of medical consultations (« 7.1.1), developed a videotape and book on *Medical Interpreting* to be used in training courses for healthcare personnel. Moreover, involving staff from prospective user institutions in role-play-based training sessions for dialogue interpreters has been described as an effective way of both raising clients' understanding of interpreter-mediated encounters and creating more realistic interpreting scenarios in the classroom (e.g. Metzger 2000).

12.5.4 Research Training

In his influential efforts to promote higher scientific standards in interpreting research, Daniel Gile (« 2.4.1) identified research training as a crucial requirement for progress in interpreting studies. Mindful of the lacunae in this respect even in graduate-level university curricula for interpreter education, Gile has played a leading role in a number of initiatives designed to develop methodological expertise among interpreting scholars. In 1993 he did so as the appointed chair in what is now the **CETRA** Research Summer School in Translation Studies, which inspired the **Aarhus Seminar** on interpreting research, organized at the Aarhus School of Business in 1997 (« 2.5.1). Aside from an earlier summer course at the University of **Granada** and the inter-disciplinary workshops for researchers convened by Barbara Moser-Mercer in **Ascona**, the Aarhus Seminar was a milestone in the promotion of young scholars in interpreting studies. More recently, Heriot-Watt University launched the **Edinburgh** Interpreting Research Summer School, which similarly caters to the needs of PhD students for guidance as well as networking in the inter-preting studies community. These events, together with publications such as the collective volume emanating from the Aarhus Seminar (Gile et al. 2001), the methodology textbook by Hale and Napier (2013) and recent reference volumes offering convenient access to the state of the art, constitute a solid foundation for further progress toward higher levels of scientific excellence in research on interpreting.

Further Reading

Curriculum

See EDUCATION and CURRICULUM in Pöchhacker (2015).

Selection

See PERSONALITY, APTITUDE TESTING, PSYCHOMETRIC TESTS and CLOZE in Pöchhacker (2015).

Teaching

See PEDAGOGY, NOTE-TAKING, PRE-INTERPRETING EXERCISES, SHADOWING and ROLE PLAY in Pöchhacker (2015).

Assessment

See ASSESSMENT in Pöchhacker (2015).

Further Education

See PEDAGOGY in Pöchhacker (2015).

Part III

Directions

13 Directions

This chapter, which is offered as a conclusion to the survey of interpreting studies presented in Parts I and II, reviews major trends in the evolution of the field to date, and identifies some of the critical issues that have been confronting the young discipline for some time. With a look to the future, attention is drawn to a number of developments which are likely to shape the professional practice of interpreting as well as the theoretical and methodological foundations of its systematic study. In view of the old and new challenges for research and the various directions it may take, the final section is an attempt to provide would-be researchers with some more concrete orientation for taking their first steps and actively contributing to this field of study.

The **main points** covered in this chapter are:

- aspects of growth and expansion in interpreting studies as a discipline
- individual, institutional and international manifestations of convergence
- obstacles and opportunities for disciplinary progress
- socio-cultural and technological developments shaping the future course of research
- theoretical and methodological perspectives for the development of the field
- basic guidance for those 'getting started' in interpreting studies

13.1 Trends

Looking back over the development of research on interpreting since the mid-twentieth century, one easily appreciates that the field has expanded in various ways and developed a more broadly shared sense of identity. Since the early 1990s, in particular, the overall trends of growth and convergence have manifested themselves on various levels and in a range of different dimensions.

13.1.1 Growth and Diversification

The most important growth trend underlying the evolution of interpreting studies as a discipline has been the **academization of training**, primarily for the domain of international conference interpreting (« 2.1.3). From a dozen or so committed professionals writing in the 1950s and 1960s to pass on their know-how to the next generation of practitioners, the **number of authors** contributing to the systematic study of (conference) interpreting has increased manifold, mainly as a result of the growing recognition of academic work as a complement to profession-oriented training in university-level T/I schools. Aside from a large number of MA-level **graduation theses**, the literature has been enriched especially by doctoral dissertations. The field's global output of **PhD research** has clearly been on the rise.

The **diversification** of the field, which began to make itself felt in the 1980s and had become widely acknowledged by the turn of the millennium (« 2.5.2), has brought new **interpreting types and settings** into the researcher's purview. In the legal domain alone, examples range from asylum settings and police interviews to interpreting in prisons; interpreting in healthcare includes such specialties as pediatrics, speech pathology and mental health; media settings have seen the emergence of new forms of practice; educational settings, long a major domain of signed language interpreting, may now also involve spoken-language interpreters; and interpreting in religious settings, often on a non-professional basis, has attracted increasing interest. This diversification has extended the range of **theoretical and methodological approaches**, as researchers seek to address new objects of study with new conceptual tools, often adopted from related or relevant disciplines. Thus, interpreting studies has received a major impetus from various **discourse-analytical approaches** to the analysis of interpreting as situated social interaction (Chapter 8). With a more quantitative outlook, **corpus-based interpreting studies** has acquired a stronger profile, as has qualitative research with an **ethnographic orientation**. Taken together, these developments have significantly broadened and diversified the field's disciplinary foundations.

No less importantly, growth and diversification have gone hand in hand with continued **internationalization**, as reflected in the pursuit of postgraduate interpreting research in an increasing number of academic **institutions** throughout the world. More and more international **journals** and publications are available to the global interpreting studies community in English, the field's international language since the 1990s.

As in many other fields, the use of a **common language** for academic communication and exchange, together with worldwide **electronic access** via the Internet, has opened up new channels for networking and cooperation. These communicative links have been essential to turning quantitative progress – more authors, 'centers,' theses, domains, approaches, countries, and so on – into qualitative changes in the field's structure and interrelations.

13.1.2 Convergence and Consolidation

Growth and diversification often come with the risk of fragmentation along diverging lines of specialization, but this is rather a 'natural' process in the evolution of human science – witness, for instance, the development of linguistics from Saussure's lectures in the early twentieth century to the conglomerate of subdisciplines and applied extensions a hundred years later. For a field as small and specialized as the study of interpreting, however, institutional development (which is still in its early stages) is first of all a matter of **growing together** rather than growing apart. While an overall assessment of convergence or divergence is also a matter of attitude and perspective (i.e. of preferring to see the glass half full or half empty), it is nevertheless possible to note a pattern of convergence at an individual and institutional, as well as an international level: more and more authors with a home base in conference interpreting are also doing and promoting research on **community-based** domains; interaction between research and researchers in the fields of **signed and spoken-language** interpreting has intensified, not least within the Critical Link community but also involving scholars of the Paris School and other CIUTI institutions; several members of the interpreting studies community have made substantial contributions to the field in more than one of its **paradigms**; a number of leading (conference) interpreting researchers have forged **interdisciplinary** ties with non-interpreter specialists in fields like cognitive psychology and neuroscience while maintaining and asserting a sense of identity for their own field; more and more T/I schools, whose teaching staff and students constitute the main intellectual infrastructure for interpreting studies, have opened up their **training programs** for newly emerging professional domains; international **conferences** on interpreting have increasingly featured a broader range of interpreting types, questioning the dominant perspective of what former UN chief interpreter Sergio Viaggio self-critically called the 'boothed gentry'; *Interpreting*, the field's dedicated international **journal**, has proved an open forum for work on all types of interpreting, vindicating the broad scope envisaged by its founders; and conferences and publication projects in Asian countries (e.g. China, Korea) have sought the active involvement of 'Western' scholars, who have in turn benefited from the momentum generated by **East–West cooperation**.

Such highlights in the process of expansion and convergence notwithstanding, there remain a number of critical areas in which growth and development will be needed if interpreting studies is to continue its progress in the future. A number of critical factors that may manifest themselves as either obstacles or opportunities are examined below, in an overview of the issues entailed.

13.1.3 Critical Issues

To facilitate a summary discussion of problem areas and weaknesses that have plagued interpreting studies as a discipline, six critical issues can be singled out and examined with regard to their mutual impact and interdependence (Figure 13.1).

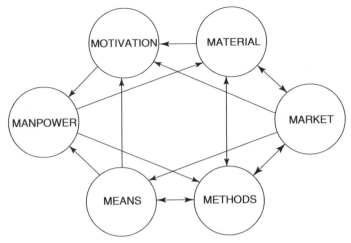

Figure 13.1 Critical issues for progress in interpreting studies (from Pöchhacker 2000a: 106)

The essential prerequisite for the field's continued capacity to generate research is an intellectual labor force with the requisite knowledge and skills. Such **manpower** (or, rather, 'womanpower,' considering the female pre-dominance in this field) is mainly available in academic institutions for (translator and) interpreter training, where teaching staff are called on to further their understanding of the subject, and students are initiated into the discipline by guided reflection on their skill-oriented practice. Instructors as well as established professionals may decide to undertake research toward a higher academic degree, joining graduate students committed enough to continue their studies up to doctoral level. It is easy to see how such factors as curricular requirements, tuition fees, charismatic role models, research funding and scholarships, employment opportunities, and so on may var-iously affect not only the **motivation** for engaging in research but also the **means** (in terms of time and money) available for sustaining a research project over several months or years.

A key to expanding the pool of able and willing research workers is what has been labeled in Figure 13.1 as '**market**' – that is, a sense that research is indeed needed to address a particular problem in the 'real world,' and that those sponsoring such research will get their money's worth. In the broadest sense, this applies to the interest of society at large in cultivating state-of-the-art academic expertise in any field of learning, hence the existence of T/I departments in (often publicly funded) universities. Academics, in interpreting studies as in other disciplines, claim an object of study for which they are best placed to conduct 'basic' (rather than applied) research. Even so, most of the perceived research needs – and much of the research output addressing them – have been of an educational nature, ultimately geared to the question of how interpreting can best be taught. There has been substantial interest in the process of (simultaneous) interpreting as a human skill to be developed through training, based on the underlying question: 'How does it work?' By contrast, the communicative and institutional implications of interpreting as a social practice have been explored only more recently. Indeed, the increasing prominence of community-based interpreting has opened up a wide field for research on the function, effect and (cost-)effectiveness of interpreting in various institutional contexts. This broadens the market for interpreting research to include institutional 'stakeholders' such as courts, hospitals, broadcasters, and advocacy groups for migrants and deaf people, and also generates educational research needs for previously neglected types of practice such as whispered interpreting, over-the-phone interpreting and sight translation. By the same token, institutional users of conference interpreter services as well as the conference interpreting profession have a growing need for research findings on the effects of new technology-based forms of practice on performance quality and working conditions. And yet, the major studies commissioned by AIIC and DG-SCIC have so far been entrusted to social science research consultants rather than interpreting scholars, possibly for lack of confidence in the methodological expertise of the latter. Admittedly, the research **methods** used in many individual studies, often involving simple experimental designs, small samples of student subjects, and single-judge output analysis, leave plenty of room for innovation and improvement. The fact that several international research training initiatives have been undertaken since the 1990s shows that the interpreting studies community is aware of the challenge and has recognized methodology as vital to the future progress of the discipline (« 12.5.4). Moreover, the emergence of new research problems in new areas of study is likely to facilitate methodological diversification, including the honing of computer-supported analytical tools on a broader range of **material**. Here again, the problem of access to data, 'subjects' and informants 'in the field,' which has long been regarded as a critical bottleneck in conference interpreting research, may be resolved as the need for 'applied research,' once accepted, leads various kinds of stakeholders to offer more support and cooperation.

The six critical issues for progress in the discipline, which have been discussed here only in very general terms without fully exploring their multiple interrelations, can serve as a framework for the analysis of past and present trends as well as an assessment of future potential, on a global, national and institutional level. A broader view of future directions will be taken in the next section, which examines some overarching developments for their potential impact on the future course of interpreting studies.

13.2 Perspectives

Although it seems reasonable to project the trends of diversified growth and disciplinary convergence into the foreseeable future, the variable interplay of the factors shaping the academic infrastructure and research environment of the field makes it difficult to predict its future direction(s). Indeed, much more powerful variables, such as globalization and technological progress, need to be reckoned with as well. These 'mega-trends' are likely to have a forceful impact on the development of interpreting studies, both via changes in the profession and by their more direct implications for theory and methodology. The latter will in turn be subject to some strong currents in the postmodern context of scientific endeavor which have begun to steer the field toward the social sciences and qualitative methods of inquiry.

13.2.1 Globalization

In line with the basic assumption that interpreting must be viewed first and foremost with regard to the social context of interaction (« 1.3.1), the ubiquitous theme of globalization is of prime relevance to interpreting studies. For international conference interpreting, itself an early example of a 'global profession,' globalization is a mixed blessing. While the trend to carry out transactions in business, politics, arts, and science on a worldwide scale could be assumed to boost the role of interpreters in international communication, the spread of **English as a lingua franca** (mentioned above as a boon to interpreting studies) largely offsets this potential need. As much as the official language policy, and **interpreting policy**, of the EU will preserve Europe's heritage as the heartland of multilateral conference interpreting, the spread of international English is likely to shrink the market for conference interpreters there as well.

At the same time, the related trend of 'localization' makes more international (usually English) informational input available to more local and diverse recipients (as in the case of 'glocalized' training of sales personnel). This tends to sustain the need for conference interpreting services, either in bilingual meetings involving English and the local language, or in events with asymmetrical (one-to-many) language arrangements. The former case highlights the role of **bidirectional interpreting**, not only in the traditional **liaison** mode but especially in the **simultaneous** mode (including simultaneous dialogue interpreting). In the case of meetings with only English spoken on the floor and interpreted into a range of languages, more fundamental issues of **power relations** and **cultural adaptation** arise, as captured in Vincent Buck's (2002) valid concern that interpreters may be "relegated to mere localisers of dominant ideologies."

Another significant development of a global nature is the increasing presence of China and other Asian countries on the international stage. Although subject to the same pattern of language policy as already described, **developments in Asia** have some broader implications for interpreting practice and interpreting studies. These include the enormous quantitative growth potential of the profession, and hence of training (and research); more pronounced cross-cultural, and not least ideological, differences in interpreter-mediated interaction; and particular cross-linguistic challenges which are likely to give a more prominent role in interpreting research to specialists in linguistics, foreign-language teaching and bilingualism studies.

Beyond the spread of a global language and the worldwide movement of goods, services and capital, globalization of course also applies to the movement, or **migration**, of people, which manifests itself in increasingly multi-ethnic and linguistically diverse societies. As witnessed in recent decades, public institutions in host countries are thus faced with a growing need for intercultural communication. The overwhelming pressure on European (and Asian) countries to care for – and communicate with – asylum seekers is the most obvious case in point. In the short as well as the longer term, countries and public institutions require **policies** to ensure **access**, regardless of language or cultural background, for those entitled to their services or under their jurisdiction. Subject to complex political, ideological and economic constraints, the **role** of interpreting and interpreters in a given context and setting is constantly in need of definition and analysis. Evaluating the **effectiveness** and implications of interpreting services will thus command particular interest and attention, not least with regard to efficiency and cost compared to other institutional arrangements. To the extent that policy-makers envisage a role for professional interpreters, new **training needs** would suggest an acute demand for research, mainly in the form of 'action research' by teachers on such issues as student selection and assessment as well as effective methods of instruction.

The relative effectiveness of interpreting services presents itself as a major research challenge in community-based and international settings alike. Speakers with a limited command of the host-country language or of international English, respectively, may try to get by without relying on an interpreter. At technical conferences, in the reception of foreign-language broadcasts, or in institutional settings such as courts and hospitals, the crucial question is whether **limited-proficiency speakers** can achieve a sufficient **degree of understanding** for their communicative purpose. This, apart from various pragmatic considerations, will decide whether there is a role for an interpreter in a given encounter – and a role for professional interpreting in a given socio-cultural context.

13.2.2 Technologization

The role of technology is no less a long-standing issue in interpreting than is globalization. Indeed, the field might not exist as such if it had not been for the use of electro-acoustic transmission equipment to allow for simultaneous interpreting in the 1920s. Half a century later, advances in telecommunications and digital data processing technology began to usher in developments which stand to profoundly transform the way interpreting is practiced in the twenty-first century. The most visible manifestation of 'the technologizing of interpreting,' to adapt Ong's (1982) phrase, is **remote interpreting**, of various types, as used in international conference settings and, even more so, in community-based institutional contexts. The effect of videoconference-based remote interpreting arrangements (« 11.2.2) on the quality of service delivery and on interpreters' working conditions, and standards of professional practice in general, will be a focus of research for years to come, with issues such as **stress, visual access** and **psycho-social factors** requiring particular attention. Moreover, the impact of digital tools for terminology management, instant knowledge access and speech recognition on the **ergonomics** of interpreting awaits further research, as does the potential of portable wireless equipment.

In communication involving **deaf** and hearing-impaired persons, the increasing availability of **audiovisual communication technologies** has allowed the spread of video relay service and video remote interpreting; at the same time, more efficient technologies for converting speech to text, and written (or even manually coded) input into spoken output, may favor the use of script-based communication, with interpreters working as **respeakers**. As in the limited-proficiency spoken mode, research will need to establish the comparative effectiveness of one mode or another for a given interactional purpose. In the long term, advanced prosthetic technology (cochlear implants) made available to – or imposed on – deaf people may well make the community of signed-language users even more heterogeneous, and the market for sign language interpreters more fragmented.

A trend toward more script-based communication may also take hold in spoken-language interpreting when respeaking-based subtitling is done inter-lingually. Such **speech-to-text** interpreting relies first and foremost on efficient speech recognition systems, which are also crucial to **machine interpreting**. The latter may become increasingly common as a substitute for human interpreters in routine institutional communication (e.g. administrative information, appointment scheduling).

Whatever the direction and impact of technological progress, and however it is taken up in the profession, there can be little doubt that the increasing role of technology will have strong repercussions on interpreter **training**, including the need to introduce would-be conference interpreters to the efficient use of state-of-the-art electronic equipment in and outside the booth; the need to prepare trainees for various types of remote interpreting arrangements; and the deployment of digital training stations and web-based source-text archives for classroom instruction as well as self-study. These and other pedagogical innovations ought to be accompanied by a concerted effort at action research by interpreting teachers, so as to assess needs and effects on an ongoing basis.

Not only will technology transform intercultural communication arrangements and professional practice – which will in turn generate new phenomena requiring systematic study – interpreting researchers will also benefit directly from the availability of new equipment and **tools** to enhance the efficiency of empirical **data collection and analysis**. Survey research, for instance, is increasingly done over the Internet, and powerful software facilitates the processing of quantitative as well as qualitative data. Fieldwork involving discourse data can rely on digital, and less obtrusive, **recording** equipment, and subsequent **transcription** is aided by specialized software and speech recognition systems. This also enhances the feasibility of applying corpus-linguistic methods to **large corpora** of source, target and comparable texts from authentic communicative events. Aside from high-volume discourse data processing, computer equipment and software for digitized speech data analysis permit investigations of **paralinguistic phenomena** such as intonation and pauses with incomparably more precision than the measurements taken by the pioneers of experimental interpreting research. Indeed, some of the present-day experimental methods for the study of interpreting, particularly from the realm of cognitive neuropsychology, stand to benefit most spectacularly from the application of imaging technologies pioneered in biomedical research, provided that interdisciplinary collaboration can be developed and sustained. This will ensure the viability of cognitive **neuroscience** approaches to interpreting, and permit unprecedented insights into its neurophysiological underpinnings.

13.2.3 'Gone Social'

The two main 'perspectives' on future developments discussed so far – technology and socio-cultural transformations – are variously interdependent, and their combined effect on future research needs and approaches in interpreting studies is difficult to gauge. The impact of technology has been shown to be pervasive, as a driver of new forms of professional practice, teaching methods and research techniques. Likewise, social change, often through **migration** in response to economic and political pressures, has been transforming the nature of the communities whose members interpreters are ready to serve in enabling communication. The most defining characteristic in this regard is probably heterogeneity: cultural groups and identities are no longer neatly defined (if they ever were) in terms of citizenship and national languages, and **multilingualism** is as common as 'monolingual' communication practices in a third language. The role and **status** of interpreting, and interpreters, is bound to be affected by these changes – and has already been affected by them for quite some time, as reflected, for instance, in the many manifestations of **non-professional interpreting**. Where some level of bilingual or multilingual proficiency is common, interpreting will seem more mundane, and less worthy of great appreciation. This hypothesis, put forward by FIT President Henry Liu in the year of the organization's sixtieth anniversary, remains to be investigated on a longitudinal basis.

As a result of these overarching changes, and given the diversity of national contexts and institutional settings, questions regarding the *raison d'être* of interpreting – that is, where, for whom and for what purpose interpreters are needed and how they are employed – receive different answers today than 40 years ago, when (professional) interpreting became an object of systematic academic study. Two prototypical domains can nevertheless be discerned: one is communication on a supranational level, where highly specialized content is negotiated through interpreters based on political imperatives; the other is highly personal communication within social institutions, often lacking a solid foundation in public policy. The former domain, which foregrounds the efficient transmission of information (typically in simultaneous mode) corresponds to the well-established field of **conference interpreting**; the latter might be subsumed under the broad notion of **community interpreting**, which is several decades younger and has yet to emerge as a professional entity in some regions and countries. Each of these two broad domains has distinct theoretical and methodological orientations, but they share a wide 'middle ground' and various areas of interface.

Where simultaneous interpreting is used for high-speed information processing, the main source of theoretical inspiration has been the **cognitive sciences**, a cluster of disciplines with various subfields, which has become increasingly interrelated with neuroscience. By contrast, areas of the **social sciences** (social psychology, sociology, sociolinguistics) are relied upon where dialogue interpreting is used in talk between individuals and representatives of a public institution about highly personal and often emotional matters relating to health and legal interests. This view yields two prototypical focal points and lines of investigation: bilingual cognitive **information** processing and its neurophysiological foundations, studied experimentally with behavioral and imaging techniques; and bilingual interpreter-mediated **interaction** under personal, cultural and institutional constraints, studied observationally by examining qualitative data with discourse-analytical techniques.

This dual perspective on the main currents of research in interpreting studies could be seen as both a helpful general orientation and a gross oversimplification. Indeed, it needs to be placed in perspective through recognition of the broad middle ground taken up by topics and approaches having to do with **communication** in the widest sense. Issues such as quality, norms, function, multimodality and effect can serve to highlight this outlook, which involves the cognitive as well as the social dimensions of language use and is open to investigations of a qualitative and a quantitative nature alike. There are also some research paradigms which embody the rationale for not considering these two dimensions as mutually exclusive: one example is a current in cognitive science known as **situated cognition**, or 'embodied cognition.' This perspective, which has proved particularly valuable in the context of education, rejects the concern with mental plans and symbolic structures in favor of interaction with a given environment and social context, regarding the person and the environment as parts of a mutually constructed whole. The ethnographic study by Duflou (2016) on EU conference interpreters in their booths is a case in point. Another integrative research paradigm, which similarly views context as part of cognition, is **cognitive pragmatics**, a cognitive approach to linguistics associated with relevance theory. In its cognitive as well as linguistic ramifications, the focus is on **processes** rather than structures, and researchers prefer to observe and reconstruct dynamic changes rather than search for quantifiable categories and patterns. An illustrative example is the essentially **qualitative** study by Setton (1999), who applied the cognitive-pragmatic approach in a corpus-based analysis of simultaneous conference interpreting. In this respect, corpus-based research affords a good illustration in its own right of the current methodological convergence, including both massively quantitative corpus-linguistic studies and in-depth analyses of pragmatic meaning in a blow-by-blow account of discourse processing.

The sociological orientation in interpreting studies goes far beyond the analysis of face-to-face interaction as foregrounded in the work of Wadensjö (1998). The level of the social institution and the constraints it places on the individuals acting within it is a genuinely sociological domain, as explored, for instance, in the work of Inghilleri (2005b, 2006) on interpreting in asylum settings. She demonstrates how, on the institutional and macro-social levels, viewing interpreting as a discourse process in society foregrounds issues such as **roles, power** and **ideology**.

Looking back over the last few decades, it is fairly evident that interpreting studies has taken a **social turn** (Pöchhacker 2006b). This is reflected in the wider scope of its object of study, now including interpreting in intra-social institutions, and its theoretical and methodological approaches. Moreover, as interpreting researchers have increasingly embraced social-science techniques such as interviews and questionnaire-based surveys, research on interpreting has also taken a **qualitative turn**. Like major sectors in the social sciences, it has moved away from an empiricist belief in apparently unproblematic 'facts' toward a greater readiness to engage with qualitative data which suggest reliance on an interpretive epistemology.

It is clear from these reflections and from the review of selected models and research presented in this book that the study of interpreting does not fit neatly into any of the fields from which it has received, and continues to receive, significant input. As a disciplinary entity which is more than the sum of its parts, interpreting studies is free to develop along various pathways. As suggested earlier in this section, it is doing so, pushing forward in several directions at once without privileging one over the others. While ensuring diversified growth, these multiple orientations constitute a major challenge for those expected to master the field's methodological repertoire. Indeed, the diversity of approaches must seem daunting especially to those starting out in the field. The final section of this chapter therefore addresses some basic aspects of the need for guidance and orientation.

13.3 Orientation

Assuming that most readers of this introductory book will be rather new to the field and still acquiring experience in academic research, this section endeavors to provide those taking their first steps as researchers with some basic orientation regarding where to go and how.

13.3.1 Getting Started

Orientation for those getting started in interpreting studies is of course the fundamental purpose of this book, which is offered essentially as a **map** of the interpreting studies **landscape**. Building on the basic understanding and broad overview of the terrain provided in Part I, students and would-be interpreting researchers are pointed to areas of study which merit their attention in Part II. The following paragraphs provide more specific pointers, hopefully amounting to a sort of **compass** for scholars to get their bearings in the **field**. However, there is neither a list of particular research questions nor a description of the methods to be adopted. The field is indeed wide open, and the plurality of domains and paradigms makes it impossible to compile a systematic and balanced research agenda complete with the appropriate methodological tools.

How, then, to take one's first steps toward the goal of completing an interpreting research project? Having gained an **overview** of the territory (step 1), it is vital to find one's bearings and reflect on one's '**position**' with regard to the professional and the institutional (academic) environment (step 2). These contextual factors, particularly the prevailing research paradigm(s) together with relevant personal experience, will largely determine the **type and domain** of interpreting to be studied as well as the underlying '**model**,' or theory, to be applied (step 3). A number of illustrative case studies of this fundamental stage in the process of *Getting Started in Interpreting Research* are included in the book by that title (Gile et al. 2001), which resulted from the 1997 Aarhus Seminar on Interpreting Research.

In the present volume, the thematic organization of Part II, with its section headings and subheadings, should be instrumental in choosing a **topic** (step 4). There are of course many additional and related concepts and issues on which to build a research idea. The structure offered in this book is meant to serve only as a scaffolding for further access, not as a rigidly constraining grid. A comprehensive overview of topics in interpreting research is also provided in the *Routledge Encyclopedia of Interpreting Studies* (Pöchhacker 2015). As indicated at the end of chapters in Part II, the articles in the *Encyclopedia* constitute the primary source of 'further reading' for the topics covered in this textbook, and also point to the most important bibliographic references.

In any research project, thorough **reading** (step 5) is vital in order to observe that fundamental principle of science, as a collective and cumulative process, which requires the researcher to build on and add to the state of the art. The sources listed in this book and, much more comprehensively, in the bibliography of the *Encyclopedia* should facilitate the compilation of an initial reading list. Purposeful reading of the literature is a significant part of a researcher's specialized skills. It requires both the sound intellectual processing of content, the critical appraisal of the author's perspective, aims, and methodology, and an appropriate way of documenting the information and insights gained from one's sources. The chapter on "critical reading" in Gile et al. (2001) provides valuable guidance and advice.

The reading process is essential to formulating a specific **research question** (step 6) and considering ways in which it might be addressed. It is at this (early) stage that the way to proceed hinges on one's basic choice of **methodological approach** (step 7), which is really not so much a stage in the research process as a fundamental orientation to 'doing science' (« 3.3.1): it concerns the choice or awareness of an epistemological position; a focus on data in search of a theory ('induction') vs theories from which to derive testable hypotheses ('deduction'); the preference for quantitative (numerical) vs qualitative data; and the overall purpose to be achieved in the scientific endeavor.

Deciding on a **research design** (step 8) will differ accordingly, depending on the researcher's main concern – such as testing a causal hypothesis in a laboratory as opposed to understanding how participants behave in a real-life event. In the former case, a number of standard designs with certain types of experimental conditions, subjects, materials and methods may be available to **choose** from. In the latter, preparing to gain 'access' and 'go into the field' may require a complex process to **develop** an appropriate design under a particular set of (often unknown) circumstances and constraints. The **context** of research, broadly speaking, includes a number of factors which may have a significant influence on the design of a study.

This basic orientation to issues of methodology, and the present book as a whole, mainly address the interaction between conceptual contexts (foundations, models, theories) and research questions within a particular environment. There is no scope for offering hands-on advice on more concrete questions of methodology, such as **planning** and organizing one's study (step 9), **implementing** the research design by collecting, processing and analyzing various types of data (step 10), **evaluating** and interpreting the findings in relation to the research question and the underlying theoretical framework (step 11), and **reporting** the study in an appropriate way, be it in the form of a conference presentation, a journal article, or an academic thesis (step 12). Help with these more detailed and practical issues in the process of empirical research is readily available from a variety of publications and sources, as indicated by way of conclusion below.

13.3.2 Getting Help

Ideally, students of interpreting can acquire the necessary research skills in graduate-level seminars under the guidance of an experienced researcher and teacher. Where curricular provisions and staff resources fall short of this ideal, there are several ways for would-be interpreting researchers to get help. As mentioned above, the volume by Gile et al. (2001) on *Getting Started* is a rich source of information and advice tailored especially to the needs of graduate students and PhD candidates. The initial chapter by Gile on "selecting a topic" and the report by Čeňková on "MA theses in Prague" offer helpful guidance on the early stages of developing a research project. The book also contains several illustrative examples of PhD research in interpreting studies, with particular emphasis on methodological problems and solutions. Content along these lines can also be found in the edited volume by Nicodemus and Swabey (2011), which includes insightful reports on *Inquiry in Action*, most of them on research in signed language interpreting. Moreover, the *Routledge*

Encyclopedia of Interpreting Studies (Pöchhacker 2015) includes a number of articles providing authoritative and concise presentations of major research approaches and methodologies, from action research and corpus-based research to ethnographic methods, and from experimental research to interviews, mixed methods and survey research.

The most detailed source of hands-on methodological guidance for interpreting researchers, however, is the textbook by Hale and Napier (2013) on *Research Methods in Interpreting*. Written in a highly accessible style, with many exercises and examples, this *Practical Resource* is ideally tailored to the needs of those embarking on research in interpreting studies, and can be seen as a perfect complement to the present overview of basic concepts and research topics in this field. With a similar purpose but a focus on translation, Saldanha and O'Brien (2013) offer an introduction to *Research Methodologies in Translation Studies*.

As mentioned above and at the end of Chapter 12, the induction of researchers into the field of interpreting studies is promoted by personal contacts and advice as much as by the reading of books. Seminars in the curriculum and summer schools and similar research training measures (« 12.5.4) offer an ideal environment for developing and sharing ideas, in line with the principle that 'doing science' is both an individual and a collective endeavor. This book is fundamentally designed to lay the foundations for such productive exchanges, making sure that everyone is roughly 'on the same page.' Based on a thorough understanding of the nature of the field and a solid grasp of the state of the art, those studying interpreting should find it possible to raise and answer new questions, thus ensuring that progress in interpreting studies will continue.

Bibliography

Ahrens, B. (2005) "Prosodic Phenomena in Simultaneous Interpreting: A Conceptual Approach and its Practical Application," *Interpreting* 7(1): 51–76.

AIIC (2002) *Interpreter Workload Study – Full Report*, Geneva: AIIC (http://aiic.net/page/657).

Albl-Mikasa, M. (2013) "ELF Speakers' Restricted Power of Expression: Implications for Interpreters' Processing," *Translation and Interpreting Studies* 8(2): 191–210.

Alexieva, B. (1985) "Semantic Analysis of the Text in Simultaneous Interpreting," in H. Bühler (ed.) *Xth World Congress of FIT: Proceedings*, Vienna: Wilhelm Braumüller, pp. 195–198.

Alexieva, B. (1994) "Types of Texts and Intertextuality in Simultaneous Interpreting," in Snell-Hornby et al. (eds) (1994), pp. 179–187.

Alexieva, B. (1997/2002) "A Typology of Interpreter-mediated Events," in Pöchhacker and Shlesinger (eds) (2002), pp. 219–233.

Alexieva, B. (1999) "Understanding the Source Language Text in Simultaneous Interpreting," *The Interpreters' Newsletter* 9: 45–59.

Altman, J. (1990) "What Helps Effective Communication? Some Interpreters' Views," *The Interpreters' Newsletter* 3: 23–32.

Álvarez Lugrís, A. and Fernández Ocampo, A. (eds) (1999) *Anovar/Anosar estudios de traducción e interpretación*, vol. 1, Vigo: Universidade de Vigo.

Alvstad, C., Hild, A. and Tiselius, E. (eds) (2011) *Methods and Strategies of Process Research: Integrative Approaches in Translation Studies*, Amsterdam: John Benjamins.

Anderson, L. (1994) "Simultaneous Interpretation: Contextual and Translation Aspects," in Lambert and Moser-Mercer (eds) (1994), pp. 101–120.

Anderson, R.B.W. (1976) "Perspectives on the Role of Interpreter," in Brislin (ed.) (1976b), pp. 208–228.

Anderson, R.B.W. (1976/2002) "Perspectives on the Role of Interpreter," in Pöchhacker and Shlesinger (eds) (2002), pp. 209–217.

Andres, D. (2002) *Konsekutivdolmetschen und Notation*, Frankfurt: Peter Lang.

Andres, D. (2013) "History of Interpreting," in C.A. Chapelle (ed.) *The Encyclopedia of Applied Linguistics*, Oxford: Blackwell, pp. 2512–2521.

Andres, D. and Behr, M. (eds) (2015) *To Know How to Suggest. … Approaches to Teaching Conference Interpreting*, Berlin: Frank & Timme.

Andres, D., Boden, S. and Fuchs, C. (2015) "The Sense and Senselessness of Preparatory Exercises for Simultaneous Interpreting," in Andres and Behr (eds) (2015), pp. 59–73.

Angelelli, C.V. (2000) "Interpreting as a Communicative Event: A Look through Hymes' Lenses," *Meta* 45(4): 580–592.

Angelelli, C.V. (2004a) *Medical Interpreting and Cross-cultural Communication*, Cambridge: Cambridge University Press.

Angelelli, C.V. (2004b) *Revisiting the Interpreter's Role: A Study of Conference, Court, and Medical Interpreters in Canada, Mexico, and the United States*, Amsterdam: John Benjamins.

Angelelli, C.V. (2006) "Validating Professional Standards and Codes: Challenges and Opportunities," *Interpreting* 8(2): 175–193.

Arjona, E. (1978) "Intercultural Communication and the Training of Interpreters at the Monterey Institute of Foreign Studies," in Gerver and Sinaiko (eds) (1978), pp. 35–44.

Arjona, E. (1984) "Issues in the Design of Curricula for the Professional Education of Translators and Interpreters," in McIntire (ed.) (1984), pp. 1–35.

Arjona-Tseng, E. (1994) "A Psychometric Approach to the Selection of Translation and Interpreting Students in Taiwan," in Lambert and Moser-Mercer (eds) (1994), pp. 69–86.

Babbie, E. (1999) *The Basics of Social Research*, Belmont, CA: Wadsworth.

Baddeley, A. (2000) "Working Memory and Language Processing," in Englund Dimitrova and Hyltenstam (eds) (2000), pp. 1–16.

Baigorri-Jalón, J. (2004) *Interpreters at the United Nations: A History* (trans. A. Barr), Salamanca: Ediciones Universidad de Salamanca.

Baigorri-Jalón, J. (2006) "Perspectives on the History of Interpretation: Research Proposals," in G. Bastin and P. Bandia (eds) *Charting the Future of Translation History*, Ottawa: University of Ottawa Press, pp. 101–110.

Baigorri-Jalón, J. (2014) *From Paris to Nuremberg: The Birth of Conference Interpreting* (trans. H. Mikkelson and B.S. Olsen), Amsterdam: John Benjamins.

Baigorri-Jalón, J. (2015a) "The History of the Interpreting Profession," in Mikkelson and Jourdenais (eds) (2015), pp. 11–28.

Baigorri-Jalón, J. (2015b) "Spain," in Pöchhacker (ed.) (2015), pp. 393–396.

Bajo, M.T., Padilla, F. and Padilla, P. (2000) "Comprehension Processes in Simultaneous Interpreting," in A. Chesterman, N. Gallardo San Salvador and Y. Gambier (eds) *Translation in Context. Selected Papers from the EST Congress, Granada 1998*, Amsterdam: John Benjamins, pp. 127–142.

Baker, M. (1997) "Non-cognitive Constraints and Interpreter Strategies," in K. Simms (ed.) *Translating Sensitive Texts: Linguistic Aspects*, Amsterdam and Atlanta, GA: Rodopi, pp. 111–129.

Baker, M. and Saldanha, G. (eds) (2009) *Routledge Encyclopedia of Translation Studies*, 2nd edn, London and New York: Routledge.

Baker-Shenk, C. (ed.) (1990) *A Model Curriculum for Teachers of American Sign Language and Teachers of ASL/English Interpreting*, Silver Spring, MD: RID Publications.

Balzani, M. (1990) "Le contact visuel en interprétation simultanée: resultats d'une expérience (Français–Italien)," in Gran and Taylor (eds) (1990), pp. 93–100.

Bao, C. (2015) "Pedagogy," in Mikkelson and Jourdenais (eds) (2015), pp. 400–416.

Baraldi, C. and Gavioli, L. (2012a) "Understanding Coordination in Interpeter-mediated Interaction," in Baraldi and Gavioli (eds) (2012b), pp. 1–21.

Baraldi, C. and Gavioli, L. (eds) (2012b) *Coordinating Participation in Dialogue Interpreting*, Amsterdam: John Benjamins.

Barik, H.C. (1972) "Interpreters Talk a Lot, Among Other Things," *Babel* 18(1): 3–10.

Barik, H.C. (1973) "Simultaneous Interpretation: Temporal and Quantitative Data," *Language and Speech* 16(3): 237–270.

Barik, H.C. (1975/2002) "Simultaneous Interpretation: Qualitative and Linguistic Data," in Pöchhacker and Shlesinger (eds) (2002), pp. 79–91.

Barsky, R. (1996) "The Interpreter as Intercultural Agent in Convention Refugee Hearings," *The Translator* 2(1): 45–63.

Bartłomiejczyk, M. (2006) "Strategies of Simultaneous Interpreting and Directionality," *Interpreting* 8(2): 149–174.

Beaugrande, R. de (1980) *Text, Discourse, and Process*, Norwood, NJ: Ablex.

Beaugrande, R. de and Dressler, W.U. (1981) *Introduction to Text Linguistics*, London: Longman.

Bendazzoli, C., Sandrelli, A. and Russo, M. (2011) "Disfluencies in Simultaneous Interpreting: A Corpus-based Analysis," in Kruger et al. (eds) (2011), pp. 282–306.

Berk-Seligson, S. (1988/2002) "The Impact of Politeness in Witness Testimony: The Influence of the Court Interpreter," in Pöchhacker and Shlesinger (eds) (2002), pp. 279–292.

Berk-Seligson, S. (1990) *The Bilingual Courtroom: Court Interpreters in the Judicial Process*, Chicago, IL and London: The University of Chicago Press.

Berk-Seligson, S. (2000) "Interpreting for the Police: Issues in Pre-trial Phases of the Judicial Process," *Forensic Linguistics* 7(2): 212–237.

Boéri, J. and de Manuel Jerez, J. (2011) "From Training Skilled Conference Interpreters to Educating Reflective Citizens: A Case Study of the Marius Action Research Project," *The Interpreter and Translator Trainer* 5(1): 41–64.

Bolden, G.B. (2000) "Toward Understanding Practices of Medical Interpreting: Interpreters' Involvement in History Taking," *Discourse Studies* 2(4): 387–419.

Bontempo, K. and Malcolm, K. (2012) "An Ounce of Prevention is Worth a Pound of Cure: Educating Interpreters about the Risk of Vicarious Trauma in Healthcare Settings," in L. Swabey and K. Malcolm (eds) *In Our Hands: Educating Healthcare Interpreters*, Washington, DC: Gallaudet University Press, pp. 105–130.

Bot, H. (2003) "Quality as an Interactive Concept: Interpreting in Psychotherapy," in Collados Aís et al. (eds) (2003), pp. 33–45.

Bot, H. (2005) *Dialogue Interpreting in Mental Health*, Amsterdam and New York: Rodopi.

Bot, H. (2015) "Interpreting in Mental Health Care," in Mikkelson and Jourdenais (eds) (2015), pp. 254–264.

Bowen, D. and Bowen, M. (eds) (1990) *Interpreting: Yesterday, Today, and Tomorrow*, Binghamton, NY: SUNY.

Bowen, M. (2012) "Interpreters and the Making of History," in J. Delisle and J. Woodsworth (eds) *Translators through History*, rev. edn, Amsterdam: John Benjamins, pp. 247–282.

Braun, S. (2007) "Interpreting in Small-Group Bilingual Videoconferences: Challenges and Adaptation," *Interpreting* 9(1): 21–46.

Braun, S. (2013) "Keep Your Distance? Remote Interpreting in Legal Proceedings: A Critical Assessment of a Growing Practice," *Interpreting* 15(2): 200–228.

Braun, S. (2015) "Remote Interpreting," in Mikkelson and Jourdenais (eds) (2015), pp. 352–367.

Braun, S. and Slater, C. (2014) "Populating a 3D Virtual Learning Environment for Interpreting Students with Bilingual Dialogues to Support Situated Learning in an Institutional Context," *The Interpreter and Translator Trainer* 8(3): 469–485.

Braun, S. and Taylor, J.L. (eds) (2012) *Videoconference and Remote Interpreting in Criminal Proceedings*, Cambridge: Intersentia.

Braun, S. and Taylor, J.L. (eds) (2015) *Advances in Videoconferencing and Interpreting in Legal Proceedings*, Cambridge/Antwerp: Intersentia.

Brennan, M. (1999) "Signs of Injustice," *The Translator* 5(2): 221–246.

Brislin, R.W. (1976a) "Introduction," in Brislin (ed.) (1976b), pp. 1–43.

Brislin, R.W. (ed.) (1976b) *Translation: Applications and Research*, New York: Gardner Press.

Broadbent, D.E. (1952) "Speaking and Listening Simultaneously," *Journal of Experimental Psychology* 43: 267–273.

Buck, V. (2002) "One World, One Language?" in *Communicate!* April–May 2002 (http://www.aiic.net/page/732).

Bühler, H. (1985) "Conference Interpreting – a Multichannel Communication Phenomenon," *Meta* 30(1): 49–54.

Bühler, H. (1986) "Linguistic (Semantic) and Extra-linguistic (Pragmatic) Criteria for the Evaluation of Conference Interpretation and Interpreters," *Multilingua* 5(4): 231–235.

Carr, S.E. and Steyn, D. (2000) "Distance Education Training for Interpreters: An Insurmountable Oxymoron?" in Roberts et al. (eds) (2000), pp. 83–88.

Carr, S.E., Roberts, R., Dufour, A. and Steyn, D. (eds) (1997) *The Critical Link: Interpreters in the Community. Papers from the First International Conference on Interpreting in Legal, Health, and Social Service Settings (Geneva Park, Canada, June 1–4, 1995)*, Amsterdam: John Benjamins.

Carroll, J.B. (1978) "Linguistic Abilities in Translators and Interpreters," in Gerver and Sinaiko (eds) (1978), pp. 119–129.

Castillo, P. (2015) "Interpreting for the Mass Media," in Mikkelson and Jourdenais (eds) (2015), pp. 280–301.

Cencini, M. and Aston, G. (2002) "Resurrecting the Corp(us|se): Towards an Encoding Standard for Interpreting Data," in Garzone and Viezzi (eds) (2002), pp. 47–62.

Čeňková, I. (1988) *Teoretické aspekty simultánního tolumočení*, Prague: Charles University.

Chabasse, C. and Kader, S. (2014) "Putting Interpreting Admissions Exams to the Test: The MA KD Germersheim Project," *Interpreting* 16(1): 19–33.

Chang, C.-C. and Wu, M.M.-C. (2009) "Address Form Shifts in Interpreted Q&A Sessions," *Interpreting* 11(2): 164–189.

Chang, C.-C. and Wu, M.M.-C. (2014) "Non-native English at International Conferences: Perspectives from Chinese–English Conference Interpreters in Taiwan," *Interpreting* 16(2): 169–190.

Chernov, G.V. (1978) *Teoriya i praktika sinkhronnogo perevoda* [*Theory and Practice of Simultaneous Interpretation*], Moscow: Mezhdunarodnyye otnosheniya.

Chernov, G.V. (1979/2002) "Semantic Aspects of Psycholinguistic Research in Simultaneous Interpretation," in Pöchhacker and Shlesinger (eds) (2002), pp. 99–109.

Chernov, G.V. (1994) "Message Redundancy and Message Anticipation in Simultaneous Interpretation," in Lambert and Moser-Mercer (eds) (1994), pp. 139–153.

Chernov, G.V. (2004) *Inference and Anticipation in Simultaneous Interpreting: A Probability-Prediction Model* (ed. R. Setton and A. Hild), Amsterdam: John Benjamins.

Chesterman, A. (1993) "From 'Is' to 'Ought': Laws, Norms and Strategies in Translation Studies," *Target* 5(1): 1–20.

Chesterman, A. (1997) *Memes of Translation: The Spread of Ideas in Translation Theory*, Amsterdam: John Benjamins.

Chesterman, A. and Arrojo, R. (2000) "Shared Ground in Translation Studies," *Target* 12(1): 151–160.

Cheung, A. (2003) "Does Accent Matter? The Impact of Accent in Simultaneous Interpretation into Mandarin and Cantonese on Perceived Performance Quality and Listener Satisfaction Level," in Collados Aís et al. (eds) (2003), pp. 85–96.

Chiang, Y. (2010) "Foreign Language Anxiety and Student Interpreters' Learning Outcomes: Implications for the Theory and Measurement of Interpretation Learning Anxiety," *Meta* 55(3): 589–601.

Chiaro, D. (2002) "Linguistic Mediation on Italian Television. When the Interpreter Is Not an Interpreter: A Case Study," in Garzone and Viezzi (eds) (2002), pp. 215–225.

Chiaro, D. and Nocella, G. (2004) "Interpreters' Perception of Linguistic and Non-linguistic Factors Affecting Quality: A Survey through the World Wide Web," *Meta* 49(2): 278–293.

Christoffels, I.K., de Groot, A.M.B. and Kroll, J.F. (2006) "Memory and Language Skills in Simultaneous Interpreters: The Role of Expertise and Language Proficiency," *Journal of Memory and Language* 54(3): 324–345.

Clark, H.H. (1996) *Using Language*, Cambridge: Cambridge University Press.

Clifford, A. (2005) "Putting the Exam to the Test: Psychometric Validation and Interpreter Certification," *Interpreting* 7(1): 97–131.

Cokely, D. (1992a) *Interpretation: A Sociolinguistic Model*, Burtonsville, MD: Linstok Press.

Cokely, D. (ed.) (1992b) *Sign Language Interpreters and Interpreting*, Burtonsville, MD: Linstok Press.

Cokely, D. (2000) "Exploring Ethics: A Case for Revising the Code of Ethics," *Journal of Interpretation* 2000: 25–57.

Collados Aís, A. (1998/2002) "Quality Assessment in Simultaneous Interpreting: The Importance of Nonverbal Communication," in Pöchhacker and Shlesinger (eds) (2002), pp. 327–336.

Collados Aís, A., Fernández Sánchez, M.M. and Gile, D. (eds) (2003) *La evaluación de la calidad en interpretación: Investigación*, Granada: Comares.

Collados Aís, A., Pradas Macías, E.M., Stévaux, E. and García Becerra, O. (eds) (2007) *La evaluación de la calidad en interpretación simultánea: Parámetros de incidencia*, Granada: Comares.

Cooper, C.L., Davies, R. and Tung, R.L. (1982) "Interpreting Stress: Sources of Job Stress among Conference Interpreters," *Multilingua* 1(2): 97–107.

Corina, D.P. and Vaid, J. (1994) "Lateralization for Shadowing Words versus Signs: A Study of ASL–English Interpreters," in Lambert and Moser-Mercer (eds) (1994), pp. 237–248.

Corsellis, A. (1997) "Training Needs of Public Personnel Working with Interpreters," in Carr et al. (eds) (1997), pp. 77–89.

Corsellis, A. (1999) "Training of Public Service Interpreters," in Erasmus (ed.) (1999), pp. 197–205.

Corsellis, A. (2000) "Turning Good Intentions into Good Practice: Enabling the Public Services to Fulfil their Responsibilities," in Roberts et al. (eds) (2000), pp. 89–99.

Cowan, N. (1995) *Attention and Memory: An Integrated Framework*, New York and Oxford: Oxford University Press.

Cronin, M. (2002) "The Empire Talks Back: Orality, Heteronomy and the Cultural Turn in Interpreting Studies," in Pöchhacker and Shlesinger (eds) (2002), pp. 387–397.

Dam, H.V. (1993) "Text Condensing in Consecutive Interpreting," in Gambier and Tommola (eds) (1993), pp. 297–313.

Dam, H.V. (1998/2002) "Lexical Similarity vs Lexical Dissimilarity in Consecutive Interpreting," in Pöchhacker and Shlesinger (eds) (2002), pp. 267–277.

Dam, H.V. (2001) "On the Option Between Form-based and Meaning-based Interpreting: The Effect of Source Text Difficulty on Lexical Target Text Form in Simultaneous Interpreting," *The Interpreters' Newsletter* 11: 27–55.

Dam, H.V. (2004) "Interpreters' Notes: On the Choice of Language," *Interpreting* 6(1): 3–17.

Dam, H.V. and Zethsen, K.K. (2013) "Conference Interpreters – the Stars of the Translation Profession? A Study of the Professional Status of Danish EU Interpreters as Compared to Danish EU Translators," *Interpreting* 15(2): 229–259.

Danks, J.H., Shreve, G.M., Fountain, S.B. and McBeath, M.K. (eds) (1997) *Cognitive Processes in Translation and Interpreting*, Thousand Oaks, CA, London and New Delhi: Sage.

Davidson, B. (2002) "A Model for the Construction of Conversational Common Ground in Interpreted Discourse," *Journal of Pragmatics* 34: 1273–1300.

Davitti, E. (2013) "Dialogue Interpreting as Intercultural Mediation: Interpreters' Use of Upgrading Moves in Parent–Teacher Meetings," *Interpreting* 15(2): 168–199.

de Bot, K. (2000) "Simultaneous Interpreting as Language Production," in Englund Dimitrova and Hyltenstam (eds) (2000), pp. 65–88.

de Groot, A.M.B. (1997) "The Cognitive Study of Translation and Interpretation: Three Approaches," in Danks et al. (eds) (1997), pp. 25–56.

de Groot, A.M.B. (2015) "Bilingualism," in Pöchhacker (ed.) (2015), pp. 31–35.

Déjean le Féal, K. (1982) "Why Impromptu Speech is Easy to Understand," in Enkvist (ed.) (1982), pp. 221–239.

Déjean le Féal, K. (1990) "Some Thoughts on the Evaluation of Simultaneous Interpretation," in Bowen and Bowen (eds) (1990), pp. 154–160.

Déjean le Féal, K. (1997) "Simultaneous Interpretation with 'Training Wheels'," *Meta* 42(2): 616–621.

Denzin, N.K. and Lincoln, Y.S. (2000) *Handbook of Qualitative Research*, 2nd edn, Thousand Oaks, London and New Delhi: Sage.

Dillinger, M. (1994) "Comprehension during Interpreting: What Do Interpreters Know that Bilinguals Don't?" in Lambert and Moser-Mercer (eds) (1994), pp. 155–189.

Dingfelder Stone, M. (2015) "The Theory and Practice of Teaching Note-Taking," in Andres and Behr (eds) (2015), pp. 145–169.

Diriker, E. (2004) *De-/Re-Contextualizing Conference Interpreting: Interpreters in the Ivory Tower?*, Amsterdam: John Benjamins.

Dodds, J.M. (1990) "On the Aptitude of Aptitude Testing," *The Interpreters' Newsletter* 3: 17–22.

Dodds, J.M. and Katan, D. (1997) "The Interaction between Research and Training," in Gambier et al. (eds) (1997), pp. 89–107.

Dollerup, C. and Appel, V. (eds) (1996) *Teaching Translation and Interpreting 3: New Horizons*, Amsterdam: John Benjamins.

Dollerup, C. and Loddegaard, A. (eds) (1992) *Teaching Translation and Interpreting: Training, Talent and Experience*, Amsterdam: John Benjamins.

Dollerup, C. and Lindegaard, A. (eds) (1994) *Teaching Translation and Interpreting 2: Aims, Insights, Visions*, Amsterdam: John Benjamins.

Donovan, C. (2011) "Ethics in the Teaching of Conference Interpreting," *The Interpreter and Translator Trainer* 5(1): 109–128.

Donovan-Cagigos, C. (1990) *La fidélité en interprétation*, doctoral dissertation, Université de la Sorbonne Nouvelle/Paris III.

Duflou, V. (2016) *Be(com)ing a Conference Interpreter: An Ethnography of EU Interpreters as a Professional Community*, Amsterdam: John Benjamins.

Edwards, R., Temple, B. and Alexander, C. (2005) "Users' Experiences of Interpreters: The Critical Role of Trust," *Interpreting* 7(1): 77–95.

Englund Dimitrova, B. (1997) "Degree of Interpreter Responsibility in the Interaction Process in Community Interpreting," in Carr et al. (eds) (1997), pp. 147–164.

Englund Dimitrova, B. and Hyltenstam, K. (eds) (2000) *Language Processing and Simultaneous Interpreting: Interdisciplinary Perspectives*, Amsterdam: John Benjamins.

Enkvist, N.E. (ed.) (1982) *Impromptu Speech: A Symposium*, Åbo: Åbo Akademi.

Erasmus, M. (ed.) (1999) *Liaison Interpreting in the Community*, Pretoria: Van Schaik.

Ericsson, K.A. (2000) "Expertise in Interpreting: An Expert-Performance Perspective," *Interpreting* 5(2): 187–220.

Ericsson, K.A. and Kintsch, W. (1995) "Long-term Working Memory," *Psychological Review* 102(2): 211–242.

Ervin, S.M. and Osgood, C.E. (1965) "Second Language Learning and Bilingualism," in C.E. Osgood and T.A. Sebeok (eds) *Psycholinguistics: A Survey of Theory and Research Problems*, Bloomington, IN and London: Indiana University Press, pp. 139–146.

Fabbro, F. and Gran, L. (1994) "Neurological and Neuropsychological Aspects of Polyglossia and Simultaneous Interpretation," in Lambert and Moser-Mercer (eds) (1994), pp. 273–317.

Fabbro, F. and Gran, L. (1997) "Neurolinguistic Research in Simultaneous Interpretation," in Gambier et al. (eds) (1997), pp. 9–27.

Fabbro, F., Gran, L., Basso, G. and Bava, A. (1990) "Cerebral Lateralization in Simultaneous Interpretation," *Brain and Language* 39: 69–89.

Fant, L. (1990) *Silver Threads: A Personal Look at the First Twenty-five Years of the Registry of Interpreters for the Deaf*, Silver Spring, MD: RID Publications.

Fantinuoli, C. (2013) *InterpretBank: Design and Implementation of a Terminology and Knowledge Management Software for Conference Interpreters*, Berlin: epubli.

Feldweg, E. (1996) *Der Konferenzdolmetscher im internationalen Kommunikationsprozeß*, Heidelberg: Groos.

Fernández-Ocampo, A. and Wolf, M. (eds) (2014) *Framing the Interpreter: Towards a Visual Perspective*, London and New York: Routledge.

Feuerstein, M., Carosella, A.M., Burrell, A.L., Marshall, L. and DeCaro, J. (1997) "Occupational Upper Extremity Symptoms in Sign Language Interpreter: Prevalence and Correlates of Pain, Function, and Work Disability," *Journal of Occupational Rehabilitation* 7(4): 187–205.

Fowler, Y. (2013) "Business as Usual? Prison Video Link in the Multilingual Courtroom," in Schäffner et al. (eds) (2013), pp. 225–248.

Frishberg, N. (1990) *Interpreting: An Introduction*, rev. edn, Silver Spring, MD: RID Publications.

Fukuii, H. and Asano, T. (1961) *Eigotsûyaku no jissai* [*An English Interpreter's Manual*], Tokyo: Kenkyusha.

Gaiba, F. (1998) *The Origins of Simultaneous Interpretation: The Nuremberg Trial*, Ottawa: University of Ottawa Press.

Gambier, Y. and Tommola, J. (eds) (1993) *Translation and Knowledge: SSOTT IV*, Turku: University of Turku, Centre for Translation and Interpreting.

Gambier, Y. and van Doorslaer, L. (eds) (2014) *Handbook of Translation Studies* (4 vols), Amsterdam: John Benjamins.

Gambier, Y., Gile, D. and Taylor, C. (eds) (1997) *Conference Interpreting: Current Trends in Research*, Amsterdam: John Benjamins.

Garber, N. and Mauffette-Leenders, L.A. (1997) "Obtaining Feedback from Non-English Speakers," in Carr et al. (eds) (1997), pp. 131–143.

García-Beyaert, S. (2015) "Key External Players in the Development of the Interpreting Profession," in Mikkelson and Jourdenais (eds) (2015), pp. 45–61.

García-Landa, M. (1981) "La 'théorie du sens', théorie de la traduction et base de son enseignement," in J. Delisle (ed.) *L'enseignement de l'interprétation et de la traduction: de la théorie à la pédagogie*, Ottawa: University of Ottawa Press, pp. 113–132.

García-Landa, M. (1998) "A Theoretical Framework for Oral and Written Translation Research," *The Interpreters' Newsletter* 8: 5–40.

Garzone, G. (2003) "Reliability of Quality Criteria Evaluation in Survey Research," in Collados Aís et al. (eds) (2003), pp. 23–30.

Garzone, G. and Viezzi, M. (eds) (2002) *Interpreting in the 21st Century: Challenges and Opportunities*, Amsterdam: John Benjamins.

Garzone, G., Mead, P. and Viezzi, M. (eds) (2002) *Perspectives on Interpreting*, Bologna: CLUEB.

Gehman, H.S. (1914) *The Interpreters of Foreign Languages Among the Ancients: A Study Based on Greek and Latin Sources*, PhD dissertation, University of Pennsylvania.

Gentile, A., Ozolins, U. and Vasilakakos, M. (1996) *Liaison Interpreting: A Handbook*, Melbourne: Melbourne University Press.

Gerver, D. (1969/2002) "The Effects of Source Language Presentation Rate on the Performance of Simultaneous Conference Interpreters," in Pöchhacker and Shlesinger (eds) (2002), pp. 53–66.

Gerver, D. (1971) *Aspects of Simultaneous Interpretation and Human Information Processing*, DPhil thesis, Oxford University.

Gerver, D. (1974a) "Simultaneous Listening and Speaking and Retention of Prose," *Quarterly Journal of Experimental Psychology* 26(3): 337–341.

Gerver, D. (1974b) "The Effects of Noise on the Performance of Simultaneous Interpreters: Accuracy of Performance," *Acta Psychologica* 38(3): 159–167.

Gerver, D. (1975) "A Psychological Approach to Simultaneous Interpretation," *Meta* 20(2): 119–128.

Gerver, D. (1976) "Empirical Studies of Simultaneous Interpretation: A Review and a Model," in Brislin (ed.) (1976b), pp. 165–207.

Gerver, D. and Sinaiko, H.W. (eds) (1978) *Language Interpretation and Communication. Proceedings of the NATO Symposium, Venice, Italy, September 26–October 1, 1977*, New York and London: Plenum Press.

Gerver, D., Longley, P.E., Long, J. and Lambert, S. (1989) "Selection Tests for Trainee Conference Interpreters," *Meta* 34(4): 724–735.

Giambruno (Miguélez), C. (2008) "The Role of the Interpreter in the Governance of Sixteenth- and Seventeenth-century Spanish Colonies in the 'New World': Lessons from the Past for the Present," in Valero-Garcés and Martin (eds) (2008), pp. 27–49.

Gile, D. (1984) "Les noms propres en interprétation simultanée," *Multilingua* 3(2): 79–85.

Gile, D. (1985) "Le modèle d'efforts et l'équilibre en interprétation simultanée," *Meta* 30(1): 44–48.

Gile, D. (1990a) "Scientific Research vs. Personal Theories in the Investigation of Interpretation," in Gran and Taylor (eds) (1990), pp. 28–41.

Gile, D. (1990b) "L'évaluation de la qualité de l'interprétation par les délégués: une étude de cas," *The Interpreters' Newsletter* 3: 66–71.

Gile, D. (1992a) "Predictable Sentence Endings in Japanese and Conference Interpretation," *The Interpreters' Newsletter*, Special Issue 1: 12–23.

Gile, D. (1992b) "Basic Theoretical Components for Interpreter and Translator Training," in Dollerup and Loddegaard (eds) (1992), pp. 185–194.

Gile, D. (1993) "Translation/Interpretation and Knowledge," in Gambier and Tommola (eds) (1993), pp. 67–86.

Gile, D. (1994a) "Opening Up in Interpretation Studies," in Snell-Hornby et al. (eds) (1994), pp. 149–158.

Gile, D. (1994b) "Methodological Aspects of Interpretation and Translation Research," in Lambert and Moser-Mercer (eds) (1994), pp. 39–56.

Gile, D. (1995a) *Regards sur la recherche en interprétation de conférence*, Lille: Presses Universitaires de Lille.

Gile, D. (1995b) *Basic Concepts and Models for Interpreter and Translator Training*, Amsterdam: John Benjamins.

Gile, D. (1997) "Methodology," in Gambier et al. (eds) (1997), pp. 109–122.

Gile, D. (1997/2002) "Conference Interpreting as a Cognitive Management Problem," in Pöchhacker and Shlesinger (eds) (2002), pp. 163–176.

Gile, D. (1998) "Observational Studies and Experimental Studies in the Investigation of Conference Interpreting," *Target* 10(1): 69–93.

Gile, D. (1999a) "Doorstep Interdisciplinarity in Conference Interpreting Research," in Álvarez Lugrís and Fernández Ocampo (eds) (1999), pp. 41–52.

Gile, D. (1999b) "Testing the Effort Models' Tightrope Hypothesis in Simultaneous Interpreting – a Contribution," *Hermes. Journal of Linguistics* 23: 153–172.

Gile, D. (1999c) "Variability in the Perception of Fidelity in Simultaneous Interpretation," *Hermes. Journal of Linguistics* 22: 51–79.

Gile, D. (2000) "The History of Research into Conference Interpreting: A Scientometric Approach," *Target* 12(2): 297–321.

Gile, D. (2003) "Quality Assessment in Conference Interpreting: Methodological Issues," in Collados Aís et al. (eds) (2003), pp. 109–123.

Gile, D. (2009) *Basic Concepts and Models for Interpreter and Translator Training*, 2nd edn, Amsterdam: John Benjamins.

Gile, D. (2015) "Effort Models," in Pöchhacker (ed.) (2015), pp. 135–137.

Gile, D., Dam, H.V., Dubslaff, F., Martinsen, B. and Schjoldager, A. (eds) (2001) *Getting Started in Interpreting Research: Methodological Reflections, Personal Accounts and Advice for Beginners*, Amsterdam: John Benjamins.

Glémet, R. (1958) "Conference Interpreting," in Smith (ed.) (1958), pp. 105–122.

Goffman, E. (1981) *Forms of Talk*, Oxford: Basil Blackwell.

Goldman-Eisler, F. (1967) "Sequential Temporal Patterns and Cognitive Processes in Speech," *Language and Speech* 10(3): 122–132.

Goldman-Eisler, F. (1972/2002) "Segmentation of Input in Simultaneous Translation," in Pöchhacker and Shlesinger (eds) (2002), pp. 69–76.

Gomes, M. (2002) "Digitally Mastered Consecutive: An Interview with Michele Ferrari," *Lingua Franca: Le Bulletin de L'Interprétation au Parlement Européen* 5(6): 6–10.

González, R.D., Vásquez, V.F. and Mikkelson, H. (2012) *Fundamentals of Court Interpretation: Theory, Policy, and Practice*, 2nd edn, Durham, NC: Carolina Academic Press.

Gorm Hansen, I. and Shlesinger, M. (2007) "The Silver Lining: Technology and Self-Study in the Interpreting Classroom," *Interpreting* 9(1): 95–118.

Gran, L. and Dodds, J. (eds) (1989) *The Theoretical and Practical Aspects of Teaching Conference Interpretation*, Udine: Campanotto.

Gran, L. and Taylor, C. (eds) (1990) *Aspects of Applied and Experimental Research on Conference Interpretation*, Udine: Campanotto.

Gran, L., Carabelli, A. and Merlini, R. (2002) "Computer-Assisted Interpreter Training," in Garzone and Viezzi (eds) (2002), pp. 277–294.

Green, A., Vaid, J., Schweda Nicholson, N., White, N. and Steiner, R. (1994) "Lateralization for Shadowing vs. Interpretation: A Comparison of Interpreters with Bilingual and Monolingual Controls," in Lambert and Moser-Mercer (eds) (1994), pp. 331–355.

Gringiani, A. (1990) "Reliability of Aptitude Testing: A Preliminary Study," in Gran and Taylor (eds) (1990), pp. 42–53.

Grosjean, F. (2001) "The Bilingual's Language Modes," in J.L. Nicol (ed.) *One Mind, Two Languages: Bilingual Language Processing*, Oxford and Malden, MA: Blackwell, pp. 1–22.

Gumperz, J.J. and Hymes, D. (1972) *Directions in Sociolinguistics*, New York: Holt, Rinehart and Winston.

Gumul, E. (2006) "Explicitation in Simultaneous Interpreting: A Strategy or a By-product of Language Mediation?" *Across Languages and Cultures* 7(2): 171–190.

Hale, S.B. (1997) "The Interpreter on Trial: Pragmatics in Court Interpreting," in Carr et al. (eds) (1997), pp. 201–211.

Hale, S.B. (2004) *The Discourse of Court Interpreting: Discourse Practices of the Law, the Witness and the Interpreter*, Amsterdam: John Benjamins.

Hale, S.B. (2006) "Themes and Methodological Issues in Court Interpreting Research," in Hertog and van der Veer (eds) (2006), pp. 205–228.

Hale, S.B. (2007) *Community Interpreting*, Basingstoke: Palgrave Macmillan.

Hale, S.B. (2011) *Interpreter Policies, Practices and Protocols in Australian Courts and Tribunals: A National Survey*, Melbourne: The Australasian Institute of Judicial Administration Incorporated.

Hale, S.B. and Napier, J. (2013) *Research Methods in Interpreting: A Practical Resource*, London and New York: Bloomsbury Academic.

Hale, S.B., Ozolins, U. and Stern, L. (eds) (2009) *The Critical Link 5: Quality in Interpreting – a Shared Responsibility*, Amsterdam: John Benjamins.

Halliday, M.A.K. (1985) *An Introduction to Functional Grammar*, London: Edward Arnold.

Hamers, J.F. and Blanc, M.H.A. (2000) *Bilinguality and Bilingualism*, 2nd edn, Cambridge: Cambridge University Press.

Hamidi, M. and Pöchhacker, F. (2007) "Simultaneous Consecutive Interpreting: A New Technique Put to the Test," *Meta* 52(2): 276–289.

Hansen, G., Chesterman, A. and Gerzymisch-Arbogast, H. (eds) (2008) *Efforts and Models in Interpreting and Translation Research: A Tribute to Daniel Gile*, Amsterdam: John Benjamins.

Harris, B. (1990) "Norms in Interpretation," *Target* 2(1): 115–119.

Harris, B. and Sherwood, B. (1978) "Translating as an Innate Skill," in Gerver and Sinaiko (eds) (1978), pp. 155–170.

Hatim, B. and Mason, I. (1997) *The Translator as Communicator*, London and New York: Routledge.

Hatim, B. and Mason, I. (1997/2002) "Interpreting: A Text Linguistic Approach," in Pöchhacker and Shlesinger (eds) (2002), pp. 255–265.

Herbert, J. (1952) *The Interpreter's Handbook: How to Become a Conference Interpreter*, Geneva: Georg.

Herbert, J. (1978) "How Conference Interpretation Grew," in Gerver and Sinaiko (eds) (1978), pp. 5–9.

Hermann, A. (1956/2002) "Interpreting in Antiquity," in Pöchhacker and Shlesinger (eds) (2002), pp. 15–22.

Hertog, E. and van der Veer, B. (eds) (2006) *Taking Stock: Research and Methodology in Community Interpreting* (*Linguistica Antverpiensia* – *New Series 5*), Ghent: Communication & Cognition.

Hervais-Adelman, A.G., Moser-Mercer, B. and Golestani, N. (2011) "Executive Control of Language in the Bilingual Brain: Integrating the Evidence from Neuroimaging to Neuropsychology," *Frontiers in Psychology 2* (15 September), Art. 234, 1–8.

Hervais-Adelman, A., Moser-Mercer, B., Michel, C.M. and Golestani, N. (2014) "fMRI of Simultaneous Interpretation Reveals the Neural Basis of Extreme Language Control," *Cerebral Cortex*. First published online July 17, 2014, doi: 10.1093/cercor/bhu158.

Hiebl, B. (2011) *Simultanes Konsekutivdolmetschen mit dem Livescribe Echo Smartpen*. MA thesis, University of Vienna.

Hlavac, J. (2013) "A Cross-National Overview of Translator and Interpreter Certification Procedures," *Translation & Interpreting* 5(1): 32–65.

Hoffman, R.R. (1997) "The Cognitive Psychology of Expertise and the Domain of Interpreting," *Interpreting* 2(1/2): 189–230.

Hokkanen, S. (2012) "Simultaneous Church Interpreting as Service," *The Translator* 18(2): 291–309.

Holmes, J.S (1972/2000) "The Name and Nature of Translation Studies," in Venuti (ed.) (2000), pp. 172–185.

Holub, E. (2010) "Does intonation Matter? The Impact of Monotony on Listener Comprehension," *The Interpreters' Newsletter* 15: 117–126.

Hsieh, E. (2007) "Interpreters as Co-diagnosticians: Overlapping Roles and Services between Providers and Interpreters," *Social Science & Medicine* 64: 924–937.

Humphrey, J.H. (2000) "Portfolios. One Answer to the Challenge of Assessment and the 'Readiness to Work' Gap," in Roy (ed.) (2000c), pp. 153–175.

Hung, E. (ed.) (2002) *Teaching Translation and Interpreting 4: Building Bridges*, Amsterdam: John Benjamins.

Ilg, G. and Lambert, S. (1996) "Teaching Consecutive Interpreting," *Interpreting* 1(1): 69–99.

Inghilleri, M. (2005a) "The Sociology of Bourdieu and the Construction of the 'Object' in Translation and Interpreting Studies," *The Translator* 11(2): 125–145.

Inghilleri, M. (2005b) "Mediating Zones of Uncertainty: Interpreter Agency, the Interpreting Habitus and Political Asylum Adjudication," *The Translator* 11(1): 69–85.

Inghilleri, M. (2006) "Macro-Social Theory, Linguistic Ethnography and Interpreting Research," in Hertog and van der Veer (eds) (2006), pp. 57–68.

Ingram, R.M. (1978) "Sign Language Interpretation and General Theories of Language, Interpretation and Communication," in Gerver and Sinaiko (eds) (1978), pp. 109–118.

Ingram, R.M. (1985) "Simultaneous Interpretation of Sign Languages: Semiotic and Psycholinguistic Perspectives," *Multilingua* 4(2): 91–102.

Ingram, R.M. (1992) "Interpreters' Recognition of Structure and Meaning," in Cokely (ed.) (1992b), pp. 99–119.

Isham, W.P. (1994) "Memory for Sentence Form after Simultaneous Interpretation: Evidence Both For and Against Deverbalization," in Lambert and Moser-Mercer (eds) (1994), pp. 191–211.

Isham, W.P. and Lane, H. (1994) "A Common Conceptual Code in Bilinguals: Evidence from Simultaneous Interpretation," *Sign Language Studies* 85: 291–317.

Jacobsen, B. (2008) "Interactional Pragmatics and Court Interpreting: An Analysis of Face," *Interpreting* 10(1): 128–158.

Jansen, P. (1995) "The Role of the Interpreter in Dutch Courtroom Interaction: The Impact of the Situation on Translational Norms," in Tommola (ed.) (1995), pp. 11–36.

Jekat, S. and Klein, A. (1996) "Machine Interpretation: Open Problems and Some Solutions," *Interpreting* 1(1): 7–20.

Jiang, H. (2013) "The Interpreter's Glossary in Simultaneous Interpreting: A Survey," *Interpreting* 15(1): 74–93.

Jones, R. (1998) *Conference Interpreting Explained*, Manchester: St Jerome Publishing.

Jörg, U. (1997) "Bridging the Gap: Verb Anticipation in German–English Simultaneous Interpreting," in M. Snell-Hornby, Z. Jettmarová and K. Kaindl (eds) *Translation as Intercultural Communication*, Amsterdam: John Benjamins, pp. 217–228.

Jumpelt, W. (1985) "The Conference Interpreter's Working Environment under the New ISO and IEC Standards," *Meta* 30(1): 82–90.

Kade, O. (1967) "Zu einigen Besonderheiten des Simultandolmetschens," *Fremdsprachen* 11(1): 8–17.

Kade, O. (1968) *Zufall und Gesetzmäßigkeit in der Übersetzung*, Leipzig: Verlag Enzyklopädie.

Kade, O. and Cartellieri, C. (1971) "Some Methodological Aspects of Simultaneous Interpreting," *Babel* 17(2): 12–16.

Kadrić, M. (2001) *Dolmetschen bei Gericht. Erwartungen, Anforderungen, Kompetenzen*, Vienna: WUV-Universitätsverlag.

Kadrić, M. (2014) "Giving Interpreters a Voice: Interpreting Studies Meets Theatre Studies," *The Interpreter and Translator Trainer* 8(3): 452–468.

Kalina, S. (1992) "Discourse Processing and Interpreting Strategies – an Approach to the Teaching of Interpreting," in Dollerup and Loddegaard (eds) (1992), pp. 251–257.

Kalina, S. (1998) *Strategische Prozesse beim Dolmetschen: Theoretische Grundlagen, empirische Fallstudien, didaktische Konsequenzen*, Tübingen: Gunter Narr.

Kalina, S. (2002) "Quality in Interpreting and its Prerequisites: A Framework for a Comprehensive View," in Garzone and Viezzi (eds) (2002), pp. 121–130.

Karlik, J. (2010) "Interpreter-mediated Scriptures: Expectation and Performance," *Interpreting* 12(2): 160–185.

Karttunen, F. (1994) *Between Worlds: Interpreters, Guides, and Survivors*, New Brunswick, NJ: Rutgers University Press.

Kaufert, J.M. and Koolage, W.W. (1984) "Role Conflict among 'Culture Brokers': The Experience of Native Canadian Medical Interpreters," *Social Science & Medicine* 18(3): 283–286.

Kaufert, J.M. and Putsch, R.W. (1997) "Communication through Interpreters in Healthcare: Ethical Dilemmas Arising from Differences in Class, Culture, Language, and Power," *Journal of Clinical Ethics* 8(1): 71–87.

Kautz, U. (2000) *Handbuch Didaktik des Übersetzens und Dolmetschens*, Munich: Iudicium.

Keiser, W. (1978) "Selection and Training of Conference Interpreters," in Gerver and Sinaiko (eds) (1978), pp. 11–24.

Keiser, W. (1999) "L'Histoire de l'Association Internationale des Interprètes de Conférence (AIIC)," *Interpreting* 4(1): 81–95.

Kellett, C.J.M. (1995) "Video-aided Testing of Student Delivery and Presentation in Consecutive Interpretation," *The Interpreters' Newsletter* 6: 43–66.

Kelly, A.M. (2000) "Cultural Parameters for Interpreters in the Courtroom," in Roberts et al. (eds) (2000), pp. 131–148.

Kim, N.H. (2015) "Korea," in Pöchhacker (ed.) (2015), pp. 224–228.

Kintsch, W. (1998) *Comprehension: A Paradigm for Cognition*, Cambridge: Cambridge University Press.

Kintsch, W. and van Dijk, T.A. (1978) "Toward a Model of Text Comprehension and Production," *Psychological Review* 85(5): 363–394.

Kirchhoff, H. (1976) "Das dreigliedrige, zweisprachige Kommunikationssystem Dolmetschen," *Le Langage et l'Homme* 31: 21–27.

Kirchhoff, H. (1976/2002) "Simultaneous Interpreting: Interdependence of Variables in the Interpreting Process, Interpreting Models and Interpreting Strategies," in Pöchhacker and Shlesinger (eds) (2002), pp. 111–119.

Kitano, H. (1993) "La traduction de la langue parlée," in A. Clas and P. Bouillon (eds) *La traductique: Études et recherches de traduction par ordinateur*, Montréal: Presses de l'Université de Montréal. pp. 408–422.

Knapp-Potthoff, A. and Knapp, K. (1986) "Interweaving Two Discourses – the Difficult Task of the Non-professional Interpreter," in J. House and S. Blum-Kulka (eds) *Interlingual and Intercultural Communication*, Tübingen: Gunter Narr, pp. 151–168.

Knapp-Potthoff, A. and Knapp, K. (1987) "The Man (or Woman) in the Middle: Discoursal Aspects of Non-professional Interpreting," in K. Knapp and W. Enninger (eds) *Analyzing Intercultural Communication*, The Hague: Mouton, pp. 181–211.

Ko, L. (2008) "Teaching Interpreting by Distance Mode: An Empirical Study," *Meta* 53(4): 814–840.

Ko, L. and Chen, N.-S. (2011) "Online Interpreting in Synchronous Cyber Classrooms," *Babel* 57(2): 123–143.

Kohn, K. and Kalina, S. (1996) "The Strategic Dimension of Interpreting," *Meta* 41(1): 118–138.

Kolb, W. and Pöchhacker, F. (2008) "Interpreting in Asylum Appeal Hearings: Roles and Norms Revisited," in Russell and Hale (eds) (2008), pp. 26–50.

Kondo, M. (1988) "Japanese Interpreters in Their Socio-cultural Context," *Meta* 33(1): 70–78.

Kondo, M. (1990) "What Conference Interpreters Should Not Be Expected To Do," *The Interpreters' Newsletter* 3: 59–65.

Kondo, M. (2003) "3-Party 2-Language Model of Interpreting Revisited," *Forum* 1(1): 77–96.

Kondo, M. and Tebble, H. (1997) "Intercultural Communication, Negotiation, and Interpreting," in Gambier et al. (eds) (1997), pp. 149–166.

Kopczyński, A. (1980) *Conference Interpreting: Some Linguistic and Communicative Problems*, Poznań: A. Mickiewicz University Press.

Kopczyński, A. (1982) "Effects of Some Characteristics of Impromptu Speech on Simultaneous Interpreting," in Enkvist (ed.) (1982), pp. 255–266.

Kopczyński, A. (1994) "Quality in Conference Interpreting: Some Pragmatic Problems," in Snell-Hornby et al. (eds) (1994), pp. 189–198.

Köpke, B. and Nespoulous, J.L. (2006) "Working Memory Performance in Expert and Novice Interpreters," *Interpreting* 8(1): 1–23.

Krouglov, A. (1999) "Police Interpreting: Politeness and Sociocultural Context," *The Translator* 5(2): 285–302.

Kruger, A., Wallmach, K. and Munday, J. (eds) (2011) *Corpus-Based Translation Studies: Research and Applications*, London and New York: Continuum.

Kuhn, T.S. (1962/1996) *The Structure of Scientific Revolutions*, 3rd edn, Chicago, IL and London: The University of Chicago Press.

Kurz, I. (1985) "The Rock Tombs of the Princes of Elephantine: Earliest References to Interpretation in Pharaonic Egypt," *Babel* 31(4): 213–218.

Kurz, I. (1989) "The Use of Video-tapes in Consecutive and Simultaneous Interpretation Training," in Gran and Dodds (eds) (1989), pp. 213–215.

Kurz, I. (1992) "'Shadowing' Exercises in Interpreter Training," in Dollerup and Loddegaard (eds) (1992), pp. 245–250.

Kurz, I. (1993/2002) "Conference Interpretation: Expectations of Different User Groups," in Pöchhacker and Shlesinger (eds) (2002), pp. 313–324.

Kurz, I. (1994) "A Look into the 'Black Box' – EEG Probability Mapping during Mental Simultaneous Interpreting," in Snell-Hornby et al. (eds) (1994), pp. 199–207.

Kurz, I. (1996) *Simultandolmetschen als Gegenstand der interdisziplinären Forschung*, Vienna: WUV-Universitätsverlag.

Kurz, I. (2001) "Conference Interpreting: Quality in the Ears of the User," *Meta* 46(2): 394–409.

Kurz, I. (2002a) "Physiological Stress Responses during Media and Conference Interpreting," in Garzone and Viezzi (eds) (2002), pp. 195–202.

Kurz, I. (2002b) "Interpreting Training Programmes: The Benefits of Coordination, Cooperation, and Modern Technology," in Hung (ed.) (2002), pp. 65–72.

Kurz, I. (2007) "The Fictional Interpreter," in Pöchhacker et al. (eds) (2007), pp. 277–289.

Kurz, I. (2008) "The Impact of Non-native English on Students' Interpreting Performance," in Hansen et al. (eds) (2008), pp. 179–192.

Kurz, I. and Basel, E. (2009) "The Impact of Non-native English on Information Transfer in Simultaneous Interpretation," *Forum* 7(2): 187–213.

Kurz, I. and Pöchhacker, F. (1995) "Quality in TV Interpreting," *Translatio. Nouvelles de la FIT – FIT Newsletter* N.s. 14(3/4): 350–358.

Kurz, I., Basel, E., Chiba, D., Patels, W. and Wolfframm, J. (1996) "Scribe or Actor? A Survey Paper on Personality Profiles of Translators and Interpreters," *The Interpreters' Newsletter* 7: 3–18.

Lamberger-Felber, H. (2003) "Performance Variability among Conference Interpreters: Examples from a Case Study," in Collados Aís et al. (eds) (2003), pp. 147–168.

Lambert, S. (1989) "Information Processing among Conference Interpreters: A Test of the Depth-of-Processing Hypothesis," in Gran and Dodds (eds) (1989), pp. 83–91.

Lambert, S. (1991) "Aptitude Testing for Simultaneous Interpretation at the University of Ottawa," *Meta* 36(4): 586–594.

Lambert, S. and Moser-Mercer, B. (eds) (1994) *Bridging the Gap: Empirical Research in Simultaneous Interpretation*, Amsterdam: John Benjamins.

Lambert, W.E. (1978) "Psychological Approaches to Bilingualism, Translation and Interpretation," in Gerver and Sinaiko (eds) (1978), pp. 131–143.

Lambert, W.E., Havelka, J. and Gardner, R.C. (1959) "Linguistic Manifestations of Bilingualism," *American Journal of Psychology* 72(1): 77–82.

Lang, R. (1978) "Behavioral Aspects of Liaison Interpreters in Papua New Guinea: Some Preliminary Observations," in Gerver and Sinaiko (eds) (1978), pp. 231–244.

Laplace, C. (1994) *Théorie du langage et théorie de la traduction. Les concepts-clefs de trois auteurs: Kade (Leipzig), Coseriu (Tübingen), Seleskovitch (Paris)*, Paris: Didier Érudition.

Laster, K. and Taylor, V. (1994) *Interpreters and the Legal System*, Leichhardt, NSW: The Federation Press.

Lawrance, B.N., Osborn, E.L. and Roberts, R.L. (eds) (2006) *Intermediaries, Interpreters and Clerks: African Employees in the Making of Colonial Africa*, Madison, WI: The University of Wisconsin Press.

Lederer, M. (1978/2002) "Simultaneous Interpretation – Units of Meaning and Other Features," in Pöchhacker and Shlesinger (eds) (2002), pp. 131–140.

Lederer, M. (1981) *La traduction simultanée – Expérience et théorie*, Paris: Minard Lettres Modernes.

Lederer, M. (1990) "The Role of Cognitive Complements in Interpreting," in Bowen and Bowen (eds) (1990), pp. 53–60.

Lee, J. (2009) "Conflicting Views on Court Interpreting Examined through Surveys of Legal Professionals and Court Interpreters," *Interpreting* 11(1): 35–56.

Lee, J. (2015) "Court Interpreting," in Mikkelson and Jourdenais (eds) (2015), pp. 186–201.

Lee, S.-B. (2015) "Developing an Analytic Scale for Assessing Undergraduate Students' Consecutive Interpreting Performances," *Interpreting* 17(2): 226–254.

Lee, T. (1999) "Simultaneous Listening and Speaking in English into Korean Simultaneous Interpretation," *Meta* 44(4): 560–572.

Levelt, W.J.M. (1989) *Speaking: From Intention to Articulation*, Cambridge, MA: MIT Press.

Linell, P. (1997) "Interpreting as Communication," in Gambier et al. (eds) (1997), pp. 49–67.

Liu, M. (2011) "Methodology in Interpreting Studies: A Methodological Review of Evidence-based Research," in Nicodemus and Swabey (eds) (2011), 85–119.

Liu, M. (2013) "Design and Analysis of Taiwan's Interpretation Certification Examination," in Tsagari and van Deemter (eds) (2013), pp. 163–178.

Liu, M. and Chiu, Y.-H. (2009) "Assessing Source Material Difficulty for Consecutive Interpreting: Quantifiable Measures and Holistic Judgment," *Interpreting* 11(2): 244–266.

Liu, M., Schallert, D.L. and Carroll, P.J. (2004) "Working Memory and Expertise in Simultaneous Interpreting," *Interpreting* 6(1): 19–42.

Livingston, S., Singer, B. and Abramson, T. (1994) "Effectiveness Compared: ASL Interpretation vs. Transliteration," *Sign Language Studies* 82: 1–53.

Llewellyn-Jones, P. (1981) "Simultaneous Interpreting," in B. Woll, J. Kyle and M. Deuchar (eds) *Perspectives on British Sign Language and Deafness*, London: Croom Helm, pp. 89–104.

Llewellyn-Jones, P. and Lee, R.G. (2014) *Redefining the Role of the Community Interpreter: The Concept of Role-Space*, Lincoln: SLI Press.

Locatis, C., Williamson, D., Gould-Kabler, C., Zone-Smith, L., Detzler, I., Roberson, J., Maisiak, R. and Ackerman, M. (2010) "Comparing In-Person, Video, and Telephonic Medical Interpretation," *Journal of General Internal Medicine* 25(4): 345–350.

Longley, P. (1978) "An Integrated Programme for Training Interpreters," in Gerver and Sinaiko (eds) (1978), pp. 45–56.

Longley, P. (1989) "The Use of Aptitude Testing in the Selection of Students for Conference Interpretation Training," in Gran and Dodds (eds) (1989), pp. 105–108.

Lonsdale, D. (1997) "Modeling Cognition in SI: Methodological Issues," *Interpreting* 2(1/2): 91–117.

Lotriet, A. (2002) "Can Short Interpreter Training Be Effective? The South African Truth and Reconciliation Commission Experience," in Hung (ed.) (2002), pp. 83–98.

Lung, R. (2011) *Interpreters in Early Imperial China*, Amsterdam: John Benjamins.

LuperFoy, S. (1996) "Machine Interpretation of Bilingual Dialogue," *Interpreting* 1(2): 213–233.

Mack, G. (2002) "New Perspectives and Challenges for Interpretation: The Example of Television," in Garzone and Viezzi (eds) (2002), pp. 203–213.

Mackintosh, J. (1983) *Relay Interpretation: An Exploratory Study*, MA dissertation, Birkbeck College, University of London.

Mackintosh, J. (1985) "The Kintsch and van Dijk Model of Discourse Comprehension and Production Applied to the Interpretation Process," *Meta* 30(1): 37–43.

Mackintosh, J. (1995) "A Review of Conference Interpretation: Practice and Training," *Target* 7(1): 119–133.

Mackintosh, J. (1999) "Interpreters Are Made Not Born," *Interpreting* 4(1): 67–80.

MacWhinney, B. (1997) "Simultaneous Interpretation and the Competition Model," in Danks et al. (eds) (1997), pp. 215–232.

Mairs, R. (2015) "Rome," in Pöchhacker (ed.) (2015), pp. 361–362.

Malmkjær, K. and Windle, K. (eds) (2011) *The Oxford Handbook of Translation Studies*, Oxford and New York: Oxford University Press.

Marschark, M., Sapere, P., Convertino, C., Seewagen, R.-M. and Maltzen, H. (2004) "Comprehension of Sign Language Interpreting: Deciphering a Complex Task Situation," *Sign Language Studies* 4(4): 345–368.

Martínez-Gómez, A. (2014) "Interpreting in Prison Settings: An International Overview," *Interpreting* 16(2): 233–259.

Marzocchi, C. (1998) "The Case for an Institution-specific Component in Interpreting Research," *The Interpreters' Newsletter* 8: 51–74.

Mason, I. (2000) "Models and Methods in Dialogue Interpreting Research," in M. Olohan (ed.) *Intercultural Faultlines*, Manchester: St Jerome Publishing, pp. 215–232.

Mason, I. (ed.) (2001) *Triadic Exchanges. Studies in Dialogue Interpreting*, Manchester: St Jerome Publishing.

Mason, I. (2012) "Gaze, Positioning and Identity in Interpreter-mediated Dialogues," in Baraldi and Gavioli (eds) (2012b), pp. 177–199.

Mason, I. and Stewart, M. (2001) "Interactional Pragmatics, Face and the Dialogue Interpreter," in Mason (ed.) (2001), pp. 51–70.

Matyssek, H. (1989) *Handbuch der Notizentechnik für Dolmetscher*, Heidelberg: Groos.

McAllister, R. (2000) "Perceptual Foreign Accent and its Relevance for Simultaneous Interpreting," in Englund Dimitrova and Hyltenstam (eds) (2000), pp. 45–63.

McDermid, C. (2014) "Cohesion in English to ASL Simultaneous Interpreting," *Translation & Interpreting* 6(1): 76–101.

McIntire, M.L. (ed.) (1984) *New Dialogues in Interpreter Education. Proceedings of the Fourth National Conference of Interpreter Trainers Convention*, Silver Spring, MD: RID Publications.

Mead, P. (1999) "Interpreting: The Lexicographers' View," *The Interpreters' Newsletter* 9: 199–209.

Mead, P. (2000) "Control of Pauses by Trainee Interpreters in their A and B Languages," *The Interpreters' Newsletter* 10: 89–102.

Mead, P. (2002) "Exploring Hesitation in Consecutive Interpreting: An Empirical Study," in Garzone and Viezzi (eds) (2002), pp. 73–82.

Merlini, R. and Favaron, R. (2005) "Examining the 'Voice of Interpreting' in Speech Pathology," *Interpreting* 7(2): 263–302.

Mesa, A.-M. (2000) "The Cultural Interpreter: An Appreciated Professional," in Roberts et al. (eds) (2000), pp. 67–79.

Metzger, M. (1999) *Sign Language Interpreting: Deconstructing the Myth of Neutrality*, Washington, DC: Gallaudet University Press.

Metzger, M. (2000) "Interactive Role-plays as a Teaching Strategy," in Roy (ed.) (2000c), pp. 83–108.

Meuleman, C. and Van Besien, F. (2009) "Coping with Extreme Speech Conditions in Simultaneous Interpreting," *Interpreting* 11(1): 20–34.

Meyer, B. (2002) "Medical Interpreting: Some Salient Features," in Garzone and Viezzi (eds) (2002), pp. 159–169.

Mikkelson, H. (1996) "Community Interpreting: An Emerging Profession," *Interpreting* 1(1): 125–129.

Mikkelson, H. (1998) "Towards a Redefinition of the Role of the Court Interpreter," *Interpreting* 3(1): 21–46.

Mikkelson, H. (1999) "The Professionalization of Community Interpreting," *Journal of Interpretation* 1999: 119–133.

Mikkelson, H. (2000) "Interpreter Ethics: A Review of the Traditional and Electronic Literature," *Interpreting* 5(1): 49–56.

Mikkelson, H. and Jourdenais, R. (eds) (2015) *The Routledge Handbook of Interpreting*, London and New York: Routledge.

Millán, C. and Bartrina, F. (eds) (2013) *The Routledge Handbook of Translation Studies*. London and New York: Routledge.

Minyar-Beloruchev, R.K. (1959) *Metodika obucheniya perevodu na slukh* [*Method of Teaching Auditory Translation*], Moscow: Izdatelstvo Instituta mezhdunarodnyh otnoshenii.

Minyar-Beloruchev, R.K. (1969) *Posobie po ustnomu perevodu (Zapisi v posledova-telnom perevode)* [*Textbook of Interpreting (Notes in Consecutive Interpreting)*], Moscow: Vysshaya shkola.

Mizuno, A. (1999) "Shifts of Cohesion and Coherence in Simultaneous Interpretation from English into Japanese," *Interpreting Research* 8(2): 31–41.

Morris, R. (1995) "The Moral Dilemmas of Court Interpreting," *The Translator* 1(1): 25–46.

Morris, R. (2000) "Plus ça change …? Community Interpreters at the End of the Twentieth Century," in Roberts et al. (eds) (2000), pp. 243–264.

Moser, B. (1978) "Simultaneous Interpretation: A Hypothetical Model and its Practical Application," in Gerver and Sinaiko (eds) (1978), pp. 353–368.

Moser, P. (1996) "Expectations of Users of Conference Interpretation," *Interpreting* 1(2): 145–178.

Moser-Mercer, B. (1985) "Screening Potential Interpreters," *Meta* 30(1): 97–100.

Moser-Mercer, B. (1994a) "Paradigms Gained or the Art of Productive Disagreement," in Lambert and Moser-Mercer (eds) (1994), pp. 17–23.

Moser-Mercer, B. (1994b) "Aptitude Testing for Conference Interpreting: Why, When and How," in Lambert and Moser-Mercer (eds) (1994), pp. 57–68.

Moser-Mercer, B. (1996) "Quality in Interpreting: Some Methodological Issues," *The Interpreters' Newsletter* 7: 43–55.

Moser-Mercer, B. (1997) "Beyond Curiosity: Can Interpreting Research Meet the Challenge?" in Danks et al. (eds) (1997), pp. 176–205.

Moser-Mercer, B. (1997/2002) "Process Models in Simultaneous Interpretation," in Pöchhacker and Shlesinger (eds) (2002), pp. 149–161.

Moser-Mercer, B. (2007) "Global Cognition: Training a New Breed of Interpreter Trainers," in Pöchhacker et al. (eds) (2007), pp. 89–101.

Moser-Mercer, B., Class, B. and Seeber, K.G. (2005) "Leveraging virtual learning Environments for Training Interpreter Trainers," *Meta* 50(4), CD-ROM.

Moser-Mercer, B., Künzli, A. and Korac, M. (1998) "Prolonged Turns in Interpreting: Effects on Quality, Physiological and Psychological Stress (Pilot Study)," *Interpreting* 3(1): 47–64.

Moser-Mercer, B., Frauenfelder, U.H., Casado, B. and Künzli, A. (2000) "Searching to Define Expertise in Interpreting," in Englund Dimitrova and Hyltenstam (eds) (2000), pp. 107–131.

Moser-Mercer, B., Lambert, S., Darò, V. and Williams, S. (1997) "Skill Components in Simultaneous Interpreting," in Gambier et al. (eds) (1997), pp. 133–148.

Mouzourakis, P. (1996) "Videoconferencing: Techniques and Challenges," *Interpreting* 1(1): pp. 21–38.

Mouzourakis, P. (2006) "Remote Interpreting: A Technical Perspective on Recent Experiments," *Interpreting* 8(1): 45–66.

Munday, J. (2001) *Introducing Translation Studies: Theories and Applications*, London and New York: Routledge.

Napier, J. (2004) "Interpreting Omissions: A New Perspective," *Interpreting* 6(2): 117–142.

Napier, J. (2012) "Here or There? An Assessment of Video Remote Signed Language Interpreter-mediated Interaction in Court," in Braun and Taylor (eds) (2012), pp. 167–214.

Napier, J. and Spencer, D. (2008) "Guilty or Not Guilty? An Investigation of Deaf Jurors' Access to Court Proceedings via Sign Language Interpreting," in Russell and Hale (eds) (2008), pp. 72–122.

Ndongo-Keller, J. (2015) "Vicarious Trauma and Stress Management," in Mikkelson and Jourdenais (eds) (2015), pp. 337–351.

Nicodemus, B. and Swabey, L. (eds) (2011) *Advances in Interpreting Research: Inquiry in Action*, Amsterdam: John Benjamins.

Nida, E.A. and Taber, C.R. (1969) *The Theory and Practice of Translation*, Leiden: Brill.

Niska, H. (1995) "Just Interpreting: Role Conflicts and Discourse Types in Court Interpreting," in M. Morris (ed.) *Translation and the Law*, Amsterdam: John Benjamins, pp. 293–316.

Oléron, P. and Nanpon, H. (1965) "Récherches sur la traduction simultanée," *Journal de Psychologie Normale et Pathologique* 62(1): 73–94.

Oléron, P. and Nanpon, H. (1965/2002) "Research into Simultaneous Translation," in Pöchhacker and Shlesinger (eds) (2002), pp. 43–50.

Ong, W.J. (1982) *Orality and Literacy: The Technologizing of the Word*, London and New York: Methuen.

Orlando, M. (2010) "Digital Pen Technology and Consecutive Interpreting: Another Dimension in Note-Taking Training and Assessment," *The Interpreters' Newsletter* 15: 71–86.

Orlando, M. (2015) "Implementing Digital Pen Technology in the Consecutive Interpreting Classroom," in Andres and Behr (eds) (2015), pp. 171–199.

Ozolins, U. (2000) "Communication Needs and Interpreting in Multilingual Settings: The International Spectrum of Response," in Roberts et al. (eds) (2000), pp. 21–33.

Padilla, P., Bajo, M.T., Cañas, J.J. and Padilla, F. (1995) "Cognitive Processes of Memory in Simultaneous Interpretation," in Tommola (ed.) (1995), pp. 61–71.

Paneth, E. (1957/2002) "An Investigation into Conference Interpreting," in Pöchhacker and Shlesinger (eds) (2002), pp. 31–40.

Paneth, E. (1990) "The Future of Projected Interpretation," *The Interpreters' Newsletter* 3: 38–40.

Paradis, M. (1994) "Toward a Neurolinguistic Theory of Simultaneous Translation: The Framework," *International Journal of Psycholinguistics* 9(3): 319–335.

Paradis, M. (2000) "Prerequisites to a Study of Neurolinguistic Processes Involved in Simultaneous Interpreting: A Synopsis," in Englund Dimitrova and Hyltenstam (eds) (2000), pp. 17–24.

Peng, G. (2009) "Using Rhetorical Structure Theory (RST) to Describe the Development of Coherence in Interpreting Trainees," *Interpreting* 11(2): 216–243.

Peper, E. and Gibney, K.H. (1999) "Psychophysiological Basis for Discomfort during Sign Language Interpreting," *Journal of Interpretation* 1999: 11–18.

Petite, C. (2005) "Evidence of Repair Mechanisms in Simultaneous Interpreting: A Corpus-based Analysis," *Interpreting* 7(1): 27–49.

Petsche, H., Etlinger, S.C. and Filz, O. (1993) "Brain Electrical Mechanisms of Bilingual Speech Management: An Initial Investigation," *Electroencephalography and Clinical Neurophysiology* 86: 385–394.

Pippa, S. and Russo, M. (2002) "Aptitude for Conference Interpreting: A Proposal for a Testing Methodology Based on Paraphrase," in Garzone and Viezzi (eds) (2002), pp. 245–256.

Pöchhacker, F. (1992) "The Role of Theory in Simultaneous Interpreting," in Dollerup and Loddegaard (eds) (1992), pp. 211–220.

Pöchhacker, F. (1993) "From Knowledge to Text: Coherence in Simultaneous Interpreting," in Gambier and Tommola (eds) (1993), pp. 87–100.

Pöchhacker, F. (1994a) *Simultandolmetschen als komplexes Handeln*, Tübingen: Gunter Narr.

Pöchhacker, F. (1994b) "Simultaneous Interpretation: 'Cultural Transfer' or 'Voice-over Text'?" in Snell-Hornby et al. (eds) (1994), pp. 169–178.

Pöchhacker, F. (1994c) "Quality Assurance in Simultaneous Interpreting," in Dollerup and Lindegaard (eds) (1994), pp. 233–242.

Pöchhacker, F. (1995a) "Simultaneous Interpreting: A Functionalist Perspective," *Hermes. Journal of Linguistics* 14: 31–53.

Pöchhacker, F. (1995b) "Slips and Shifts in Simultaneous Interpreting," in Tommola (ed.) (1995), pp. 73–90.

Pöchhacker, F. (1999) "Teaching Practices in Simultaneous Interpreting," *The Interpreters' Newsletter* 9: 157–176.

Pöchhacker, F. (2000a) *Dolmetschen: Konzeptuelle Grundlagen und deskriptive Untersuchungen*. Tübingen: Stauffenburg.

Pöchhacker, F. (2000b) "The Community Interpreter's Task: Self-perception and Provider Views," in Roberts et al. (eds) (2000), pp. 49–65.

Pöchhacker, F. (2002) "Researching Interpreting Quality: Models and Methods," in Garzone and Viezzi (eds) (2002), pp. 95–106.

Pöchhacker, F. (2004) *Introducing Interpreting Studies*, London and New York: Routledge.

Pöchhacker, F. (2006a) "Research and Methodology in Healthcare Interpreting," in Hertog and van der Veer (eds) (2006), pp. 135–159.

Pöchhacker, F. (2006b) "'Going Social?' On Pathways and Paradigms in Interpreting Studies," in A. Pym, M. Shlesinger and Z. Jettmarová (eds) *Sociocultural Aspects of Translating and Interpreting*, Amsterdam: John Benjamins, pp. 215–232.

Pöchhacker, F. (2007) "Coping with Culture in Media Interpreting," *Perspectives: Studies in Translatology* 15(2): 123–142.

Pöchhacker, F. (2008) "Interpreting as Mediation," in Valero-Garcés and Martin (eds) (2008), pp. 9–26.

Pöchhacker, F. (2010a) "Interpreting," in Y. Gambier and L. van Doorslaer (eds) *Handbook of Translation Studies, Volume 1*, Amsterdam: John Benjamins, pp. 153–157.

Pöchhacker, F. (2010b) "Interpreting Studies," in Y. Gambier and L. van Doorslaer (eds) *Handbook of Translation Studies, Volume 1*, Amsterdam: John Benjamins, pp. 158–172.

Pöchhacker, F. (2011a) "Researching Interpreting: Approaches to Inquiry," in Nicodemus and Swabey (eds) (2011), pp. 5–25.

Pöchhacker, F. (2011b) "Assessing Aptitude for Interpreting: The SynCloze Test," *Interpreting* 13(1): 106–120.

Pöchhacker, F. (2012) "Interpreting Participation: Conceptual Analysis and Illustration of the Interpreter's Role in Interaction," in Baraldi and Gavioli (eds) (2012), pp. 45–69.

Pöchhacker, F. (2014) "Remote Possibilities: Trialing Simultaneous Video Interpreting for Austrian Hospitals," in B. Nicodemus and M. Metzger (eds) *Investigations in Healthcare Interpreting*, Washington, DC: Gallaudet University Press, pp. 302–325.

Pöchhacker, F. (ed.) (2015) *Routledge Encyclopedia of Interpreting Studies*, London and New York: Routledge.

Pöchhacker, F. and Kadrić, M. (1999) "The Hospital Cleaner as Healthcare Interpreter: A Case Study," *The Translator* 5(2): 161–178.

Pöchhacker, F. and Liu, M. (eds) (2014) *Aptitude for Interpreting*, Amsterdam: John Benjamins.

Pöchhacker, F. and Shlesinger, M. (eds) (2002) *The Interpreting Studies Reader*, London and New York: Routledge.

Pöchhacker, F., Jakobsen, A.-L. and Mees, I.M. (eds) (2007) *Interpreting Studies and Beyond: A Tribute to Miriam Shlesinger*, Copenhagen: Samfundslitteratur.

Pöllabauer, S. (2004) "Interpreting in Asylum Hearings: Issues of Role, Responsibility and Power," *Interpreting* 6(2): 143–180.

Pöllabauer, S. (2007) "Interpreting in Asylum Hearings: Issues of Saving Face," in Wadensjö et al. (eds) (2007), pp. 39–52.

Pöllabauer, S. (2015) "Interpreting in Asylum Proceedings," in Mikkelson and Jourdenais (eds) (2015), pp. 202–216.

Poyatos, F. (1987/2002) "Nonverbal Communication in Simultaneous and Consecutive Interpretation: A Theoretical Model and New Perspectives," in Pöchhacker and Shlesinger (eds) (2002), pp. 235–246.

Price, E.L., Pérez-Stable, E.J., Nickleach, D., López, M. and Karliner, L.S. (2012) "Interpreter Perspectives of In-Person, Telephonic, and Videoconferencing Medical Interpretation in Clinical Encounters," *Patient Education and Counseling* 87(2): 226–232.

Puebla Fortier, J. (1997) "Interpreting for Health in the United States," in Carr et al. (eds) (1997), pp. 165–177.

Putsch, R.W. (1985) "Cross-cultural Communication: The Special Case of Interpreters in Health Care," *Journal of the American Medical Association* 254(23): 3344–3348.

Pym, A. (2007) "On Shlesinger's Proposed Equalizing Universal for Interpreting," in Pöchhacker et al. (eds) (2007), pp. 175–190.

Rabin, C. (1958) "The Linguistics of Translation," in Smith (ed.) (1958), pp. 123–145.

Reithofer, K. (2010) "English as a Lingua Franca vs. Interpreting: Battleground or Peaceful Co-existence?" *The Interpreters' Newsletter* 15: 143–157.

Reithofer, K. (2013) "Comparing Modes of Communication: The Effect of English as a Lingua Franca vs. Interpreting," *Interpreting* 15(1): 48–73.

Riccardi, A. (1996) "Language-Specific Strategies in Simultaneous Interpreting," in Dollerup and Appel (eds) (1996), pp. 213–222.

Riccardi, A. (2002) "Evaluation in Interpretation: Macrocriteria and Microcriteria," in Hung (ed.) (2002), pp. 115–126.

Rinne, J.O., Tommola, J., Laine, M., Krause, B.J., Schmidt, D., Kaasinen, V., Teräs, M., Sipilä, H. and Sunnari, M. (2000) "The Translating Brain: Cerebral Activation Patterns during Simultaneous Interpreting," *Neuroscience Letters* 294: 85–88.

Roberts, R.P. (ed.) (1981) *L'interprétation auprès des tribunaux: Actes du mini-colloque tenu les 10 et 11 avril 1980 à l'Université d'Ottawa*, Ottawa: University of Ottawa Press.

Roberts, R.P. (1997) "Community Interpreting Today and Tomorrow," in Carr et al. (eds) (1997), pp. 7–26.

Roberts, R.P. (2000) "Interpreter Assessment Tools for Different Settings," in Roberts et al. (eds) (2000), pp. 103–120.

Roberts, R.P. (2002) "Community Interpreting: A Profession in Search of its Identity," in Hung (ed.) (2002), pp. 157–175.

Roberts, R.P., Carr, S.E., Abraham, D. and Dufour, A. (eds) (2000) *The Critical Link 2: Interpreters in the Community; Selected Papers from the Second International Conference on Interpreting in Legal, Health and Social Service Settings, Vancouver, BC, Canada, 19–23 May 1998*, Amsterdam: John Benjamins.

Robson, C. (1993) *Real World Research: A Resource for Social Scientists and Practitioner-Researchers*, Oxford and Malden, MA: Blackwell.

Romero-Fresco, P. (2012) "Respeaking in Translator Training Curricula: Present and Future Prospects," *The Interpreter and Translator Trainer* 6(1): 91–112.

Rosenberg, B.A. (2002) "A Quantitative Discourse Analysis of Community Interpreting," in *Translation: New Ideas for a New Century. Proceedings of the XVI FIT Congress*, Paris: FIT, pp. 222–226.

Rosenberg, B.A. (2007) "A Data-Driven Analysis of Telephone Interpreting," in Wadensjö et al. (eds) (2007), pp. 65–76.

Rothman, E.N. (2015a) "Dragomans," in Pöchhacker (ed.) (2015), pp. 119–124.

Rothman, E.N. (2015b) "Jeunes de langues," in Pöchhacker (ed.) (2015), pp. 217–220.

Roy, C.B. (1993/2002) "The Problem with Definitions, Descriptions and the Role Metaphors of Interpreters," in Pöchhacker and Shlesinger (eds) (2002), pp. 345–353.

Roy, C.B. (1996) "An Interactional Sociolinguistic Analysis of Turn-taking in an Interpreted Event," *Interpreting* 1(1): 39–67.

Roy, C.B. (2000a) *Interpreting as a Discourse Process*, Oxford: Oxford University Press.

Roy, C.B. (2000b) "Training Interpreters – Past, Present, and Future," in Roy (ed.) (2000c), pp. 1–14.

Roy, C.B. (ed.) (2000c) *Innovative Practices for Teaching Sign Language Interpreters*, Washington, DC: Gallaudet University Press.

Roy, C.B. and Napier, J. (eds) (2015) *The Sign Language Interpreting Studies Reader*, Amsterdam: John Benjamins.

Rozan, J.-F. (1956) *La prise de notes en interprétation consécutive*, Geneva: Georg.

Roziner, I. and Shlesinger, M. (2010) "Much Ado about Something Remote: Stress and Performance in Remote Interpreting," *Interpreting* 12(2): 214–247.

Rudvin, M. and Tomassini, E. (2011) *Interpreting in the Community and Workplace: A Practical Teaching Guide*, Basingstoke: Palgrave Macmillan.

Russell, D. and Hale, S. (eds) (2008) *Interpreting in Legal Settings*, Washington, DC: Gallaudet University Press.

Russo, M. (1995) "Self-Evaluation: The Awareness of One's Own Difficulties as a Training Tool for Simultaneous Interpretation," *The Interpreters' Newsletter* 6: 75–85.

Russo, M. (2011) "Aptitude Testing over the Years," *Interpreting* 13(1): 5–30.

Russo, M. (2014) "Testing Aptitude for Interpreting: The Predictive Value of Oral Paraphrasing, with Synonyms and Coherence as Assessment Parameters," *Interpreting* 16(1): 1–18.

Sacks, H., Schegloff, E. and Jefferson, G. (1974) "A Simplest Systematics for the Organization of Turn-taking in Conversation," *Language* 50: 696–736.

Saldanha, G. and O'Brien, S. (2013) *Research Methodologies in Translation Studies*, London: Routledge.

Salevsky, H. (1987) *Probleme des Simultandolmetschens. Eine Studie zur Handlungsspezifik*, Berlin: Akademie der Wissenschaften der DDR.

Salevsky, H. (1993) "The Distinctive Nature of Interpreting Studies," *Target* 5(2): 149–167.

Sanz, J. (1930) "Le travail et les aptitudes des interprètes parlementaires," *Anals d'Orientació Professional* 4: 303–318.

Sawyer, D.B. (2004) *Fundamental Aspects of Interpreter Education: Curriculum and Assessment*, Amsterdam: John Benjamins.

Schäffner, C. (ed.) (2004) *Translation Research and Interpreting Research: Traditions, Gaps and Synergies*, Clevedon: Multilingual Matters.

Schäffner, C., Kredens, K. and Fowler, Y. (eds) (2013) *Interpreting in a Changing Landscape: Selected Papers from Critical Link 6*, Amsterdam: John Benjamins.

Schjoldager, A. (1996) "Assessment in Simultaneous Interpreting," in Dollerup and Appel (eds) (1996), pp. 187–195.

Schmidt, Paul (1949) *Statist auf diplomatischer Bühne 1923–45: Erlebnisse des Chefdolmetschers im Auswärtigen Amt mit den Staatsmännern Europas*, Bonn: Athenäum.

Schuster, M. (2013) "From Chaos to Cultural Competence: Analyzing Language Access to Public Institutions," in Schäffner et al. (eds) (2013), pp. 61–82.

Schweda Nicholson, N. (1990) "Consecutive Note-taking for Community Interpretation," in Bowen and Bowen (eds) (1990), pp. 136–145.

Schweda Nicholson, N. (1994) "Professional Ethics for Court and Community Interpreters," in D.L. Hammond (ed.) *Professional Issues for Translators and Interpreters*, Philadelphia: John Benjamins, pp. 79–97.

Schweda Nicholson, N. (2005) "Personality Characteristics of Interpreter Trainees: The Myers-Briggs Type Indicator (MBTI)," *The Interpreters' Newsletter* 13: 109–142.

Schwenke, T.J., Ashby, J.S. and Gnilka, P.B. (2014) "Sign Language Interpreters and Burnout: The Effects of Perfectionism, Perceived Stress, and Coping Resources," *Interpreting* 16(2): 209–232.

Seleskovitch, D. (1962) "L'Interprétation de Conférence," *Babel* 8(1): 13–18.

Seleskovitch, D. (1968) *L'interprète dans les conférences internationales: Problèmes de langage et de communication*, Paris: Minard Lettres Modernes.

Seleskovitch, D. (1975) *Langage, langues et mémoire: Étude de la prise de notes en interprétation consécutive*, Paris: Minard Lettres Modernes.

Seleskovitch, D. (1975/2002) "Language and Memory: A Study of Note-taking in Consecutive Interpreting," in Pöchhacker and Shlesinger (eds) (2002), pp. 121–129.

Seleskovitch, D. (1976) "Interpretation, a Psychological Approach to Translating," in Brislin (ed.) (1976b), pp. 92–116.

Seleskovitch, D. (1978a) *Interpreting for International Conferences*, Washington, DC: Pen and Booth.

Seleskovitch, D. (1978b) "Language and Cognition," in Gerver and Sinaiko (eds) (1978), pp. 333–341.

Seleskovitch, D. (1999) "The Teaching of Simultaneous Interpretation in the Course of the Last 50 Years," *Interpreting* 4(1): 55–66.

Seleskovitch, D. and Lederer, M. (1984) *Interpréter pour traduire*, Paris: Didier Érudition.

Seleskovitch, D. and Lederer, M. (1989) *Pédagogie raisonnée de l'interprétation*, Paris/Brussels: Didier Érudition/OPOCE.

Seleskovitch, D. and Lederer, M. (1995) *A Systematic Approach to Teaching Interpretation* (trans. J. Harmer), Silver Spring, MD: Registry of Interpreters for the Deaf.

Setton, R. (1998/2002) "Meaning Assembly in Simultaneous Interpretation," in Pöchhacker and Shlesinger (eds) (2002), pp. 179–202.

Setton, R. (1999) *Simultaneous Interpretation: A Cognitive-Pragmatic Analysis*, Amsterdam: John Benjamins.

Setton, R. (2003) "Models of the Interpreting Process," in A. Collados Aís and J.A. Sabio Pinilla (eds) *Avances en la investigación sobre interpretación*, Granada: Comares, pp. 29–89.

Setton, R. (2011) "Corpus-based Interpreting Studies (CIS): Overview and Prospects," in Kruger et al. (eds) (2011), pp. 33–75.

Setton, R. and Dawrant, A. (2016) *Conference Interpreting: A Complete Course and Trainer's Guide* (2 vols), Amsterdam: John Benjamins.

Shackman, J. (1984) *The Right To Be Understood: A Handbook on Working with, Employing and Training Community Interpreters*, Cambridge: National Extension College.

Shannon, C.E. and Weaver, W. (1949) *The Mathematical Theory of Communication*, Urbana, IL: University of Illinois Press.

Shiryayev, A. (1979) *Sinkhronniy perevod: Deyatelnost sinkhronnogo perevodchika i metodika prepodavaniya sinkhronnogo perevoda* [*Simultaneous Interpretation: The Activity of a Simultaneous Interpreter and Methods of Teaching Simultaneous Interpretation*], Moscow: Voyenizdat.

Shlesinger, M. (1989a) "Extending the Theory of Translation to Interpretation: Norms as a Case in Point," *Target* 1(1): 111–116.

Shlesinger, M. (1989b) *Simultaneous Interpretation as a Factor in Effecting Shifts in the Position of Texts on the Oral–Literate Continuum*, MA thesis, Tel Aviv University.

Shlesinger, M. (1991) "Interpreter Latitude vs. Due Process: Simultaneous and Consecutive Interpretation in Multilingual Trials," in S. Tirkkonen-Condit (ed.) *Empirical Research in Translation and Intercultural Studies*, Tübingen: Gunter Narr, pp. 147–155.

Shlesinger, M. (1994) "Intonation in the Production and Perception of Simultaneous Interpretation," in Lambert and Moser-Mercer (eds) (1994), pp. 225–236.

Shlesinger, M. (1995a) "Shifts in Cohesion in Simultaneous Interpreting," *The Translator* 1(2): 193–214.

Shlesinger, M. (1995b) "Stranger in Paradigms: What Lies Ahead for Simultaneous Interpreting Research?" *Target* 7(1): 7–28.

Shlesinger, M. (1997) "Quality in Simultaneous Interpreting," in Gambier et al. (eds) (1997), pp. 123–131.

Shlesinger, M. (1998). "Corpus-based Interpreting Studies as an Offshoot of Corpus-based Translation Studies," *Meta* 43(4): 486–493.

Shlesinger, M. (1999) "Norms, Strategies and Constraints: How Do We Tell Them Apart?" in Álvarez Lugrís and Fernández Ocampo (eds) (1999), pp. 65–77.

Shlesinger, M. (2000a) *Strategic Allocation of Working Memory and Other Attentional Resources*, PhD dissertation, Bar-Ilan University.

Shlesinger, M. (2000b) "Interpreting as a Cognitive Process: How Can We Know What Really Happens?" in Tirkkonen-Condit and Jääskeläinen (eds) (2000), pp. 3–15.

Shlesinger, M. (2003) "Effects of Presentation Rate on Working Memory in Simultaneous Interpreting," *The Interpreters' Newsletter* 12: 37–49.

Shlesinger, M. (2004) "Doorstep Inter-subdisciplinarity and Beyond," in Schäffner (ed.) (2004), pp. 116–123.

Shlesinger, M. (2008) "Towards a Definition of Interpretese: An Intermodal, Corpus-based Study," in Hansen *et al.* (eds), 237–253.

Skaaden, H. (2013) "Assessing Interpreter Aptitude in a Variety of Languages," in Tsagari and van Deemter (eds) (2013), pp. 35–50.

Smith, A.H. (ed.) (1958) *Aspects of Translation*, Studies in Communication 2, London: Secker and Warburg.

Smith, M.B. (2015) "Interpreting in Education," in Mikkelson & Jourdenais (eds) (2015), pp. 265–279.

Snell-Hornby, M., Pöchhacker, F. and Kaindl, K. (eds) (1994) *Translation Studies: An Interdiscipline*, Amsterdam: John Benjamins.

Sperber, D. and Wilson, D. (1986/1995) *Relevance: Communication and Cognition*, Oxford: Blackwell.

Steiner, B. (1998) "Signs from the Void: The Comprehension and Production of Sign Language on Television," *Interpreting* 3(2): 99–146.

Steiner, G. (1975) *After Babel: Aspects of Language and Translation*, London: Oxford University Press.

Stenzl, C. (1983) *Simultaneous Interpretation: Groundwork Towards a Comprehensive Model*, MA thesis, Birkbeck College, University of London.

Stenzl, C. (1989) "From Theory to Practice and from Practice to Theory," in Gran and Dodds (eds) (1989), pp. 23–26.

Stewart, D.A., Schein, J.D. and Cartwright, B.E. (1998) *Sign Language Interpreting: Exploring Its Art and Science*, Boston, MA: Allyn and Bacon.

Straniero Sergio, F. (1999) "The Interpreter on the (Talk) Show," *The Translator* 5(2): 303–326.

Straniero Sergio, F. and Falbo, C. (eds) (2012) *Breaking Ground in Corpus-based Interpreting Studies*, Frankfurt: Peter Lang.

Strong, M. and Rudser, S.F. (1985) "An Assessment Instrument for Sign Language Interpreters," *Sign Language Studies* 49: 344–362.

Strong, M. and Rudser, S.F. (1992) "The Subjective Assessment of Sign Language Interpreters," in Cokely (ed.) (1992b), pp. 1–14.

Szabó, C. (2006) "Language Choice in Note-Taking for Consecutive Interpreting: A Topic Revisited," *Interpreting* 8(2): 129–147.

Takeda, K. (2010) *Interpreting at the Tokyo War Crimes Tribunal*, Ottawa: University of Ottawa Press.

Takeda, K. (2015) "Japan," in Pöchhacker (ed.) (2015), pp. 215–217.

Tate, G. and Turner, G.H. (1997/2002) "The Code and the Culture: Sign Language Interpreting – In Search of the New Breed's Ethics," in Pöchhacker and Shlesinger (eds) (2002), pp. 373–383.

Tebble, H. (1998) *Medical Interpreting: Improving Communication with Your Patients*, Geelong/Melbourne: Language Australia/Deakin University.

Tebble, H. (1999) "The Tenor of Consultant Physicians: Implications for Medical Interpreting," *The Translator* 5(2): 179–200.

Tebble, H. (2014) "A Genre-Based Approach to Teaching Dialogue Interpreting: The Medical Consultation," *The Interpreter and Translator Trainer* 8(3): 418–436.

Thieme, K., Hermann, A. and Glässer, E. (1956) *Beiträge zur Geschichte des Dolmetschens*, Munich: Isar.

Thiéry, C. (1978) "True Bilingualism and Second-language Learning," in Gerver and Sinaiko (eds) (1978), pp. 145–153.

Timarová, S. (2015) "Working Memory," in Pöchhacker (ed.) (2015), pp. 443–446.

Timarová, S. and Ungoed-Thomas, H. (2008) "Admission Testing for Interpreting Courses," *The Interpreter and Translator Trainer* 2(1), 29–46.

Timarová, S., Dragsted, B. and Hansen, I.G. (2011) "Time Lag in Translation and Interpreting: A Methodological Exploration," in Alvstad et al. (eds) (2011), pp. 121–146.

Timarová, S., Čeňková, I., Meylaerts, R., Hertog, E., Szmalec, A. and Duyck, W. (2014) "Simultaneous Interpreting and Working Memory Executive Control," *Interpreting* 16(2): 139–168.

Tirkkonen-Condit, S. and Jääskeläinen, R. (eds) (2000) *Tapping and Mapping the Processes of Translation and Interpreting*, Amsterdam: John Benjamins.

Tiselius, E. (2009) "Revisiting Carroll's Scales," in C.V. Angelelli and H.E. Jacobson (eds) *Testing and Assessment in Translation and Interpreting Studies*, Amsterdam: John Benjamins, pp. 95–121.

Tissi, B. (2000) "Silent Pauses and Disfluencies in Simultaneous Interpretation: A Descriptive Analysis," *The Interpreters' Newsletter* 10: 103–127.

Tommola, J. (ed.) (1995) *Topics in Interpreting Research*, Turku: University of Turku, Centre for Translation and Interpreting.

Tommola, J. (1999) "New Trends in Interpreting Research: Going Psycho – or Neuro?" in Álvarez Lugrís and Fernández Ocampo (eds) (1999), pp. 321–330.

Tommola, J. (2003) "Estimating the Transfer of Semantic Information in Interpreting," in Collados Aís et al. (eds) (2003), pp. 125–146.

Tommola, J. and Helevä, M. (1998) "Language Direction and Source Text Complexity: Effects on Trainee Performance in Simultaneous Interpreting," in L. Bowker, M. Cronin, D. Kenny and J. Pearson (eds) *Unity in Diversity? Current Trends in Translation Studies*, Manchester: St Jerome Publishing, pp. 177–186.

Tommola, J. and Lindholm, J. (1995) "Experimental Research on Interpreting: Which Dependent Variable?" in Tommola (ed.) (1995), pp. 121–133.

Torikai, K. (2009) *Voices of the Invisible Presence: Diplomatic Interpreters in post-World War II Japan*, Amsterdam: John Benjamins.

Toury, G. (1978/2000) "The Nature and Role of Norms in Translation," in Venuti (ed.) (2000), pp. 198–211.

Toury, G. (1995) *Descriptive Translation Studies and Beyond*, Amsterdam: John Benjamins.

Treisman, A.M. (1965) "The Effects of Redundancy and Familiarity on Translating and Repeating Back a Foreign and a Native Language," *British Journal of Psychology* 56: 369–379.

Tsagari, D. and van Deemter, R. (eds) (2013) *Assessment Issues in Language Translation and Interpreting*, Frankfurt: Peter Lang.

Tseng, J. (1992) *Interpreting as an Emerging Profession in Taiwan – a Sociological Model*, MA thesis, Fu Jen Catholic University.

Tsuruta, C. (2011) "Broadcast Interpreters in Japan: Bringing News to and from the World," *The Interpreters' Newsletter* 16: 157–173.

UN (2001) "Remote Interpretation," *The Interpreters' Newsletter* 11: 163–180.

Valdeón, R.A. (2013) "Doña Marina/La Malinche: A Historiographical Approach to the Interpreter/Traitor," *Target* 25(2): 157–179.

Valero-Garcés, C. and Martin, A. (eds) (2008) *Crossing Borders in Community Interpreting: Definitions and Dilemmas*, Amsterdam: John Benjamins.

van Dijk, T.A. (ed.) (1997a) *Discourse as Structure and Process. Discourse Studies: A Multidisciplinary Introduction*, vol. 1, London, Thousand Oaks, CA and New Delhi: Sage.

van Dijk, T.A. (ed.) (1997b) *Discourse as Social Interaction. Discourse Studies: A Multidisciplinary Introduction*, vol. 2, London, Thousand Oaks, CA and New Delhi: Sage.

van Dijk, T.A. and Kintsch, W. (1983) *Strategies of Discourse Comprehension*, New York: Academic Press.

van Hoof, H. (1962) *Théorie et pratique de l'interprétation*, Munich: Max Hueber.

Venuti, L. (ed.) (2000) *The Translation Studies Reader*, London and New York: Routledge.

Verhoef, M. and du Plessis, T. (eds) (2008) *Multilingualism and Educational Interpreting: Innovation and Delivery*, Hatfield: Van Schaik.

Vermeer, H.J. (1989/2000) "Skopos and Commission in Translational Action," in Venuti (ed.) (2000), pp. 221–232.

Vermeer, H.J. (1992) *Skizzen zu einer Geschichte der Translation*, Frankfurt: Verlag für Interkulturelle Kommunikation.

Viaggio, S. (1991) "Teaching Beginners to Shut Up and Listen," *The Interpreters' Newsletter* 4: 45–58.

Viaggio, S. (1996) "The Pitfalls of Metalingual Use in Simultaneous Interpreting," *The Translator* 2(2): 179–198.

Vidrine, J.A. (1979) *Historical Study of the Neo-professional Organization: Registry of Interpreters for the Deaf, Inc. (1964–1978)*, PhD thesis, Walden University.

Viezzi, M. (1990) "Sight Translation, Simultaneous Interpretation and Information Retention," in Gran and Taylor (eds) (1990), pp. 54–60.

Vik-Tuovinen, G.-V. (2002) "Retrospection as a Method of Studying the Process of Simultaneous Interpreting," in Garzone and Viezzi (eds) (2002), pp. 63–71.

Vuorikoski, A. (1993) "Simultaneous Interpretation – User Experience and Expectations," in C. Picken (ed.) *Translation – the Vital Link: Proceedings of the XIIIth World Congress of FIT*, vol. 1, London: Institute of Translation and Interpreting, pp. 317–327.

Vuorikoski, A. (2004) *A Voice of Its Citizens or a Modern Tower of Babel? The Quality of Interpreting as a Function of Political Rhetoric in the European Parliament*, Tampere: Tampere University Press.

Wadensjö, C. (1993/2002) "The Double Role of a Dialogue Interpreter," in Pöchhacker and Shlesinger (eds) (2002), pp. 355–370.

Wadensjö, C. (1998) *Interpreting as Interaction*, London and New York: Longman.

Wadensjö, C. (1999) "Telephone Interpreting and the Synchronization of Talk in Social Interaction," *The Translator* 5(2): 247–264.

Wadensjö, C. (2001) "Interpreting in Crisis: The Interpreter's Position in Therapeutic Encounters," in Mason (ed.) (2001), pp. 71–85.

Wadensjö, C. (2008) "In and Off the Show: Co-constructing 'Invisibility' in an Interpreter-Mediated Talk Show Interview," *Meta* 53(1): 184–203.

Wadensjö, C., Englund Dimitrova, B. and Nilsson, A.-L. (eds) (2007) *The Critical Link 4: Professionalisation of Interpreting in the Community*, Amsterdam: John Benjamins.

Wahlster, W. (ed.) (2000) *Verbmobil: Foundations of Speech-to-Speech Translation*, Berlin: Springer.

Wang, B. and Mu, L. (2009) "Interpreter Training and Research in Mainland China: Recent Developments," *Interpreting* 11(2): 267–283.

Weber, W.K. (1990) "The Importance of Sight Translation in an Interpreter Training Program," in Bowen and Bowen (eds) (1990), pp. 44–52.

Wehrmeyer, E. (2015) "Comprehension of Television News Signed Language Interpreters: A South African Perspective," *Interpreting* 17(2): 195–225.

Wiegand, C. (2000) "Role of the Interpreter in the Healing of a Nation: An Emotional View," in Roberts et al. (eds) (2000), pp. 207–218.

Wilss, W. (1978) "Syntactic Anticipation in German–English Simultaneous Interpreting," in Gerver and Sinaiko (eds) (1978), pp. 343–352.

Wilss, W. (1999) *Translation and Interpreting in the 20th Century: Focus on German*, Amsterdam: John Benjamins.

Winston, E.A. and Monikowski, C. (2000) "Discourse Mapping: Developing Textual Coherence Skills in Interpreters," in Roy (ed.) (2000c), pp. 15–66.

Witter-Merithew, A. (1986/2015) "Claiming Our Destiny," in Roy and Napier (eds) (2015), pp. 293–296.

Wolf, M. (2015) *The Habsburg Monarchy's Many-languaged Soul: Translating and Interpreting, 1848–1918* (trans. K. Sturge), Amsterdam: John Benjamins.

Wong, F.K. (1990) "Court Interpreting in a Multiracial Society – the Malaysian Experience," in Bowen and Bowen (eds) (1990), pp. 108–116.

Wu, F.S. (2013) "How Do We Assess Students in the Interpreting Examinations?" in Tsagari and van Deemter (eds) (2013), pp. 15–33.

Xiao, X., Chen, X. and Palmer, J.L. (2015) "Chinese Deaf Viewers' Comprehension of Sign Language Interpreting: An Experimental Study," *Interpreting* 17(1): 91–117.

Yagi, S.M. (1999) "Computational Discourse Analysis for Interpretation," *Meta* 44(2): 268–279.

Zimman, L. (1994) "Intervention as a Pedagogical Problem in Community Interpreting," in Dollerup and Lindegaard (eds) (1994), pp. 217–224.

Zwischenberger, C. (2010) "Quality Criteria in Simultaneous Interpreting: An International vs. a National View," *The Interpreters' Newsletter* 15: 127–142.

Zwischenberger, C. (2011) "Conference Interpreters and Their Self-Representation: A Worldwide Web-based Survey," in R. Sela-Sheffy and M. Shlesinger (eds) *Identity and Status in the Translational Professions*, Amsterdam: John Benjamins, pp. 119–133.

Author Index

Subject Index